Charles Joseph Bellamy

**An Experiment in Marriage**

A Romance

Charles Joseph Bellamy

**An Experiment in Marriage**
*A Romance*

ISBN/EAN: 9783337345365

Printed in Europe, USA, Canada, Australia, Japan

Cover: Foto ©Thomas Meinert / pixelio.de

More available books at **www.hansebooks.com**

AN

# EXPERIMENT IN MARRIAGE.

A ROMANCE,

BY
CHARLES J. BELLAMY,
AUTHOR OF "THE BRETON MILLS," "A MOMENT OF
MADNESS," ETC.

---

ALBANY BOOK COMPANY,
36 STATE STREET,
ALBANY, N. Y.
1889.

ALBANY, N.Y.,

WEED, PARSONS AND CO., PRINTERS,

1889.

# CHAPTER I.

In the dining-room of one of the fashionable clubs of New York two men were just finishing a late supper. They had taken their favorite table in the corner near the window, so that when conversation flagged there were always the busy streets to glance down upon, streets almost as light in the glare of the fierce electric light by night as by day in sunlight. Harry Vinton, the younger of the two, was intensely imaginative, or perhaps it was remarkably observing. To his mind every individual, every group in the crowded street, was a fit subject for a poem or a romance. Their stories they carried in their faces, he thought, revealed them in their gait, even in the fit of their garments. Not one story of them all was commonplace. All had their elements of tragedy, of heroic self-sacrifice, or of devilish malignity, of grand philosophy perhaps, or of despair utter and black as everlasting night.

His companion, John Ward, a professional idler, regarded Vinton as well nigh a necessity to make life endurable. Vinton was always entertaining to him, always suggestive, endowing the most ordinary scene with interest of its own, and drawing from the most prosaic surroundings hints for conversation always full of life, or varied with endless discussion and disagreement.

But on this occasion there was no need to glance down into the street for suggestions to conversation. So engaging was their topic that they left unnoticed the ices ordered to finish their meal, and those dainty

devices of modern epicureanism were slowly resolving
themselves into their most unappetizing elements un-
regarded and unregretted.

"I tell you, Ward," exclaimed the younger man,
with an emphasis all his own, "You are not looking
the situation fairly in the face. The woman question
has not been solved, and until it is solved, society will
have to stay in a bad way. Until the relations of the
sexes are properly adjusted, we can have no real reform, nor progress."

Ward laughed, glanced at the door through which
two tall gentlemen were entering, and interrupted the
reply on his lips by saying: "There is Bevan; I wish I
could catch his eye and get him over here. He's always good company. He has a stranger with him I
see, probably a business acquaintance. Bevan is always thinking of money getting."

"Never mind Bevan; if you have any thing to say
on this woman question worth listening to, say it."

"Don't be impatient, Harry, my boy. The question will wait for us. It has been waiting for a good
many hundred years. The truth is it is a hard thing
to ask of human nature, that it will behave itself. For
my part I don't expect any such consummation, so I
don't expect the woman question ever to be settled."

"There you go again with your attempts to be epi-
grammatic," retorted Vinton, impatiently. "Drop that
sort of thing, you really should, if you pretend to be a
seeker after truth. An epigram is always a lie. These
smooth sentences that round off so delightfully are
snares of the evil one, set for the unwary, I don't doubt,
by the great father of lies himself."

"You know you like them, Vinton," replied his
friend, satirically. "It is the grief of your life that you
cannot make them yourself as well as I. But, really,
what is the perversion of the sexual relation, which we
are deploring, but one of the manifestations of original
sin, or whatever you heretics may choose to call the in-

born disposition of humanity to do wrong whenever it has a chance. We steal, we cheat, we defraud, we kill, because we are bad. We are a bad lot, my boy, and I regret to say I see no promise of our improving. The faults of society are the faults of the souls and consciences belonging to the men and women who make up society. The relations of husbands to their wives, or of wives to their husbands, are so unsatisfying, so disappointing, because men and women do not cease to be men and women and become angels when they marry. Marriage is no more, as it is no less a failure than the other relations of mankind. Marriage is a failure because human nature is a failure."

"But compare lovers before marriage with the married men and women. Indeed, the very word 'lovers' is almost exclusively appropriated for the ante-nuptial period. The lover is what a man and woman might always be in relation to each other. The average marriage illustrates what they should not be."

"Carry your comparison a little farther, my dear Harry. Examine your lover at the beginning and at the end of a long engagement. He soon ceases his unselfish devotion, and exchanges his adoring attitude for one of familiar, and half-contemptuous criticism."

"Of course what is true of the married state is true of long engagements. The latter unite all the restraints with none of the consolations of marriage. But I think that there are just enough exceptions to the rule of cooling lovers, and estranged husbands and wives, to prove that it may be because the relations of the sexes are distorted that they yield so little harmony, that men and women might be to each other after marriage what lovers now dream, if —— if ——"

"If we were all angels or saints," interrupted Ward.

Then he turned half around in his chair so that he could see the table where the two gentlemen who had lately entered were sitting. "They are just finishing a Welsh rare-bit. Suppose we ask Bevan to bring his

friend over here. Four heads are better than two, and
this is a hard task we are essaying to-night."

Vinton nodded his head in assent, and Ward crossed
over to the table where Mr. Bevan and the stranger
were sitting. Vinton saw Ward bow to the stranger,
who rose from his chair with great cordiality in response to the introduction. Then the three gentlemen,
followed by the waiter with pencil and wine-card, approached the table in the corner where three vacant
chairs and one ready tongue awaited them.

For a few minutes after the addition to the party
in the corner the conversation was strictly conventional. It was of course first necessary to make Vinton
acquainted with Mr. Bevan's companion, a man of
about thirty, tall, and distinguished in bearing, and
graceful in manner. He was introduced as a dealer in
California grapes and wines, a frequent visitor to New
York, where he came to dispose of enormous quantities of those toothsome articles of merchandise.

"My friend Gillette," began Mr. Bevan, as the
waiter filled the four glasses with California Moselle,
ordered out of special compliment to the visitor —
" My friend Gillette's grapes might have been grown in
one vineyard, and his wines have come from one cellar,
they run so remarkably alike. But of course there is
no single producer who could have such an enormous
output to offer for sale. He is a very mysterious fellow, is my friend Gillette, and I understand no more
about him now than I did three years ago, when I
bought my first lot of him. It was only a tenth as
large as the invoice I took to-day, eh Gillette?"

"Next year I hope to have twice as much to sell
you. But why talk business longer?" And Gillette
cast an apologetic glance at the two gentlemen to
whom he had just been introduced. "You and I
have made our bargain, and, what is very rare in this
selfish city, are both satisfied. Why annoy these
gentlemen with our mercenary dealings?"

"I assure you," interposed Vinton with his peculiarly magnetic smile, "if there is any mystery likely to be solved there is nothing could please my friend Ward and myself more."

"Now, Gillette, is a golden opportunity for you," said Mr. Bevan. "Reveal your mystery. Do you know I always suspected you of being the dictator of some little realm in an unknown corner of our wild West, where grapes grow for the asking, and whose people work for love of you."

"If you had said for love of each other," remarked Gillette, with a peculiar inflection, "you would have better described it — that is, have better described a model state of society." Then in a sudden change of voice, "but I positively decline to constitute myself the hero of this conversation. Didn't Mr. Ward say, as he invited us to join you, that help was wanted to settle some very abstruse question?"

"We were discussing the relations of the sexes," remarked Vinton, after a short pause. Then he lifted his sparkling glass. His companions imitated him, and then waited before tasting the wine until the young man should offer the expected toast. "Here is to woman, who might be the greatest force for good and happiness." The four glasses were drained and set down as Vinton added: "But is not."

"How far have you progressed?" asked Gillette, leaning across the table with very noticeable interest. Then with a keen glance from Vinton to Ward, he added: "I am under the impression you did not come very near agreeing."

Bevan laughed. "You will have to look out for my friend Gillette. He's a great guesser, an intuitist."

Ward waited an instant for Vinton to state their respective positions, but as the latter seemed in no haste to speak, volunteered the following:

"Vinton thinks married men and women should always be to each other as the same individuals when first lovers. I say that could only be expected if we were all angels, or at least saints."

"Very good, Ward," assented the younger man, with an appreciative look at his friend. "If you can analyze and state our several positions as well when the evening is over, you will deserve to be crowned with the laurel."

"Yes," said Gillette, "Mr. Ward has set Bevan and myself on the scratch with yourself. Now, how shall we get to work? Shall we all talk at once?"

"First, let James, here, fill our glasses," interposed Vinton. "James, where are you? That's right. Now please watch these glasses, James, and see that they are kept filled. We shall, all of us, be too much absorbed in thinking what we shall say next to notice our glasses. When this bottle is empty bring another, and so on."

"As to the method of the conversation," suggested Mr. Ward, "I must say I always like decency and good order. How would it be for each one, in turn, to state his views? This is a subject upon which every one has views. This part of the programme should be free from interruptions, except when James, here, makes us sign our names to the orders for more wine. Then, after each has had his turn, let there be all the cross-questioning desired, if the night is long enough."

"Good again," said Vinton, "and let Mr. Bevan begin. He is sure to be practical, and will doubtless set a healthy pace for us."

"And you," continued Ward, looking at Vinton, "for the sake of variety, you should come next. You may safely be trusted not to agree with Bevan. Then I will follow you with all the conservative force I can muster. The place of honor, the close, we will leave for our visitor from the land of grapes and wine. Let us drink once to Mr. Gillette and his domain, and then to business."

As the glasses were set down for the attention of

the faithful James, Mr. Bevan cleared his throat, and began : "As Ward says, every man can talk on the woman question. From the time we first notice the cropping of a beard on our chins until we return to our second childhood, we devote a good share of our thoughts to women, and sometimes so much of our talk that we are ashamed of it. I think the man shows himself the most sensible who keeps poetry and romance out of his head as much as possible, where women are concerned. The biggest fool in the world is the man who falls heels over head in love. Everybody laughs at him. Everybody ridicules him, and well they may. He is stark staring mad. Even the woman he worships usually joins in the general merrymaking at his expense. She cannot but see what an idiot her pretty face, or likely enough it is a homely one, has made of the young man. Young man indeed! Why an old lover is more of a spectacle than a young one. No time of life to be sure is safe from this acute attack of insanity, and repeated attacks come usually with increased virulence. The only consoling feature of the peculiar mental derangement called love is that its duration is very short. It is cured in various ways, but the best remedy of all is continued exposure to the contagious influence. Marriage will cure the most acute case in a very few weeks. If marriage is not a convenient or practical remedy, try familiarity. Give the patient the utmost possible intimacy with the object of his insane delusion. This is one of the few diseases, one of the very few mental disturbances, for which the doctors can safely warrant a complete cure or money refunded, always provided dose is taken as ordered."

Everybody laughed, Ward heartily, Vinton grudgingly.

Then Mr. Bevan, looking somewhat pleased at the success of his effort, continued in a somewhat different vein.

2

" But if we look in a cool and healthy state of mind, and, shall I add of body? at woman, there is no occasion for us to fret ourselves over the problem. For my part I don't see any problem. When a man marries a sensible woman of similar tastes to his own, and of congenial disposition, he has simply provided himself with a housekeeper and a mother to his children. He must not expect she will want him to sit at her feet and read poetry to her when he should be at his business, and she at her marketing. He mustn't expect she will keep on telling him what a classic profile he has, or that his voice thrills her as she hears him calling up the stairs that he would like to know what the confounded women in this house have done with his hat."

"This is blasphemy," interjected Vinton with an uneasy laugh.

"No interruptions," insisted Ward, and the speaker continued.

"I am afraid I am not discussing the woman question as philosophically as my company would like," suggested Mr. Bevan, moistening his lips with the wine. "If cheap talk like mine is out of place in the presence of this awful theme, just say so, somebody, and I will yield the floor."

"You're intensely practical," remarked Gillette in a tone that attracted a sharp look from Vinton; "from your standpoint, I mean. At this stage of the discussion nothing, I think, could be more helpful."

"Go ahead, by all means," added Ward, with an amused glance at Vinton's disgusted face.

"Well," continued Mr. Bevan, " I have not much more to say. Yet there is something so alluring about the subject that I believe I could drift on all night. A husband must not expect that his wife will like all his club friends or his club jokes. She will always prefer to talk gossip, or discuss servant girls, to politics or the money market. She will always enjoy shopping, which we abhor, elaborate dressing, which we hate, and all sorts of pomps and vanities which the well organized of the male sex despise. The more thoroughly a husband recovers from the false ideas and impossible expectations born and cultivated during that brief frenzy called courtship, the better he will enjoy his wife and his home after marriage. It seems to be the proper and the necessary thing for a man to fall in love, and go daft over the imaginary goddess concealed in woman. When a man, be he young or old, married or single, is in this condition, he is to be pitied, not to be maliciously scoffed at or ridiculed, for he is sensitive, and on other subjects comparatively sane. Besides, no human being is safe from similar attacks, and the scoffer of to-day is liable to be the scoffed at of to-morrow. A man in this condition — and doubtless a woman in love is just as foolish — is likely enough to sacrifice position, fame, honor, duty, independence, every thing to his frenzy. Let us make allowances for the acts of the madman, throw a cloak over his sins. But certainly, gentlemen, there is no good reason why we should believe him when he claims that it is he who is sane, and the rest of us who are beside ourselves. Surely there is no sense in listening to his erotic ravings and maudlin rhapsodies as the true revelation as to what men and women can be and should be to each other. Bevan has spoken.''

There was silence for a moment as Mr. Bevan drained his glass, and watched James replenish it. Then Gillette remarked quite seriously: ''You are actually a worse Philistine even than I suspected. You ought to be preserved in alcohol, a curious specimen of nineteenth century civilization.''

Vinton watched Gillette with great interest as he made the remark. Ward glanced at the clock which stood over the fireplace just behind Mr. Bevan, and suddenly exclaimed: ''It is growing late. We must not waste a minute. It is your turn next, Vinton. Answer the reviler.''

Vinton waited for no second prompting, but rushed
into the subject in his own impetuous, almost impatient
fashion.   " I am glad Bevan spoke first.   He has saved
me the trouble of describing the prevailing scepticism
as to the scope and meaning of love.   He is a living,
breathing example of the shocking degradation which
the sexual ideal has reached."

# CHAPTER II.

"Our friend Bevan," continued Vinton, "is no worse than the average man. What he says about woman, the average man would say if he could express himself as well. The attitude of Bevan toward the sex is that of the average man, responded to in kind by most women. These are the facts which make the problem so serious. Society is overwhelmed with despair. Marriage is described as a lottery, love as a delusion. But I do not for a minute believe that harmonious and ennobling relations between the sexes have ceased to be possible. I believe there is such a thing as an ideal marriage. I have seen many instances of it. So must you all. I have seen husbands, who, after ten years of married life, were as much lovers as the hour they were accepted; wives to whose adoring eyes their husbands continued to be perfection; husbands and wives whose hearts always glowed at the approach of each other, whose whole natures seemed ever stimulated into their highest attributes in each other's presence. Such husbands and wives live ideal lives. Suffering and pain but serve to drive them closer to each other's arms, sorrows to teach them the rare sweetness of giving and receiving perfect consolation, misfortunes to offer complete conviction of the blessedness and all sufficiency of love. These instances are exceptional, but they prove conclusively how glorifying, how ennobling the relations of the sexes may be. It is just such a perfect relation each ardent pair of lovers expects. The failures of countless thousands go for nothing to them. They have perfect faith that their love

is purer and more eternal than that of others, that the
fond dreams of their hearts will be fulfilled, and their
married life prove an earthly paradise. Poor fools, we
say, and we watch their ardors waning with their honeymoon, we overhear their first cross words, notice the
silence that befalls when they are alone, in place of the
eager flood of talk of earlier days, the small rudenesses
and petty neglects growing more frequent with time,
the thousand signs of weariness and lack of mutual
sympathy and good will. They too have drawn blanks.
They both mean well. They both are miserable over
the wreck of their hopes of marital felicity. Nothing
would so win their gratitude as to tell them some
method to regain the elusive passion which promised to
make their two lives a pathway of flowers. A whole
school of writers wins its bread by preaching to disappointed husbands and wives, by dispensing maxims
which, if faithfully followed, will, it is claimed, coax back
the erring Cupid to gild their lives with poetry and
romance once more. But they might as well attempt to
warm into new life the body of a drowned man, to make
the cold charcoal left from yesterday's fire glow and
crackle of itself. These disappointed husbands and wives
have made dreadful mistakes, and must suffer for them
the rest of their lives. They will doubtless patch up some
new and commonplace relation of companionship, of
friendship, of partnership, but they can no more fall in
love with each other again, than they could keep so by
main force. Yet they will commonly keep up the man-
nerisms of lovers, call each other pet names, but alas, in
very matter-of-fact tones of voice, kiss each other at
meeting and parting, but what a travesty on the kiss
of love which once they exchanged."

Vinton paused for a moment, and swallowed half a
glass of wine. A peculiar solemnity had taken the
place of the merriment evoked by Mr. Bevan's little
statement of creed. Ward seemed loath to have his
friend leave the theme where it was, and inquired :

"Which do you blame, the man or the woman?"
Vinton finished his glass before replying.
"Blame for what? Because their marriage is a
failure? Why, I tell you either of them would have
been willing to give an arm if the lover's dream might
be realized for them in married life. Their vision,
however, refuses to materialize. Blame them, indeed!
They have their punishment whether they deserved
one or not. Their feelings are such as an epicure
might have, if a basket of the rarest grapes from Mr.
Gillette's vineyard were first placed before him so he
should take their perfume and his appetite be excited,
then just as he reached forth his hand to carry a cluster
of the luscious beauties to his mouth, basket and all
should be caught forever away. The epicure is not to
blame. From the perfume and appearance of the
grapes he might well count on a perfect feast. But
the basket was not for him. Those lovers who find
marriage a failure, and, accordingly, life itself pretty
nearly one, were not so mistaken in their lofty ideas of
what marriage might be. Their mistake is in their
choice. The poets tell us there is some one woman
fitted to be the perfect mate for eacu man. Very
likely there are many women in the world adapted to
make any man happy and to be made happy by him.
Marriage is so generally a failure, and the sexual relation as a force for progress and education so generally
perverted to be merely an excitant of base passions and
degrading lusts, because those who could make each
other true husbands and wives seldom, according to
the inexorable law of chances, meet under circumstances
to recognize each other."

Mr. Ward did not wait to be informed that his turn
had come, but began as follows: "Bevan and Vinton
agree as to one of their conclusions, and I cannot do
better than agree with both disputants that married
people generally cease to be lovers. Bevan thinks
this is a proper and natural course of affairs, and that

love is a sort of emotional insanity. I cannot agree
with him in this. Vinton thinks that marriage is so
generally a failure because the right people commonly
fail to marry each other. Here I cannot agree with
him. I do not say that every married man and woman
can be expected to continue lovers. There are numerous cases of utter incompatibility which necessarily result in making husband and wife a constant annoyance
to each other. But I believe that the man and woman,
who, after a reasonable acquaintance and courtship, decide to marry, convinced that they can make each other
happy, are very able to fulfill those expectations, always
provided that they show decent common sense and
proper unselfishness. The follies committed by the
young husband and wife during the first few months
of married life pass common credence. It is not so
much a wonder that they often lose their love and sentiment for each other, as that there are cases where
they always continue lovers. If we have a friend whom
we are very anxious to keep, we are a thousand times
more considerate and careful in our demeanor toward
him than the average husband is in his behavior toward
a newly-wedded wife. The manner of the young husband to his bride is a queer compound of fatuous confidence and insulting distrust. He wants her to continue to be as devoted, as reverent as in those first
dreamy days after their betrothal. But, himself, he in-
dulges in selfish weaknesses to which he never gave
way before. He treats the woman he has married as
if she were his slave, and her bondage perpetual, so
that he need no longer care to show himself at his
best. He is more like a spoiled child than a fully-
grown and disciplined man, to whom are offered new
possibilities of sympathy, appreciation, and inspiration
to a higher life. When a woman shows disappointment at the change in him whom she had thought so
god-like as her lover, he forgets his own faults, and
convinces himself that she does not love him. His

heart is filled with bitterness and despair. I used the case when the husband is the thoughtless, inconsiderate one, and the wife is the sufferer. Just as often it is the husband who is the sufferer, and the wife who ceases to be adorable. Usually both are guilty and both are sufferers. Their faults act and re-act until another marriage has become a palpable failure. As lovers they call forth what is best in each other, disclose hidden virtues, stimulate unguessed powers, undreamed. of graces. Neither may have seemed especially admirable to the world in general. It is only to the other that each one yields sweetness and light. To each other, as lovers, they are really adorable. The sudden fruition of marriage it is which seems to have changed every thing. For a few days they riot in each other's expanding natures. The whole of their lives might be the same, but on condition that both should continue to give forth only their best, that both should suppress the base, the selfish, the ignoble. They should at once educate and enjoy each other. Sexual love should be the great religious force of our existence. As Vinton says, we all of us know instances where love is all I describe to the happy married man and woman who have not been blind to its possibilities. The average human nature is not, however, fine and strong enough to endure the strain of continuing the lover attitude through life. A few weeks, with occasional lapses at that, mark the capacity of the ordinary man and woman for that ideal relation of the sexes which brings out all that is best and most satisfying in each other. When the tension is released the groveling tendency of mankind shows itself. Marriage is a failure because the man and woman nature is as yet incapable of the sustained elevation of character which comes at the beginning of sexual love, and, alas, usually goes with it."

Bevan rose suddenly to his feet, watch in hand. "It is twelve o'clock and I must positively leave you. I would like to sit here and discuss this subject all night, but I can't do it."

"I see the steward is eyeing us somewhat uneasily," exclaimed Vinton, pushing back his chair. "He apparently wants to sleep, however we may feel. To hear Mr. Gillette's views we must go elsewhere."

"Don't let me put you to so much trouble, gentlemen," urged Gillette with a pleasant smile. "Let me tell my story at my next visit to New York." By this time all the gentlemen had risen, and the steward's countenance lost its melancholy expression as they moved slowly toward the door. Bevan and Vinton were in advance, Ward and Gillette behind.

Ward laid his hand lightly on his companion's arm. "We haven't the least idea of letting you off, Mr. Gillette. I speak for Vinton and myself. Bevan there is a man of business, and social delights are mere by-play to him. Vinton, on the other hand, is a literary man, a writer of novels. To him a new idea is treasure-trove. He would willingly turn night into day for a week, if he might find one suggestion such as a man like you, with different associations from ours, will be sure to give. As for myself I am a professional idler, a searcher into all sorts of unanswerable questions, any thing to make me forget I am not busy. You can't escape us."

"But Bevan says he is going home," laughed Gillette, as he put on his tall hat, just recovered from the sleepy check clerk.

"He takes the 'elevated' at the second corner from here. Suppose we walk to the station with him, and send him home, in the pleasing but erroneous notion that he has done his whole duty. Then for some quiet 'always open' beer saloon, and the extraction of your ideas on the woman question."

Bevan and Vinton were close at hand by the time Ward had made his proposal to the visitor from the West, and so the latter had no opportunity to reply.

But he permitted Ward and Bevan to lead the way to the elevated railroad station, although his hotel lay in the opposite direction, and when Bevan had been sent steaming up-town, with a light conscience and a sense of duty performed, Mr. Gillette turned to Vinton and said·

"Your friend has betrayed you into a scrape, Mr. Vinton. He insists that you, as well as he, would like to hear my ideas on the sexual relation."

"Delightful," exclaimed Vinton with unmistakable enthusiasm. "I suspected what Bevan would say on the subject, I knew what my friend Ward would say. But you will introduce a new element into the discussion. You will say something we have not thought of. Where shall we go, Ward?"

"Excuse me," interposed Gillette before Ward could reply. "New York streets have not lost their interest for me. If you do not very much care to go inside, what do you say to walking as we talk? The streets are 'always open' too, you know."

"Let me be the pilot," said Vinton. "I am a great lover of the streets of New York. Instead of wearying me it seems as if they excited me more and more. The intensity of the life that throbs in the very air here is positive pain sometimes. But it thrills me. It gives me sensations. It breeds an endless succession of thoughts and of sympathies."

So Vinton took Gillette's right arm, and Ward his left. They then started on a walk fated to have very momentous consequences to the two gentlemen of New York.

"From what you two gentlemen have said I see that you believe what I have come to know! That is, that one of the greatest blessings in life, if not the greatest of all blessings, is sexual love. You are unhappy over the rarity of the lover in married life, causing the so common failure of marriage and the home, in this the most polished age of modern civilization and of human progress. Bevan is an unbeliever in the scope and office of this love. The modern man of the world has grown to believe that woman can only serve a man by gratifying his lusts; that love is nothing but desire for physical pleasure, and once sated dies as a matter of course. But I can see that you believe as I do, that in this love the soul finds its best expression, its religion; the mind, its best stimulus; the spirit, our real inner self, its wings. You believe this from your memory of love's young dream, its glory, its sacredness, its marvelous expanding power. When the lovers have found what should be fruition in marriage, you have seen them for the most part cease to be lovers. Yet you have faith; I believe because I have seen."

Gillette paused for an instant, and Vinton exclaimed: "You mean you have seen cases of married lovers whose passion, if you may call it so, increased with increase of years; who were eternal joys to each other, as well as inspirations. So have I, so has Ward."

"I mean more than that," answered Gillette, slowly. He seemed hesitating whether he should go further. But he continued: "I know a spot where marriage is all that it ought to be here. It is a lovers' paradise. I am willing to tell you about it if you wish it."

To say that Ward and Vinton were taken aback by this bold statement from their new acquaintance was a feeble expression. Was the man so much affected by the wine? Ward recovered his presence of mind first.

"A fancy sketch, I suppose. By all means give it to us."

"No, but a real description of a real society," answered Gillette, not without some amusement at the apparent shock he had given his companions. "Mr. Bevan, you will remember, spoke of me as selling grapes and wine in large and yearly increasing quantities. I am the eastern selling agent of a settlement which we call Grape Valley. It is on no map, but a thousand men, beside women and children, live there an ideal life, because love has its perfect work. Our numbers are constantly increasing through our propaganda. So it is that we have more grapes and wine to sell each year. With the price of our products we buy in your markets such articles as our minds and bodies may need."

"A socialistic society, of course?" queried Ward with an assumed calmness.

"As you say, of course," replied Gillette. "You may well believe that if a social system be set up *de novo* as this was, the accumulated abuses of civilization, the burden of the misdeeds of centuries would not be shouldered. One for all and all for one, is our first maxim of political economy. All our children are educated in what are really common schools. Our men and women work a small portion of each day for an equal reward, and all have leisure enough for the pleasures and entertainments to which all have access."

After a silence of almost a minute, Ward found his voice again: "If you are not insane, Mr. Gillette, I know you are philosopher enough to excuse, under the circumstances, my brutal frankness. If you are insane, your delusion appears to be a pleasing one. I should like to hear you elaborate it. Vinton here probably would say so too, but he is almost in a state of mental collapse. Some of these literary men have extremely sensitive organizations, you must know. We are nearly at the City Hall now. Let us take the Brooklyn bridge, and, when we reach the highest point, seat ourselves on the benches which we shall find there and hear this matter out if it takes until morning."

The party was well upon the bridge when Vinton found his voice: "You must see, Mr. Gillette, that what you say is naturally very startling. I can see that my friend is inclined to doubt your good faith.

But in me please behold the most credulous man in the
world. I solemnly assure you I shall believe all that
you tell me.''

"Shall I describe our economical relations to you
in detail?" asked Gillette, as they began to climb the
steps once the scene of so awful a catastrophe?

"No there is not time," answered Vinton, beginning
to show symptoms of extreme nervous excitement.
"Besides, I am in a mood to hear of nothing but miracles to-night. It is quite a matter of course that a
settlement of sensible persons should decide not to live
under the economical conditions which curse so-called
civilization. But you say you have solved the sexual
problem in Grape Valley. We will try to understand
your new economical relations when you use that
luminous adjective 'socialistic.' Devote all your powers to explaining how your settlement has been made a
lovers' paradise.''

# CHAPTER III.

There was a bright moon, a clear sky, and the air was free of fog. The view on either side and down the harbor was impressive to the point of grandeur. The glistening water far beneath bore on its bosom ships from the ends of the earth, with thousands sleeping in their depths. To their left was Brooklyn, with its hundreds of thousands of sleeping creatures, to the right New York, Jersey City and Staten Island with their millions of dreamers. Only these three and nature seemed awake. Mr. Gillette could not have asked for more fitting surroundings while he should reveal the secrets of Grape Valley.

"It is the socialistic nature of our settlement which makes a reform in sexual relations possible. Our women are personally independent, as much so as our men. The woman earns with her own hands her equal share of the necessities and luxuries of Grape Valley. If she marries, it is, therefore, with no mixed motives, but for what she thinks pure love. If she finds she is mistaken, there are no questions of maintenance to be settled. She is as independent as your married heiress here with $100,000 in her own right. There is nothing but love to keep the husband and wife in Grape Valley together. The children? Yes, our women have children. Neither do they regard their advent with fears nor anxieties as to care and expense involved. Children in Grape Valley are the wards of the State. They are cared for at the general nursery and at the schools and colleges where their parents see, visit and enjoy them. There is nothing to prevent the affectionate father and mother from spending all their leisure with their children if they desire, but a burden, a restraint, an inconvenience, a consuming care, the children of Grape Valley can never be. But the woman does not have all her development stopped when she becomes a mother; she is not forced by imperious maternal duties to neglect to be her husband's sweetheart. Now let us see how our Grape Valley husbands and wives differ from those of your civilization; first, since the wife is pecuniarily independent they are not held together by a necessity for support on her side, nor by pity and consideration on his; second, the children are no tie to hold the parents together against their will, no common burden entailing common bondage. You tell me then that I have only described conditions which weaken the ties between husband and wife? I admit it. There should be no tie between man and woman which will confine them after they have ceased to love each other. Any thing less than love uniting husband and wife is bondage. Any other relation except that founded on absorbing and controlling passion is mutual slavery. The simple means we have adopted under our socialistic institutions in Grape Valley to make it a lovers' paradise is free divorce.

"When a husband or wife is so inclined whichever desires divorce separates from the other by a certain entry in our record office. Some of the States of the Union have very broad divorce laws, as you will remind me. According to the United States Constitution each State can make its own provisions on this subject. But you have not noticed that the States with the freest divorce laws are famous for their happy homes? Nor have I. Free divorce is the key to domestic felicity only when practiced under socialistic conditions such as prevail in Grape Valley. With us the assured possession which Mr. Ward speaks of as turning the heads of husbands and wives does not exist. The husband and wife in Grape Valley are always on probation. If they love one another they continually seek to endear themselves to each other. When one or the other discovers a mistake in choice has been made, there is a speedy means of correcting it. No husband or wife in Grape Valley makes the best of a spouse who cannot confer and inspire the profoundest love. All are capable of such love; in order to achieve happy lives and insure progressive souls, all should have it. In Grape Valley every thing is favorable to the enjoyment and cultivation of sexual love. Our day's labor is but half as long as yours, so that there is ample leisure for companionship. There are no anxieties in money matters or household cares and burdens more trying still to spoil the temper and mar the features. There is none of that sense of restraint which makes the bachelor of your civilization dread marriage so much, and the average Benedict regret his old freedom, even if he finds comfort in the domestic relation."

Gillette drew three cigars from his pocket, and handing one to each of his companions, lighted the third, and puffed at it as vigorously as if he were conscious of a good deal of lost time to make up. His companions evidently expected him to resume his story, and were so much interested as not to be willing to distract even so much of their attention as should be necessary to light a cigar.

"Aren't you going to smoke?" demanded Gillette after enduring their inquiring gaze as long as he thought possible.

"Bother the cigars," exclaimed Vinton impatiently. "Finish your description. Have you really achieved general connubial felicity in what you call Grape Valley?"

"Yes."

"But tell us," insisted Ward, "tell us how the women look and act. Is your whole colony more elevated in moral and intellectual tone, owing to your system?"

4

" Yes."

Vinton and Ward looked past their new friend, suddenly became monosyllabic, into each other's disappointed faces, and then both laughed at what they saw. In a minute more there were three cigars alight, and it was only after a very significant silence that Ward said calmly :

"I conclude you have told us all you mean to."

"I wouldn't put it so baldly as that," answered Gillette. "I have told you all you would believe."

"And if we want to know the rest?" inquired Vinton.

Gillette thought for a moment. Then he answered in a hearty tone : "In that case you must come and join us. I will take you back with me."

"I will go," exclaimed Vinton impetuously. But Ward with the conservatism of years kept silent. "It will be an experience worth all the time it takes," added Vinton, for the benefit of his friend.

"Excuse me," said Gillette, after a little pause. "I have apparently not made myself understood. I did not propose to take you with me to Grape Valley merely as curious students. Those who join us are enthusiastic converts, impatient with the farce of love as it is usually rendered under your social conditions, passionately eager to enjoy our new world."

Then Ward spoke : "Nothing would please me more than a visit to Grape Valley. But I am not ready to go to that bourne from which no traveler returns. I am not so far surfeited with the luxuries and amenities of this effete civilization, cursed with abuses, reeking with corruption as I acknowledge it is, to be willing to exchange it forever even for your lovers' paradise."

Vinton suddenly burst out with : "Can't you let us try your society — say for two years? Then if one or both of us still sigh for our dear old abuses let him, or us both as may happen, return?"

"Two years is a long time, Vinton," remarked Ward significantly.

"Two years a long time? Why, what are you thinking of, Ward? If in two years we can learn something really new, we ought to consider ourselves in rare luck. A new experience! A chance to study, from the inside, new social conditions! An opportunity to examine an attempt to solve that most fascinating and baffling of earthly problems, the true sexual relations! Why, bless your heart, Ward, isn't it worth five times two years of our idle and desultory lives?"

"Yes," answered Ward in a convinced tone, "you are right. I will give two years to Grape Valley if Mr. Gillette will accept such provisional devoteeship as that."

Gillette made no reply, and Vinton, throwing away his cigar, laid his hand persuasively on his new friend's arm.

"Try us, Mr. Gillette. You know our surroundings and education have made us sceptics. A sceptic is a variety of dead sea fruit of which our civilization is proudest you know. It is left for the ignorant, the unlettered, the inexperienced to believe. The flower of our culture doubts all things. So you must make allowances for us." he concluded, scoffing at himself.

Still Gillette made no answer, and Ward took up the argument.

"Naturally you do not care to reveal to the world at large the location of your settlement. I can understand that. A new crusade would be at once organized against you. The admirers of the system of society where marriage is usually a failure, where vice and shame are triumphant, would not rest satisfied or sleep o'nights, while one of your grape vines clung to its nourishing soil. But believe me, we would not betray the approaches to your Eden."

"Make your own terms," urged Vinton, with characteristic eagerness, "put all your vows upon us. We submit in advance to all your conditions."

"Yes," added Ward, "first put in all the possible appeals to our last remnant of honor. Then surround us with all the restrictions you can invent to make assurance doubly sure. Blindfold us if you choose."

Gillette slowly rose from his seat, and stood looking thoughtfully out upon the water. In the distance the giant arm of Bartholdi's statue held up her dim torch in vain hope of enlightening the world. The symbol perhaps touched him, and turned the scale of his determination.

"My conditions would have to be hard ones," he said at last. "You are, clearly enough, neither of you disciples. But still I believe I will run the risk of taking you with me, if, indeed, there is any risk, such conditions as I must impose being accepted."

"We accept them in advance," exclaimed Vinton. "As for discipleship, please count me in. I feel assured I shall not want to return to this poor world." And the young man actually snapped his fingers at the untold wealth and luxury of the magnificent cities that slept at his feet.

Gillette smiled at the enthusiasm of his new friend, and then began to state his conditions. "First, when we reach Topeka, Kansas, some excuse must be invented for blindfolding you both, and sealing your ears. You must consent to do without two of your senses for something more than a week."

"Agreed," exclaimed Vinton; and Gillette continued:

"Then when the time of your novitiate has expired, if either of you decide to leave us, he must be similarly blindfolded and deafened until his return to Topeka is accomplished."

"Agreed." And this time Ward joined Vinton in the exclamation.

"Now for the moral restraints," continued Gillette.

"I need not explain how disastrous notoriety would be to our settlement. We should die a double death. The influx, too rapid for humanizing and elevating influences, of the vulgar crowd, would overwhelm our institutions and debase them. The bigots would arouse governments against us, and statutes would either be discovered, or quickly enacted for our extinction. You must each of you promise on your honor not to seek to know the geographical location of Grape Valley, either while there or after leaving."

"I promise," said Ward.

"I promise," echoed Vinton.

"When can we start?" asked Gillette in a more matter of fact tone. "My business is completed here. I would like to set out to return day after to-morrow, but this will probably be too short notice for you."

"Not for me," answered Ward, rising to his feet. "No one has any claims on me. I have only a few money matters to settle, and I am ready. That reminds me; it will, of course, be necessary for us to take a considerable amount of money with us."

Gillette laughed. "Apparently, my dear Mr. Ward, you are not erudite in matters socialistic. Your money would not be current in Grape Valley. But your labor and brains will doubtless be of value to the State, sufficient for your board, lodging and clothes. Take enough money with you for traveling expenses — say $200 each. That will be more than enough." Then turning to Vinton, "Can you, too, be ready to start day after to-morrow?"

Vinton laughed with some bitterness. "I don't know what preparations I have to make," he said, "unless it were a last farewell visit to the woman who jilted me for another man's millions. Very likely she would enjoy the sensation of another parting. She is quite an epicure in the way of sensations." Then he rose suddenly to his feet and said in a more genial tone: "Certainly, I will be ready." And the three men once more joined arms and retraced their steps across the silent bridge.

In another hour, after making an appointment to meet at Gillette's hotel, the Fifth Avenue, at nine o'clock the next morning but one, they had parted. They were all in bed, if not asleep, by the time the first carts with country produce began to rumble over the drowsy streets.

## Editorial Note.

It was not much after the middle of the next day that Ward and Vinton made their appearance, as they had often done before, in the editorial room of the daily paper with which I have been for many years connected. I was just putting the finishing touches to a leader entitled ' The Growing Frequency of Divorce." I was not a little proud of my effort, and proposed to take advantage of my intimate relations with my visitors to read them the article. " It is not long," I said, clearing my throat.

"Don't do it," exclaimed Vinton. "We have n't a moment to spare, and have enough to say to you to fill a book."

"Forgive us this time," pleaded Ward, satirically, as he saw a disgusted look come over my face. " Put on your hat and lunch with us at Delmonico's. Don't be sulky now. There isn't any time to waste. Vinton is right."

In half an hour we were seated in a private room in Delmonico's, ordered by Mr. Ward with perfect disregard of expense, and were enjoying what he was pleased to call a lunch, but a more royal dinner I had never sat down to. My friends did not at first tell me what they had for me to do. They were conscientious enough not to be guilty of distracting my attention from the rare viands, of which, indeed, they too partook as if in apprehension that it might be long before they had such another opportunity. It was only after the remnants of the feast had been removed and our cigars had been lighted that the waiter was told to leave the room, and I saw that the mystery of the banquet in the private room, which had been given in my honor, was about to be solved. Of course not even for a moment had I suffered myself to entertain the idea that the dinner was intended merely as a tribute to my long unappreciated virtues or talents, so I very calmly prepared to listen to what my friends had to impart. Then first one and then the other attempted to tell me of the strange conversation of the night before and its stranger outcome. What Vinton forgot, Ward supplied. So with numberless interruptions and frequent changes of point of view I was finally placed in possession of every thing said and done by Mr. Gillette, Mr. Bevan and my two friends, from ten o'clock last evening until they went to bed very early this morning. It made no difference what arguments, drawn from a broad and practical experience, I offered to dissuade them from what I called a crazy adventure. They simply laughed at my labored worldly wisdom, as they called it. Just before they shook my hand at parting, Vinton said :

"What we particularly want of you is to write up all we have told you, using imaginary names of course, and to do it at once, before you forget the details. You may never hear from either of us again. In that case we want to have what we have already told you put before the public in some shape. Give whatever title you choose to your report. Call it ' A Mysterious Disappearance' if you can think of no better title. But have it published without fail. It might do for a magazine article. Use your own judgment about that. Of course you can add as a foot-note whatever explanation you choose to offer of your part in the literary work. Yet I hope within the two years that I may be able to get into your hands some sort of a description of our actual experiences and observations in Grape Valley itself. I mean to keep a full record of all that is interesting to me, with a view to sending it to you some time. If that sketch, or whatever you may please to call it, comes·by any means into your hands, you can use what we have just given you as an introduction, you know, and publish the whole together. We want the world to get the benefit of our experience."

Of course I agreed, and the foregoing pages were written and laid away among my private papers. Shortly before the expiration of two years a thick package, addressed to me in Vinton's handwriting, was placed in my hands by a district messenger boy. Perhaps I can do no better than to let the contents of that envelope occupy the rest of the volume now ready for the printers.—[EDITOR.

# CHAPTER IV.

It was only after leaving Topeka that Gillette insisted on the use of the precautions to which Ward and I had agreed in advance. The explanation given for the benefit of the curious was that my friend Ward and I had undergone serious surgical operations upon our eyes, and were now on our way, in the charge of attendants, to our southwestern home. Inquirers were informed that the eminent Chicago specialist who performed the delicate operation had positively enjoined upon our guides that under no circumstances must we be excited by conversation. Hence it was, Gillette explained, that he had put cotton in our ears. Doubtless the expressions of sympathy for our luckless condition were numberless. Poor Gillette must have been tormented nearly to the point of insanity by pitiful woman, whose heart, careless of latitude and longitude, ever melts for the unfortunate. But we, of course, were unconscious of every thing that the two most important of our senses could have told us, and only knew that we traveled night and day, whether north, south, east or west, we could not guess; we could not even exchange impressions.

For a day and a night more we went by rail. Then there were several days' journey in wagons, and several more on horseback. It was a strange experience to me, at first extremely trying to bear, but I do not know as I regret having passed through it. At first my self-consciousness seemed intensified almost to the point of pain. All the faculties of observation, deprived of their ordinary employment, seemed turned

5

inward. I could almost see my mental operations. It was as if I discerned the dual man, myself and my self-consciousness, the spirit as something apart from the body. Then my body became of infinitely small importance to me. I became conscious of a better, a fuller, a less sordid life apart from the physical.

I was in no haste to have my eyes unbandaged, and my ears unsealed. Indeed, my first emotion as I felt some one trying to untie the handkerchief from about my head was one of impatience. I should have preferred to have been left alone with myself. It was as if profane steps had approached the shrine where I was rapt in devotion. But in a moment I felt my eyes uncovered and the bright light shining on their unwonted lids. I put my hand over them to relieve the pain, and as I did so the cotton was removed from my ears, and the sound of running water was the first that I heard. Then came Gillette's voice saying:

"Your pilgrimage is nearly over."

Then my curiosity overcame my fear of the dazzling light, and, shading my eyes with my hand, I looked around. In front of me, from almost at my very feet rose the lofty walls of a mountain, over whose heights the sun was just passing. I had never conceived, until that instant, how intensely brilliant is mere light, what a force there is in it. It was as if a keen knife pierced to my very brain.

At my side stood Ward, leaning against the horse from which he had just dismounted, and shading his dazzled eyes as I was shading mine. In that first look, too, I noticed that my friend's face had aged perceptibly since I last looked into it, and a quick sense of regret that I had ever taken him from his comforts flashed through me. On my other side stood Gillette, regarding us with an expectant smile, and just behind him a stranger.

"This is Mr. Barlow," said Gillette. "He joined us at Topeka."

" And this is Grape Valley ? " asked Ward, as his eyes becoming used to the light, he let them slowly skirt the whole horizon. My eyes followed his, and this is what I saw: in the distance a treeless prairie changing into a rolling country, then into hills, and at last into the elevated plateau on which, and at the base of the steep inaccessible acclivity of a mountain side, we now stood. At the very edge of the mountain rushed a roaring torrent, foaming in its haste to plunge, as it seemed to do almost at our feet, into the bosom of the solid rock.

" Is this Grape Valley ? " I repeated in a tone out of which I could not, with all my will force, keep an inflection of disappointment and reproach. There was no sign of human habitation in view except one small house and its barn. Where were Gillette's thousand men besides women and children ? But if this were not our destination where could it be ? Not far off, certainly, since all precautions had been abandoned and we were now permitted the free use of our eyes and ears. Yet what valley could there be to the south where the mountain range reared its bristling peaks until their outlines became dim in the distance ? Our course certainly could not be to the north or west, where the prairies stretched out as far as we could see. Could it be possible Gillette had played this profound practical joke on us, that he had rightly seen in us a pair of hare-brained enthusiasts, and perhaps in conspiracy with Bevan, had arranged for this stupendous farce ? Now that he had literally brought us up against a stone wall he would doubtless burst into loud and uncontrollable guffaws of laughter. Well it was not a bad joke on us. How New York would ring with it ! It would never do for Ward and me to live in the metropolis again. So much was certain.

Then another and even less agreeable possibility struck me. Perhaps this was a scheme of Gillette's to plunder us. What a magnificent confidence game it

was, if so; to persuade two wealthy New York men of
the world to travel thousands of miles, a part of the
distance blindfolded, by cars, by wagon and horseback,
under the guidance of an almost total stranger in search
of a will o' the wisp, a socialistic colony. How easy
it would be, now that we were disarmed, lost and without hope of a possibility of escape or of rescue, for our
guide to make his own terms for our ransom. I clap-
ped my hands suddenly to my side and found a pair
of pistols in my belt. There was of course no chance
that they were loaded. Doubtless they had been hung
at my belt only as a part of the trick. Lifting my
eyes to Gillette I saw he had seen my movement
toward the pistols. He suddenly burst into a laugh
like a school boy.

"What awful thoughts are you revolving, my dear
fellow?" he asked. "You think there is no Grape
Valley?"

"Where can it be if there is such a place?" demanded Ward, a very ugly expression coming over a
face I had never seen disturbed before. "It surely is
not there?" and he pointed to the north.

"No."

"Nor there?" and Ward moved his extended arm
so that his finger indicated the east.

"Nor there?" as he pointed to the south.

"No," answered Gillette, apparently enjoying our
ill temper, the full meaning of which, perhaps, he did
not grasp.

"And it surely is not there?" Ward snapped his
finger incredulously at the steep mountain side. "So
you must have —— "

"But it is just there," interrupted Gillette, pointing at the mountain, "and in two hours we can be in
Grape Valley. That is, all of us but our friend Barlow. His place is without."

Ward gave Gillette a disgusted look, but said no
more. He apparently believed as I did, that our guide

was telling us an untruth. Indeed, the impossibility of scaling the mountain seemed self-evident. Its sides were almost as perpendicular as a wall. But since Gillette's humor had not had its bent, as yet, we seemed to have no recourse but to fall in with it. The time for remedy had passed some days since. Our plight could be no worse for following Gillette's directions somewhat longer.

"Come with us, gentlemen," said Gillette, and leading our horses we advanced toward the point where the swollen stream seemed to plunge into the very side of the mountain. It was not until we reached the edge of the stream that I noticed a cleft in the rocky wall wide enough to admit the roaring torrent, but as far as I could see, the mountain closed up again, leaving no gorge unless it were a subterranean one.

"That is our course," said Gillette, pointing after the foaming stream. "That river leads to Grape Valley."

I confess I was too much astonished to think of a fitting reply. But my friend Ward was seldom taken at such a disadvantage.

"It looks inviting," he answered, "but I do not see your boat for the trip to the infernal regions. You surely will not ask us to swim there."

Before answering us, Gillette directed Barlow to take the horses to his stable for rest and food, and as the man led away our tired beasts, we followed them with uneasy glances. It seemed as if our condition now became more helpless than ever.

"Your eyes deceive you," said Gillette, "if they lead you to suppose that Rapid river takes a subterranean course, or that there is no roadway through these mountains. The gorge through which that torrent flows winds between the mountains with frequent twists and turns, coming out into a very pretty and well-protected valley. Where a stream can go, we can go."

"But not at the same time," retorted Ward, keenly.

"No," laughed Gillette. "You are right, not at the same time. First, we will put out this very uncompanionable stream, and then travel the road by ourselves in peace and safety."

Ward took a side look at me as if to see how this strange talk of our guide affected me. But he made no reply. The climax of the situation could not be long postponed.

By this time Barlow had rejoined us, and Gillette, warning us to keep close by his side, stepped along to the point where the river turned from its southerly course and took the greater descent to the west. They seemed searching for something, and soon lifted up a temporary bridge made of light wood and leather, which, being thrown over the stream, Barlow crossed.

Ward and I had by this time recovered our interest in the situation, and were watching the mysterious proceedings of Gillette and his assistant with the intensest curiosity.

"Are they crazy?" demanded Ward in a low tone. "Both of them? Or are we?"

I had no time to make answer, for Gillette beckoned us to come closer still to his side, and forgetting our sullenness of a moment or two since, we obeyed with alacrity. As we followed the sharp turn of the stream I noticed that we were stepping over the gravel bottom of a former river bed, which ran to the south, skirting instead of entering the mountain range. Rapid river, or perhaps a branch of it, may in time of spring freshets have once taken that course. If the river were to take that course now instead of running to the west and through the mountains, it was plain enough the gorge would be left free for us. Perhaps Gillette was not so crazy after all. But no sooner had the idea formed itself in my mind, than it was realized. Barlow had raised some sort of a gate on the opposite side of the stream, and a solid and water-tight dam, running apparently in grooves at the bottom, was shot across Rapid river. The course of the torrent was suddenly changed from a westerly to a southerly direction; our retreat was now cut off, but the gorge through the range of mountains was ready for the astonished travelers.

"Our promenade is prepared," said Gillette, enjoying the surprise he had given us. Then he turned to Barlow: "How long a time do you allow for the walk down the cañon and into the valley?"

"Two hours is more than enough," answered Barlow. "But let us compare watches to make sure there is no disagreement in time."

These precautions were certainly suggestive of very possible dangers, and gave Ward and me some uneasiness. I, for one, was much relieved when Gillette said:

"Well, you say two hours is ample for us to make the trip; now, if you do not pull up the dam for three hours, we shall certainly have a good deal more than ample time. It is now two o'clock." Ward and I drew out our watches and set the hands to Gillette's time, as he continued: "Let the water on at five. That will be safe enough surely."

"Safe!" echoed Barlow. "I should think so; if you are not out of the gorge in three hours, you never will be."

# CHAPTER V.

With this somewhat ominous remark of Barlow's echoing in our ears, Gillette, Ward and I set out on our peculiar journey down the bed of the stream, which had given place to us, as our guide had promised. For a dozen rods the stream had run due west, then suddenly the mountains seemed cleft again, and between two towering walls of frowning rock, Rapid river had rushed north for twice that distance. Then a westerly course was resumed, and the awful walls of rock drew back, so that for a while our surroundings were less fearful.

Perhaps it was to give Ward and me an opportunity for a brief exchange of opinions and reflections that Gillette just now put a few rods between himself and us. At any rate we were not slow to avail ourselves of the precious privilege.

"My faith in the reality of Grape Valley is restored," said Ward. "As for its being a lovers' paradise my infidelity is unchanged, however. It is human nature which renders such a thing impossible. Mere difference in latitude and longitude cannot achieve miracles."

"But," I answered, "human nature develops very diversely, according to conditions and surroundings. Most of our criminals, I suppose every one admits, are made such by circumstances."

"Still," he continued, "I cannot believe that your friend Gillette and his company can have discovered or created conditions under which lovers cease to grow cold, and passion no longer changes to indifference or revulsion."

"If I understand Gillette," I said, "he admits the disease but offers a cure for it. His panacea is the removal of restrictions which in our society bind together those who have discovered themselves mismated. But since we are within two hours' walk of Grape Valley I am willing to entirely suspend judgment upon its institutions until we behold them in operation."

At this point in our conversation, the bed of the stream which we were following took another turn, this time to the south, and once more our surroundings were, to say the least, portentous. Beneath our feet was a thin coating of alluvial soil and pebbles, while occasionally the edge of primeval rock jutted out, over which the torrent, which a few minutes before poured where we were now walking, must have foamed and roared magnificently. The bed of the stream was, however, in this place, and wherever the mountains came close together, chiefly rock, shaped into a trough, the sides, polished by the water, inclining inward so that the level space, on which we found our path, was very narrow, sometimes not wide enough for two to walk abreast. On the glistening face of the mountain, at either side, we could see the mark left by the stream turned, but a few moments since, from its ancient course, for our accommodation. In many places this water mark was considerably above our heads. In others where the cañon was somewhat wider, the wet line along the rock was not higher than our waists. Gillette, having given us, as he thought, sufficient time to exchange confidences, now waited for us to overtake him.

"We are doing finely," he said, as he glanced at his watch. "We are one-third of the way into the valley, and have only used up a sixth part of our allotted three hours."

6

Ward and I looked at our watches and found it was half-past two.

"Mr. Barlow was to raise the gates at five, I believe," remarked Ward. "Have you any idea how long it would take the torrent to overtake us, if we should loiter past the appointed hour and minute?"

"Don't breathe such a thought," I exclaimed, looking fearfully at the steep walls of the cañon which, at this point, rose a thousand feet without a break. "Why, if the water overtook us here, there would be no possible escape for us. It is as hopeless a death-trap as I ever saw."

"Never fear," responded Gillette. "We shall have been out of this cañon a full hour before Rapid river flows in its bed again. Barlow is absolutely to be depended upon. I would stake my life that he would not raise the gates one second before the appointed time. Please remember, too, that I made the time a full hour more than it ever takes to make the trip."

"How far is it from start to finish?" I asked.

"A trifle less than seven miles."

"Now," suggested Ward, sarcastic as ever, "perhaps my sensitive young friend will permit you to answer my question."

"As to the speed of Rapid river you mean?" asked Gillette.

"The name of the stream is rather significant," I again interrupted. "Too much so, I don't like it."

"Well," continued Gillette, "it takes the river just seven minutes to make the run from the gate where Barlow stands to the valley. I estimate we are now a third of the distance through the cañon. It would take the water a little less than two minutes and a half to overtake us here."

"A pleasing thought," commented Ward, quickening his pace, perhaps unconsciously. "In two minutes and a half from the instant the first roar of the torrent breaks upon our ears the water will be over our heads."

"The roar and the deluge would be far nearer together than two minutes and a half. You could not hear the water very much farther than you could see it," answered Gillette.

Ward looked mystified. "Certainly a stream dashing over a rocky bed and at the rate of an express train must make a loud noise. I hope I may never hear it."

"So it does; an awful and never-to-be-forgotten roaring. But you must remember the mountain separates you from the cañon you have just passed through, at its first turn. The mountain, in the same way, acts as an additional barrier every turn the erratic stream makes. 'Sound cannot turn short corners to advantage you know. So if Rapid river gets on our track you will not have time to say your shortest prayer between the time its first terrible roar falls upon your ears and the instant that the flying wall of water strikes you like a tidal wave, and —— and ——"

"And what?" demanded Ward rather sternly. "It is surely a small thing to ask that I may know what manner of death I must die."

Gillette had grown serious in spite of himself. His imagination had been forced to work, and shadows of the pictures it was drawing were upon his face as he replied.

"If the river overtook us in such a spot as this," he answered slowly, as he glanced up the scarce divided walls of rock to the thin patch of sky above, which looked so wonderfully bright and beautiful, "it would be almost instant death. Our brains would be dashed out against these walls of rock before we had time to begin to be drowned. In some portions of the course, where the river is less confined, and so less angry, we might have the alternative of a death from drowning."

"There would be one satisfaction at least," I suggested. "We would have every inducement to die like the philosophers we fancy ourselves."

"How so?" demanded Ward, gloomily.

"Simply because we should not be distracted by frantic efforts to save ourselves." This closed our conversation for perhaps an hour. We set our faces in dogged determination, and walked as fast as the uneven nature of the river bed would permit. When the narrow cañon succeeded a more open stretch it was as if the pitiless walls of fate were visibly closing in upon us. Perhaps I felt something as soldiers do when ordered to charge upon an earthwork bristling with hostile artillery about to vomit forth flame and death. As we made our way through these terrible gorges, the rocky walls of what might be our tomb seemed, to my gloomy fancy, to be cast into a strange semblance to some pitiless and malignant monster. Vain as the movement, we often turned to look behind us to see if the waters were not at our heels, then glancing at each other expected to be mocked. To have been derided would have been a relief, but not one of us was yet free from terror of what seemed each moment more horrible a fate. When such dismal cañons were nearly penetrated and we could see before us the walls spreading out, and the river bed growing wider, a pressing weight seemed for the moment lifted from our brains.

Suddenly Gillette glanced at his watch and closed it with a snap. Then he gave a hearty laugh. Ward and I stopped short in our tracks and looked at him in astonishment.

"Why, cheer up," he exclaimed. "It is only half-past three, and our journey is almost over."

"You don't say so," said Ward, stupidly.

"Only half an hour's brisk walking," continued Gillette, "is now between us and Grape Valley."

Ward's face relaxed. The tense strain left his arms and legs. Then he laughed as I thought in a somewhat silly fashion, though I immediately did the same.

"I'm tired," he said. "As long as we have an hour and a half to make a half hour's trip let us rest a little."

Then he added as he looked from one to the other of us: " I am conscious of having made a very cowardly exhibition of myself."

Gillette and I very considerately permitted Ward to be the common scapegoat, and also to lead the way to a suitable spot for rest. It so happened that at this point the river did not occupy the whole of the gorge. We saw another cleft in the mountains, and another gorge on a slightly different level, but running in the same general direction.

" Perhaps the ancient course of a river," suggested Ward. "Why here is a spring now. It is actually gushing out of the solid rock."

" Nonsense," exclaimed Gillette, " that is only a pool left by Rapid river. The river comes up to this level; you can see the water marks on the rock."

So we had our laugh at Ward, and then climbing higher still to the opening of the second gorge, threw ourselves on the ground for sadly-needed rest.

" While we are resting, why not answer a few questions?" suggested Ward, looking at Gillette. " It cannot be you bring your grapes and wine for export up this narrow and uneven river bed ? "

" No, we do not," answered Gillette. " This river bed and cañon serve us merely as an entrance from the west. For exit, and for the transportation of produce and merchandise, both ways, we use a different route. Grape Valley furnishes a very varied topography, by the way. Between the northerly parts of our little country and the extreme southerly districts there is almost as much difference in climate and landscape as between Northern and Southern California, although of course our valley is numbered by only a few square miles. This difference in climate is made partly by the variation in elevation and in rain-fall, and partly by the fact that south of us is a sand desert, which seems to absorb every particle of the sun's heat only to give it forth in double intensity. In the upper portion of our valley there is good pasture for cattle and suitable soil for ordinary agriculture, while in the lower districts grapes only can be grown to an advantage. It is through the desert that our main avenue of entrance and exit lies. The desert is, too, a better guard and outpost than ten thousand armed men. The outside world does not dream that a fertile valley lies at one edge of it, much less that a happy colony of thousands of souls have there found practical solution for some of the hardest problems that ever vexed the human mind."

"But I should not think grape culture would yield profit enough to enable you to supply the colony with the necessities as well as the luxuries of life."

Gillette smiled. "In the first place, my dear Vinton, we do not require the most expensive of the luxuries of so-called civilization, created in response to finical appetites and forced tastes. We find joy in living. But then, please remember that, in our varied climate, we can produce such plain food as we may want in our valley. The products of our vineyards and the treasures of our wine cellars ought certainly to be sold for enough to supply us with clothes, books and whatever other articles are necessary to supply reasonable demands. But I may as well tell you now, since there is no occasion to keep further secrets from you, that we have still another source of what, in your political economy, may be called wealth. The gold we find in the Grape Valley placer mines serves excellently well to barter with the silly outside world for really useful articles in abundance. To us the gold is of no value except as we impose on your nineteenth century folly to procure what you produce and we do not."

"You have placer mines you say?" asked Ward.

"Yes, mines of the good, old-fashioned sort. We shovel the pay dirt into the sluices, turn on the water, and lo, there is the glistening gold left on the riffles beneath. If all the world were as sensible as we of

Grape Valley, the shining stuff would be of little more value than so much iron. But since we are the only socialistic settlement on the continent, our gold mines are a decided benefit to us."

" And when all America has become one grand socialistic community," suggested Ward, satirically, " I suppose there will still remain the slow-moving old world to barter its wares for your gold. It will be a long time before gold and silver cease to have a value far above their uses simply as material for manufacture."

As Ward spoke he took up a handful of the soil and held it up: " Supposing this were what you call ' pay dirt.' If it were rich with gold I imagine we would suddenly go out of our senses with greed. We none of us need more wealth than we have, yet we would doubtless go as mad with lust of gold if we made a discovery here as any of the half-starved and wholly desperate ' forty-niners.' "

Gillette cast an amused glance at Ward's handful of dirt, and seemed on the point of making a bright repartee. But what he was about to say, the world can never know. His attention was so completely distracted, that he quite forgot it himself. The smile on his face gave place to unmistakable surprise. He bent forward and catching Ward's wrist he fixed his eyes intently on the handful of yellow earth.

" Great heavens, man," he exclaimed after a moment of vivid silence, " that looks like ' pay dirt.' Perhaps you have discovered a placer mine."

" Is that gold ? " I demanded, leaping up, and forgetting every thing in the world except the boundless fortune that might be at our feet. " You can't mean it." The announcement seemed too glorious to be true. I had left all the comforts of civilization and the easy competence provided for me, to make a pilgrimage to an ideal colony where a higher law than selfishness controlled the division of property, but at the exciting thought that before me lay the treasure which, perhaps, would make me immensely rich, my devotion vanished. My philosophical spirit was supplanted by the insensate hunger for gold as ancient as history, as old as our race.

But Gillette did not appear to hear me. He had suddenly snatched his hat from his head and begun to take from Ward's hand the last grain of earth. Then he cried in a shrill voice:

" Where was it you found this dirt? show me the very spot, the very spot."

Before Ward, however, could do his bidding, Gillette's keen eyes had sought out the place where the soil had been disturbed, and falling upon his knees he immediately caught up two more handfuls resembling the first in appearance, and deposited them in his hat, and then more, until his hat was nearly full.

" What are you going to do ? " almost gasped Ward, apparently nearly unbalanced by the sudden influx of new ideas. I, however, had already guessed the meaning of the actions of my companion, and had my hat half filled with the same precious earth by the time he rose to his feet.

" Come and see for yourself," answered Gillette, without looking around, as he started to the little pool of water which we had passed as we climbed from the river bed. I followed him hat in hand, and Ward watched us both in amazement.

# CHAPTER VI.

In a moment more Gillette had dipped his hat into the pool and filled it brimfull of water. I followed his example and then imitated him as he shook the improvised pan so as to thoroughly wet the earth, and turned it so as to throw a little of it out at a time. Then we refilled our hats with water and resumed the shaking and tipping process until the few handfuls of earth in each receptacle were reduced to less than a tablespoonful. Then we threw more of the earth into our hats and returned to the pool.

By this time Ward had recovered enough of his senses to understand what we were about, and he stood between us looking first into one extemporized pan and then into another with an excited interest not a particle less than our own.

"Be careful," he cried, as first Gillette and then I filled our hats for the last time at the pool. "Be very careful or you will lose it all."

No need to warn us. No starving beggar could be more careful with his last crust of bread. No trembling miser could be more cautious as he hides the coin he worships. Gently we shook our hats until the water became discolored again with the dissolving earth. Slowly and with many a nervous recovery, we poured out the muddy water.

The last drop of water was emptied and Ward peered eagerly into Gillette's hat. I dared not look yet for the result of my own experiment. I waited for Ward to return the verdict of success or failure. I thought

7

to read it on his face. If he saw the hoped for grains of gold, I should see a sudden lighting up of his countenance. A smile would relieve the stern lines of his mouth. But his face did not change. I could see his eyelids move as his glance wandered from side to side of the bottom of the hat. My heart sank within me. I did not need to wait for words. It was a failure. Gillette had been deceived in thinking there was gold in the vile earth. A sudden despair of life seized upon me. I dreaded the thought of existence without the boundless fortune of which I had imagined myself already the possessor. Then a hot indignation for Gillette burned in my heart. I could have killed him where he stood, white-faced and agonized at the catastrophe. Now came Ward's dreaded words:

"There is no gold here." Then he added, fiercely, voicing my madness: "Curse you for a fool." In a sudden frenzy I threw my shapeless hat to the ground and stamped upon it.

"I feel more like a devil than a man," I cried, half conscious of my degradation, though unable to rise above it. As for Gillette, he gave Ward, and then me, a dazed look, and in a moment more, aimlessly, as it seemed, lifted his hat and peered into it. Suddenly he gave a veritable scream of delight, and reaching out his hand, fairly dragged Ward to him.

"This is gold, man, real gold," he said. "Were you blind?"

I looked over Ward's shoulder, as drawing back a fold of the lining of the hat, Gillette showed a little pinch of gold dust.

"Look at yours now," exclaimed Gillette, his pallor giving place to a vivid flush on either cheek. And as I stood, half stunned at the sudden transition from despair to triumph, he took up my hat and looked into it.

"Better yet," he cried. "Half a salt spoonful of gold." And he held the shapeless piece of felt forward for us to look into it.

"If you had only looked closer," he added, "you would have saved us all an awful moment of suffering."

But Ward had no sooner seen the second little pinch of gold than he tore his hat from his head, and rushing to the spot where we had made the beginning of an excavation, fell upon his knees and dug his nails deep into the earth. Then he too hurried to the pool and began to wash for the remnant of gold, as Gillette and I had done, who now stood watching him as he had watched us.

"I have more than either of you," he cried with a delight that was almost ferocious, as he examined for results. "Now, where shall we put what we have, while we wash for more?"

Gillette drew from his pocket a large handkerchief and spread it on the ground near the pool. "We might scrape our savings into this," he said, and suiting the action to the word he turned his hat inside out, and its contents made a pretty little yellow heap on the white linen. Instead of using the common receptacle proposed, Ward, however, made a separate treasure-house for himself, and I, although struggling with a not wholly lost sense of shame, also made a little heap of my own. Then, without even looking each other in the face again, we returned to the place where we had first filled our hats, and threw in the proper amount of the precious soil. From the new-found mine we again went to the pool, and, standing on different sides, filled and refilled our strange basins, shook, and dipped and poured without a word, but with ill-concealed rivalry, until the pinch of gold was discovered at the bottom. Then each betook himself to the spot where lay his own handkerchief and scraped out the yellow metal, most potent of all created poisons to set friends at variance and make even brothers hate each other.

Again and again, and many times again we filled our hats with the gold-tainted earth, until, where Ward

had caught up that first handful, with most apt philosophy, there was a hole deep enough to bury a child.
The little piles of gold in the handkerchief, over which
each of us gloated as he made a new deposit, grew
lustily, Ward's most of all, much to the envy of Gillette and myself. So intent were we in gathering
treasure, that we did not notice that our pool of water
was rapidly disappearing. At last, however, Gillette
had just with difficulty dipped enough water into his
hat to advance its contents another stage toward reduc-
tion, when Ward bent forward, looked into the hollow
where the pool had been and exclaimed :

"The water is all gone."

His voice sounded strange and harsh, breaking a
long silence.

I had just finished with a washing and was examining, with contemptible joy, the pinch of gold which
was my last prize. Gillette was busily shaking and
twirling his hat, and made no response. He was only
anxious to make the most of the water which he had
just taken.

"See here," continued Ward, fiercely, "you had
no right to take the last drop in the pool."

"Why not as much right as you would have?"
retorted Gillette, pouring off some muddy water,
watched by Ward as thirsty castaways might watch a
glittering raindrop.

"Because another hatful of water would have cleaned
my dust, and it has done you no good," insisted Ward.

By this time Gillette had poured off the water from
his hat, and saw that the remaining contents had as yet
very little resemblance to gold.

"Your success wouldn't have helped me," he answered, and then he turned his hat inside out upon
the ground in disgust, as he added : "Any more than
this does."

Ward looked almost ready to spring upon Gillette,
so maddened was he with disappointed covetousness.

But instead, thrusting his hand into his hat he drew out its contents and threw them at his feet.

"We have loitered here long enough," I said with returning reason. "It is fortunate the water gave out when it did."

"Yes," exclaimed Gillette hurriedly, "we can come back; there is a fortune for us all here."

In five minutes more each of us had taken up his handkerchief with its burden of gold, and put it in his pocket, and we were all hurrying down the river bed on our interrupted course. For a few rods we kept silence, and then Ward remarked:

"That mine comes at the beginning of another cañon, you remember. Do you suppose that it leads to your valley?"

"I haven't the least idea," answered Gillette. "It looks like an ancient river bed, but whether it leads to Grape Valley or to the south, I cannot even guess. We can explore it sometime."

A very unpleasant impression had been growing upon me for some minutes. It was that more time had passed while we had been searching for gold than we had been conscious of. We had had an hour and a half to get to Grape Valley when we sat down to rest, and only a half hour's walk before us. We still had a trip to take which would require half an hour. The query kept presenting itself to my mind, how much of that hour and a half was left to us? Again and again I put my hand on my watch, determined to know the worst. But each time I faltered.

We were apparently now going at nearly our best speed. If there were time to get out of the cañon before the fateful hour of five, when Rapid river was to resume its course, why we should be saved. If not, what need to anticipate the death agony? But if it were no later than half-past four, we were safe. If it were twenty minutes to five, by hurrying we might still make our escape. At this point in my reasoning I

would see how important it might be for us to know
the exact time at once. There might be only a matter
of a few hasty strides, at the last, between us and
death.

But then the thought would strike me that I might
find the threatening hands at fifteen minutes to five, or
even nearer still to that hour. My hand again faltered. Perhaps it was even past five. Perhaps Rapid
river was already rushing upon our track with murderous haste. Gillette had told us that it took but seven
minutes for the water to make the whole seven miles.
To reach the spot where we now were would require
less than six minutes. If it were five minutes past five
our doom was already sealed. In an instant more a
terrible roar would burst upon our ears. It seemed to
me I already heard the sound of the rushing waters.

I stopped short and looked behind me.

When I made this significant movement, my companions turned too, and the color forsook their cheeks,
as it had doubtless forsaken mine. But there was no
foaming tide of water pouring between the lofty walls.
There was not a sound. Then we looked each other
in the face, and Gillette slowly drew out his watch.

"We are all thinking of the same thing," he said in
an unsteady voice. "It will be better to know the
truth."

It seemed a full minute before he pressed the spring
which opened his hunting-case. The case rose as slowly
as if it were an immense weight being raised by a der-
rick.

Then Gillette's lips moved, and he gave us the time.
"Four minutes to five."

For a moment we stood still. The awful suspense
was over. We knew the worst. There were less than
eleven minutes between Rapid river and us, but, perhaps, there was a chance for us to escape from the cañon
before the water swept through it — just a chance.
Then Gillette's voice sounded out, shrill and tense :

"Run for your lives."

We needed no second call. As Gillette spoke, he turned and led the way down the gloomy gorge at a fast trot, followed first by Ward, and then by me. I was but four years out of the college where I had been a famous football player, and I was sure I could have outstripped Gillette if I had chosen. But Ward was my senior by a dozen years, and a man entirely unaccustomed to violent exercise. I felt required by common humanity to keep behind my friend so as to help him to his feet if he fell, to keep up his courage, too, and banish the thought that he was far in the rear and alone.

The probabilities were we should be overtaken by the furious waters, but I thought that to live with the ever present consciousness of being a coward would be more unpleasant and infinitely less inspiring than an honorable death. As I, perhaps, made clear some pages back, the river bed was a most uneven and uncertain path. Sometimes the sides of the cañon came so close together that there was scarce room for two men to pass abreast between them. Sometimes huge bowlders obstructed the way. More often ragged ledges of rock projected up from beneath, or inward from the sides. A more difficult course for runners could not have been made by design. We could hardly plant both feet on a level plane. It was hard enough for a college athlete only a trifle out of practice, but for poor Ward it could have been little less than intolerable agony. It was only indomitable will that could have kept him at all in this well nigh hopeless race for life.

Gillette passed out of our sight at the first turn of the gorge, and we saw him no more. A pang of dismay shot through me as he disappeared. A new hopelessness came over me, and I know over Ward. But immediately I ceased to blame him. He could not have helped us by sacrificing his own chances for life.

It could be no consolation to Ward and me, when the
mad waters should, in a very few minutes, overwhelm
us, that a third victim should be also sacrificed. I think
we were both magnanimous enough even in our own
despair to wish our former comrade's escape.

The wonderful endurance of my friend, Ward, compelled an admiration greater than I had ever before
entertained for him.   Here was a darling of fortune,
a pet of destiny, who had never until now known a
discomfort or suffered an inconvenience.   He had not
so much as suspected that he had muscles such as the
less favored use for hard work.   He fell over projecting rocks, and rose bleeding, but it was only to rush on
the faster.   He staggered against bowlders, until I
thought he must have broken every bone in his tormented body, but he did not utter more than the first
inarticulate groan. His breathing was as loud as that of a
"roaring" horse, but still he pressed on in an unsteady
trot, his hands bleeding from his almost continual falls,
his face bruised from frequent collisions with the pitiless rock.   His spirit was mighty still, and whipped on
the poor, broken, but unflagging body.   I shall always
feel that it was more for my sake than to save his own
life, that Ward made such a sublime battle.   He had
too much honor himself not to know that it was impossible for me to desert him.   He must have longed
most intensely to throw himself face downward in the
fatal cañon, and wait for the death that was already on
our track, whose damp breath was already in the air.
For my sake, not for his own, he made a struggle and
endured an agony to which sudden death could not but
seem a pleasure by comparison, and endured it too on
a bare chance of thus saving my life.

So we ran on our devious course turning again and
again on itself as took us around the mountains.   Beside us still rose the walls of our narrow cell, thousands
of feet to the sky, before us what seemed a solid face of
rock, opening as we drew nearer for the narrow gorge

to make another turn. Then it came over us that our time must have elapsed. I drew out my watch, and found it was three minutes past five.

"We have but three minutes to live," I cried. "Let us sit down and die in peace." Certainly it would have been a short death agony. The cañon was very narrow at this place, and the raging waters, half their way down the course by this time, would have come upon us with almost the force of a battering ram.

But Ward shook his head and still pressed on. He stumbled over a projecting stone and fell his full length. I raised him to his feet and tried to stay him. It seemed almost infamous to struggle so frantically in a hopeless fight for life. The blood flowed from new cuts on his face, become positively dreadful with its fierce determination to vanquish fate and death, and in its startling contrast of marble like whiteness and the crimson tint of his bleeding wounds. But he threw my hand from his arm with a strength I could not have believed he retained, and still staggered on. And it is to his unconquerable determination that, as it happened, we both owe our lives. At the very next turn of the river course the longed for Grape Valley lay open before us and a paradise it certainly seemed to our eyes. In the distance at the south were vast areas of vineyards, while to the north were green fields and verdant pastures with cattle. In the middle, on the banks of a placid stream that flowed from the north, were the houses and streets of a little city. The promised land was before us, and we had been permitted to see its beauties, but as I remembered how few seconds separated the pursuing river from us, I saw little reason to believe we should ever enter that city alive.

Still we ran on. The mountains drew farther apart at every step, and if we could have had but two minutes more of time, we should have reached a point where to clamber up a gentle slope would have placed us out of danger. I was running now by Ward's side, hold-

8

ing his hand in mine, and we had almost reached the
spot we struggled for. But my companion's feet seemed
like lead; his limbs to be stricken with paralysis; I had
fairly to drag him along.

Then came an awful roar behind us, as if a thousand
fierce Numidian lions had broken loose, and the resist-
less waters of Rapid river sprang upon their prey.

# CHAPTER VII.

When I recovered consciousness I was in a bed. So much I knew without opening my eyes. A real earthly bed! After enjoying for a few minutes, with a new zest, the sense of existence, I opened my eyes. Above me, as I might have expected, was a ceiling, not of plaster, however. Since plaster had always seemed to me one of the worst of the bad features of our effete civilization I at once congratulated myself on having found a place where it was not; undoubtedly Grape Valley. But how did I come here?

The last clear remembrance I had was of seeing the valley as it spread out most alluringly before my despairing eyes, and of doing my best to get out of the course of Rapid river. Then came the dreadful roar behind us, and I knew no more. Yes, I had a vague remembrance of a sense of cold, and a sudden shock. Now I awake to find myself in Grape Valley after all. But how I came here was quite beyond even my ready powers of speculation. I am sure I need not pause to explain at length why it was I was convinced I was in Grape Valley. At last accounts I was in the course of Rapid river. Rapid river was on its way to Grape Valley, and I must either be in Grape Valley or in the other world. The other world hypothesis was quite absurd and untenable.

Having inspected the ceiling to my satisfaction I decided to turn on my side, and change my point of view. But what a pain there came into the back of my head when I attempted to move! I shall feel that pain by association of ideas whenever I call to my mind that moment, all the rest of my life. I groaned aloud, and decided not to incur further painful experiences. If lying still prevented them, I would lie still indefinitely. When the pain in my head stopped I was disposed to resume my study of the ceiling, and so I opened my eyes again.

But this time I did not see the ceiling at all. An object was interposed, nothing else than a beautiful woman's face. It seemed to me the most lovely face I had ever seen, although I was always staring at women from boyhood. It was framed and crowned with red gold hair which glistened in the light. Her skin was as fair as a child's, but her gentle and tender blue eyes seemed to bless me as they looked into mine. Then her lips parted in a smile, and I caught her breath, like that of a rose before the morning's dew has left it.

"You are better?" she said softly, as only a woman can speak to the sick. "But you must not move your head, it was badly hurt." Then I felt her hands readjusting the pillows at my side and smoothing the coverlet. I tried to speak, but my lips and throat were so parched the voice refused to come. Her quick eyes noticed my plight.

"You are thirsty?" and in a moment more she held a teaspoonful of liquid to my mouth.

"Who is it?" I murmured.

"Oh, I am Kate," she smiled. "But you must not talk, the doctor says." She added : "You must try not even to think." Then she drew herself back, and I could not tell whether she remained in the room or not.

I did very little thinking for some days to come. I was conscious of seeing something very beautiful when Kate's face came between mine and the ceiling. I was soothed by her gentle voice and tender tones, and was quite too sick a man to care to understand or to investigate more than was necessary. I rather preferred mystery, as it helped to muddle my brain, and to put me into the delightful naps which I have coveted ever since. I wondered vaguely whether Gillette had escaped entirely without injury, and bestowed a somewhat misty regret on my poor friend Ward, who I concluded must have been lost. Ward was a good fellow. I should never have such another friend. But the realities were indistinct in those hours of sickness, all but the sweet and winning beauty of Kate's face as I saw it come between mine and the ceiling at intervals, the length of which I was unable to estimate.

But at last I grew better. My brain seemed to have resumed its ordinary powers. - I knew I was myself again because I began to be impatient at confinement, to fret and worry over the mystery which enveloped me. I wondered where my nurse was. How neglectful it was of her to leave me! I refused to consider that nurses must eat and sleep like other mortals. I became particularly anxious to give her a scolding. I was surely getting into the normal state of man very fast. Then I heard a light step across the room and the fair face bent over mine with an almost maternal movement. A true woman is as much a mother as a sweetheart. How fresh her face, how limpid her large eyes, how divinely her lips parted as if for a kiss; no, it was a smile she gave me, bright and gracious as a mother's for her waking child. My impatience left me. I tried to think of a new and most tender of names for her.

"I have good news for you," she said, in her clear, full tones, "you can turn in your bed and look around."

"Is that all, Kate?" and. I too essayed a winning smile. But I was conscious of a dead failure.

"Who told you my name was Kate?" she demanded, with a light laugh that disclosed two glistening rows of teeth. "Oh, I remember, I did myself. What? You want more privileges? Well, perhaps bye and bye you can talk a little."

Then she moved my pillows, while I turned upon

my side. The pain had left the back of my head, but
how weak I was. I had never been sick before, and
had perhaps not been able to properly sympathize with
invalids. But I shall not soon forget the sullen mutiny
of my muscles, enervated as they were by fever, when
my still healthy will commanded them to work. A
sudden light of compassion illumined the woman's
face, and she bent and passed her round arms about my
shoulders, and put her strength with mine. Her golden hair brushed my forehead, then her cheeks, firm,
soft and warm, touched my unshaven face. My
heart gave a great throb, and pumped the dull blood
into each startled vein and artery. For an instant I
was strong. But Kate had suddenly released me, and
her face was turned away, as she busied herself in adjusting the medicines on the table by the bed. Was
that a flush which seemed to be spreading over her
neck and averted cheek, or was it the pink light from
the window curtain? What had I done? Could it be
I had kissed that perfumed cheek as it touched my
face? If she became offended with me, I must then
plead as extenuation some remnant of the fever clinging
to my brain. Surely a man as sick as I had been was
not wholly responsible.

But whether my brain was disordered or not, I retained enough of the good judgment upon which I once
had prided myself, to know better than to launch at
once into conversation. There is no social rule
more safe to follow than this: when you don't know
what to say, say nothing. From my changed position
in the bed, I could see what then seemed to me almost
enough of the world. Every movement of the beautiful woman, who permitted me to call her Kate, was
beneath my eyes. Opposite me was an open window,
with a pot of fragrant flowers at either side, and with
out were green fields, a glistening river and a summer
sky. This world seemed excellent to me at that moment, almost perfect. How stupid of mankind to turn it

into a place of torment. But this was Grape Valley, the people of which, as Gillette had assured me, had agreed on a reasonable existence; had consented to work together instead of at cross purposes, to help to build up instead of to destroy all that is worth living for. Alas! for poor Ward. His thirst for knowledge had cost him his life, a life which he could have spent in a spot where it was made possible for men to be happy.

"Kate," I called, and she turned toward me. If she had been blushing there was no sign of it now on her calm, fair face. If she had been angry there was no hint of wrath or indignation now in her wide, open eyes, or in the gentle curves of her mouth. "I want to ask you about my friend, Mr. Ward." My voice was faint and my breath a little uncertain, but it was a relief to speak even thus. "Did they find his body?"

"Oh, yes," she answered, with a quiet laugh. I experienced a sense of shock at her lack of seriousness. But perhaps the people of Grape Valley had a religion which can indeed rob death of its terrors, the grave of its gloom. It would be as well worth studying as its social innovations. "They found his body," Kate continued, "and its spirit had not left it."

"You don't mean to say Ward is alive?" I exclaimed, in excitement.

"He was not as seriously injured as you were, although he may be confined to his bed longer. He was badly bruised, but his injuries were not on his head."

"Why," I exclaimed, "it was little less than a miracle that we both should be saved."

"No," she answered, drawing a chair up to the bedside, "not a miracle at all. It happened in this way. Mr. Gillette had given the alarm to a number of us who were returning to the city with a load of grapes. You were both of you taken from the water within five minutes of the time the river overtook you."

"Gillette — where is he now?"

"He was obliged to start almost immediately on another business trip. It will be a fortnight before he will return."

I relapsed into silence. I was alone, then, among strangers, sick and alone. The sun, which a moment ago had been shining so cheerfully into the window, went under a cloud. The river, in the distance, lost its sheen, and took on the appearance to my eye of a black, baleful serpent of monstrous proportions. Even the woman by my side, I fancied, had a distrait expression on her face. Doubtless she wished herself rid of the burden of the sick stranger.

"How did I come here?" I asked, wearily.

She rose and bent over me, taking my hot hands between her cool palms. "But you are getting feverish. You must stop talking and worrying at once. If I answer this one question, will you promise faithfully to go to sleep?"

I nodded my head. She did not seat herself, but still stood cooling my hands with hers.

"I told you that I was with a party from the vineyards, which Mr. Gillette called to the rescue. When you were taken from the river limp and white as death itself, though without disfiguring wounds or bruises, I took your head in my lap, and dried your face with my handkerchief. It was I who forced the few drops of brandy between your lips which made you breathe again. The others had thought you dead, but I could not believe that death looked so beautiful —— I mean ——," and her hands trembled, I fancied, as they touched mine. "I thought that the spirit had not left your body yet, and when you gave the first sign of life, nothing would suit me but to be permitted to nurse you back to health. So you were brought here, and here you are recovering. Now to sleep," and, without so much as a look behind her, Kate left the room.

But my sense of loneliness had gone. In its place

was a sweet peace and satisfaction which I did not care to analyze. A delightful languor distilled through my veins, and I dropped away into such sleep as opium-eaters describe.

9

# CHAPTER VIII.

In another week the physician gave the long-craved permission for me to be dressed, and the young man from the hospital who had assisted Kate in her self-appointed task, really made me look quite presentable. He even shaved me, and when my gentle nurse came into the chamber to find me sitting by the window and looking much like other men, she seemed as delighted as a child. I always have had a particular contempt for an ungrateful man, and I certainly felt myself under great obligations to the assistant from the hospital. Still I knew my strength was limited and I could not consent to waste any of it talking with him, when I had so much to say to my nurse and to hear from her. He had told me that I could sit up this first time only an hour, and fifteen minutes of it had slipped away before he made the first movement toward leaving me with Kate. I hope that I did not bid him goodbye too eagerly, but I certainly was very much pleased as he closed the door behind him.

Kate was pleased also, or I am no judge of female character. She had been busying herself in little nothings while he remained, mere pretenses in the way of occupation. She pulled the curtain down somewhat lower, straightened the pictures on the wall, changed a few vases on the mantel, moved the chair out of the corner and set it back again. When the young man stood in the doorway saying his long-desired farewell, she half turned toward him as if interrupted in something vitally important. "Are you going so soon? Well you must be back at eleven promptly to put the sick man to bed again."

But no sooner had he closed the door behind him and my eyes turned eagerly to her, than she dropped her brush broom into the nearest chair, and hurried to me as if she thought I was in peril. She touched my hands and gently pressed them, to learn if I were feverish, and then cooled my forehead with something very much like a caress. She bent over and looked me in the face, and if my eyes were misty with an unshed tear or two I do not know as I need be ashamed to confess it. I was still weak and my nerves were unstrung, and she was so sweet and compassionate. Her eyes shone with tears of joy and pity. I could not help feeling a little pity for myself.

" How happy I am," she said simply. Then she brought a low stool and seated herself at my feet. " I am going to talk with you for the whole of three-quarters of an hour. This will be my last forenoon with you."

I gave a startled movement which made her laugh. " But not my last afternoon. I resume work to-morrow forenoon. I have taken as long a vacation as I can."

" So women work in Grape Valley !" I exclaimed, rather scornfully.

" Here we draw wages too; that is where we have another advantage over the women of civilization."

" I should think it would be better for the men, either as husbands or as fathers, to support the women," persisted I.

" That isn't the way in Grape Valley. Every man or woman does a share of the necessary work and draws a corresponding share of the returns. The women of Grape Valley are dependents or pensioners on no man's bounty."

" But," I urged, " I should think the men would prefer to provide for the women they love. A father.

for instance, must certainly take pleasure in feeding and clothing his grown-up daughter."

"But why should he support her if she is able to support herself, any more than a grown-up son? There is nothing to admire in idleness. Besides he would be forced to carry an extra burden by so doing, and more working hours would be required than are necessary now that each woman bears her own burden. A day's work is but four hours in Grape Valley, because all except the children and the sick bear a hand."

"But,——" I began.

"Wait a minute," she interrupted, eagerly. "There is another reason why fathers do not support their grown-up daughters here. If a daughter were a charge upon her father, when the father died the daughter would be left dependent on some one's else bounty. If she married and her husband died or left her, she would be once more left to charity, or to the chance of commending herself to a second's husband's favor. By giving her work to do, our policy secures her freedom after so many centuries of bondage."

"But," I continued, "I should think the husbands of Grape Valley would prefer their wives should be at home."

"What good would it do even such fond husbands" demanded Kate, "for their wives to be at home when they themselves are away at work? As long as the wife is at home when the husband is there, he ought to be satisfied."

"But aside from that," I urged, "you must remember man's pride. He likes to feel that it is he who provides the woman he loves with the necessities and luxuries of existence. It is usually supposed, too," I added, "that the loving wife enjoys her blessings doubly when bestowed by her husband's hand."

"A grown woman should not have such silly ideas," exclaimed Kate with a curl of her red lips, "and a sensible man should be above any such pride as you speak of, which it would cost so much to indulge. It would cost her independence, which is essential if there is to be the true and passionate relation between them, rather than the mutually degrading relation of owner and slave."

"Not if they love each other," I insisted.

But Kate would not let me talk. "If they love each other, this mercenary relation which you admire so much, corrupts, taints, and tends to destroy the emotion. Love is not bought and sold. But supposing they love each other very little, or, as is often the case, not at all, what then becomes of the pleasure of the proud husband in providing for her, and of her sweet humility in accepting his begrudged bounty?"

I said nothing, and Kate seemed very glad of the opportunity to answer her own question.

"Why, their union then becomes shameful as well as painful. She eats her bread in bitterness, which he throws to her in contempt. He is under a sort of bondage to her in the continued obligation to support one who cannot provide for herself, and she is an unwilling pensioner for her board and clothes. Common honor and decency constrain him; absolute and gross hunger and want constrain her."

"But you have true love matches here?" I suggested.

"Since the women of this valley are independent, there are no marriages here for support, no marriages for money. Love, pure and simple, or what they think to be love, draws men and women together, and their relation after marriage is the same as in courtship, based on passion, physical and spiritual, and giving that passion its perfect course."

When any woman talks of love it is apt to make a man's pulses beat somewhat faster. But when she was beautiful, young and gentle, and when she talked with such fervor, such enthusiasm, what wonder that my heart throbbed wildly, and hot words of passion rushed to my trembling lips? It must have been that Kate perceived my emotion, and desired, for some good reason of her own, to check it. She rose suddenly from her stool, and taking her place by my side, pointed out of the window and down the valley.

"You see those fields of a peculiar green?"

I could not yet trust my voice. She doubtless knew why. Women are all clairvoyants where matters of the heart are concerned. So she continued without waiting for an answer: "Those are the vineyards. That district is on a lower level than this part of the valley, and is much hotter and dryer. See how brown and parched the land looks, except where occupied by the vines; Grapes would not grow to advantage in this district; It is too cool and moist here. But we have green grass instead, something the southerly end of the valley does not have."

"You surely do not pick the grapes yourself?" I exclaimed in something like my natural voice, although I could not hide the admiration in my eyes as I turned them toward her fair cheeks.

"Oh, no, the men do that. I sometimes go down to see them, as fortunately I had been doing that day when I first saw you. My work is packing the grapes in boxes for the market." She extended her closed hands toward me, and then slowly opened them. "Look, you can see the stains on my fingers. I have hidden them before."

I caught her hands in mine to bring them closer to my eyes for examination. Yes, they were stained at the tips.

"Ah, you will not admire them any more," she cried, with a sweet mingling of coquetry and reproach in her voice and on her face. But when in an instant more she felt my burning kisses, and heard my breath come in quick sighs, she snatched her hands from me almost furiously, and was half way across the room as the door opened to admit the young man from the hospital.

"The hour is up," he said, smiling pleasantly at us. Then he approached me. "Ah, our patient looks feverish again. I am afraid he has talked too long."

The next morning a little before eight o'clock, Kate stood in the doorway of my chamber for an instant.

"I am going to get some more stains on these fingers," she said, kissing the tips of them to me in what I quite justly considered the most exasperating manner. The four hours between eight and twelve that she would be absent I passed in bed, alternately studying the condition of my heart, and taking short naps. The naps were more satisfactory than the self-examinations. I woke refreshed each time, and resumed the mental analysis until, confused and tired, I fell asleep again.

So far as I am able to condense the results of my meditations, I will give them. I was quite unable to decide whether or not Kate was the most beautiful woman I had ever seen, the brightest or the sweetest. I was unable to recall with sufficient clearness my past experiences to positively decide whether I had ever before been as much thrilled in a woman's presence; whether I had ever liked as well to look in any other woman's face; whether I had ever been as fond of the touch of another woman's hand. I was unable to find data to prove that I should always feel toward Kate as I felt now, or that she was and always would be to me the ideal woman, or even that she was the first or the only woman I had ever met who could inspire in me an enduring passion. Before noon, however, I had admitted to mysel. that long before I could get away from this house I should have made a complete surrender of myself and all I was to Kate; that I should have made as absolute a devotee of myself as a nineteenth century lover can be.

I tried to be philosophical, and to look at my case from an indifferent standpoint. I had come to Grape Valley to study its institutions and morals. By falling

in love was I not willfully blinding myself to a proper
study of the situation ?　At first I was disposed to admit that I was doing just that.　But later I recollected
that nothing usually opens a man's eyes like marriage.
Perhaps, even if I had not been led to it by force of
circumstances, it would have been my duty as a student
of social dynamics to have sought the experience of a
Grape Valley marriage.　What teacher like experience ?
Marriage alone could make me an adept.　But even if
it had not been in the plain line of my duty, it clearly
was my manifest destiny.　What other possible de-.
nouement could there be to my drama ?　A sick and
weak man is nursed by a beautiful and charming girl.
His fancy is fitful and feverish, his senses impression-
able as newly-heated wax.　It was for me to thank fortune that this girl was remarkably beautiful and charming.　My cold philosophy would not let me deny that
I should probably have fallen just as hopelessly in love
under the same fatal conditions with a woman many
degrees less worthy.

Shortly after twelve o'clock when the young man
from the hospital came, he was accompanied by the
doctor.　The latter felt of my forehead and looked in
my eyes, took my temperature, and counted my pulse in
a most solemn fashion.　Then his countenance relaxed.

" Why the patient is a good deal better and stronger
than he was yesterday," said the doctor.

" Of course I am," I remarked, adding jocularly :
" Who said I wasn't ? "

The young man from the hospital looked surprised.
" Then you think it would not hurt him to be dressed
and sit up for an hour to-day ? "

" He can sit up all the afternoon if he wants to," answered the doctor, with the bluff address affected by
the profession, both in and out of effete civilization.

" But yesterday when I came to undress him," insisted the young man, "his face was very much
flushed and his pulse bounding."

"Nonsense, nonsense, my boy. Why, Mr. Vinton, here, can take a walk outside by day after to-morrow."

So the doctor paid me his last visit, and the assistant, in a most disheartened manner, proceeded to dress me. He had lost all the geniality and sprightliness which had made him so engaging. I was really sorry for him. And I knew so well just how he came to make that mistake about my condition. When he entered the room the previous forenoon, to be sure my face was flushed and my pulse bounding. In the interest of science I suppose I should have given him the true explanation of my excitement. He may in his future career lose some far more important patient than I, owing to neglect of symptoms of high fever, such as he thought he saw in me. Even out of common friendliness I ought to have told him that it was love, not disease, which caused the acceleration of pulse, which he correctly diagnosed. I ought to have admitted that it really was a fever which affected me, a fever which frequently deranges the body and always unbalances the mind. But I concluded that the young man would not keep my confidences to himself. He would feel impelled to tell the doctor in charge what I had told him, if for no other reason than to justify his report of feverish symptoms. The doctor would repeat the sentimental tale to his professional brethren, and each of them to his best patient, until Kate and I should become the center of interest for the whole settlement.

So it was that, after the young man had rolled my easy chair into position by the window, and had helped me to it, although, in fact, I hardly felt the need of his assistance, I permitted him to go with only a "thank you." Considering the ill turn I had done him, I felt he was quite excusable for not putting a table within my reach, and for misarranging the pillows so that by no possible position of the human form could I adapt my back and neck to them. But his malice turned to my benefit. In a minute more I heard Kate's step in the hall, and her gentle knock at the door.

"Can I do any thing for you?" she asked, and I was able to answer:

"Oh, yes, lots of things," proceeding to explain what was wrong, and she to put it aright, with many a word of undeserved abuse for the absent assistant, and of pity for me, who, she was convinced, had been shamefully treated.

She had taken her lunch at the work-room, as was the custom, and so had nothing more important to do than spend a happy afternoon with me. From the very instant Kate entered the room and gave me her first look, I abandoned myself to the inevitable. I knew that, unless for some direct interposition of fate, I should, before we separated again, offer myself to her. But I determined that whatever small amount of will power I possessed should be exerted to postpone the inevitable for two hours at least. I was loth to sacrifice the charming piquancy there is in the relations of two undeclared lovers. I wanted to make the most of the delicious mystery which envelops the woman one loves before she confesses a like passion and makes haste to reveal her inmost soul. I always had the disposition and taste of an epicure in matters intellectual as well as physical. I was resolved to extract and enjoy the last drop of sweetness there was in the first and undetermined period of love, before passing into the second, that of sweet assurance. Charming and beatific as the first act might be, I almost dreaded to bid good-bye forever to the prelude.

But as soon as Kate, instead of taking the stool at my feet as she had done yesterday, drew a chair up to my side, I knew my determination was all for naught. I confessed to myself that if Kate was not in my arms within five minutes, it would be because she did not return my passion.

" Have you missed me ? " she gently asked, bending forward to look in my face.

But without answering I reached out my hand and took hers. It gave one tug as if seeking escape, and then lay still.

" Oh, you want to see if my fingers are stained still ? " and she tried to laugh, but the color left her face, her eyes had fallen to her lap, and I shall remember as long as I live the bewitching quiver of the lashes on her cheek. She knew as well as I that the supreme moment was at hand.

" Kate, I love you."

I had thought it certain that this woman loved me. But it suddenly came over me now that I might have been mistaken. I would not have been the first conceited fool to have been convinced that a woman was in love with him simply because she had a kind heart.

What, it suddenly burst upon me, was there in me to inspire a passion ? Since my illness I was not even good-looking. I had been unable to talk very much, so it could not be I had been interesting. My social accomplishments, which had not been wholly amiss in Eastern drawing-rooms, had no field or occasion here. My wealth and position were not only unknown to the woman to whom I was just offering myself, but utterly out of account in this colony.

All these thoughts passed through my mind in the pause which followed my declaration, and I was suddenly plunged into the despair which should be the condition of the true lover's soul. There is something unchivalrous in a lover who counts it only necessary for him to speak to be accepted, for him to ask in order to receive unconditional surrender of the fortress which he should be willing to risk his life to win. I forgot I was weak or had ever been ill. I sprang to my feet and stood before her.

" Kate," I cried, " do not say you have only pitied me ; that you only cared for me as a good angel might care for any suffering human being. I want your love."

She, too, must have forgotten that I had been very ill, for she seemed to see nothing surprising in the fact that I was standing. She rose too, and suddenly lifting her downcast lids, let her great blue eyes shine into mine with all the splendor of awakening passion. The warm blood rushed back into her cheeks, and tearing her hand from mine she threw both her arms around my neck and laid her beautiful head upon my shoulder.

This was surely answer enough, but what triumphant lover but would have wanted more.

"Then, you love me, Kate?" And I put my arm about her waist. "Tell me. Say so, then."

Without lifting her head from my shoulder she turned her face toward mine and smiled like an angel. A woman's passion makes her almost divine. Her dewy lips parted:

"I love you —— " she began, and then my lips met hers in a kiss which is the true confession of love.

# CHAPTER IX.

Then Kate seemed to discover that her patient had been on his feet, and altogether behaving himself like a well man. Nothing would satisfy her but that I take my easy chair again. In vain I assured her that my happiness had completely restored me to health. In vain I argued that a tonic was all that I had required to make me well, explaining that while the doctor had failed to find the proper agent, and was leaving me to the slow recuperative influences of nature, she had offered me the elixir of life, and lo, I was restored.

But at last I had to yield to Kate's inflexible commands and return to my easy chair, while she, drawing her chair nearer to mine, for consolation laid her head upon my shoulder.

So every thing was amicably arranged at last, and, without further loss of time, we started upon those mutual confidences which always come at the beginning of love affairs, and usually cease all too soon. Kate told me that it was while she looked down upon my face as it lay in her lap, death-stricken as it seemed to be, she had first fallen in love.

As the reader has not my photograph by which to confirm or correct Kate's fond description, I will not give in detail her language concerning what nothing shall ever again convince me are not Grecian features of most classic mould. I may forget the criticisms of my enemies, or the half compliments of my friends, but although I am too much afraid of being ridiculous to write here the words Kate used, I shall never forget one adjective of them all. All men are vain, and if we do not suspect your sincerity, believe me, dear readers, since I speak from my own experience, when I say it, you can please one of us more by praises of our physical graces and facial beauties, half or wholly imaginary though they may be, than by any amount of ascriptions to our virtues or to our talents. We feel perhaps that others may not see the virtues or admire the talents, but a handsome face or a fine figure can be appreciated by everybody.

But Kate told me, too, that I was so patient with my pain that it would have been a heart of stone not to have softened for me. "Most men," she said, "are brutes when they are sick." And when I began to recover, and called her by name, and seemed pleased to have her near me, she said she first knew what pure happiness was. But then came the fear lest I should not love her, or worse still, if when I grew better I asked her to marry me, it might be out of gratitude and not out of true love.

"Are you sure you love me?" Her voice came in a more subdued tone from my shoulder where her head rested.

"Tell me what you think love is."

I tried to make her lift her head, so I could watch her face as she answered. But women seem half ashamed of the intensity of their feelings.

"No," she said, "you must not make me look at you now."

Then she continued: "A man who loves should never want to leave the woman he has chosen, should think only of how he can make her happy, should, when in her presence, feel a tender warmth always about his breast. When she comes his heart should give a bound of delight. When she leaves him, if only for a moment, it should be as if the light were taken from the room. Her smiles should be reward enough for every effort, her continued favor a solace for every misfortune. All that is best, noblest and most unselfish in him should be stimulated by her presence, every thing base, covetous or unjust, should find stifling the atmosphere of his passion for her. He should feel that life without her would be a blank, and death with her a delight. This is the way a man should love a woman. Like that, I think, is my love for you."

"Why do you say 'I think'?" I demanded, reproachfully.

"Because we cannot be sure," she answered, sadly. "I have described love as it is in its own nature. If a man and woman are not fitted for each other they find it out in time. When they cease to love as I have described, then they cease to love at all."

Then it was for me to tell her how I had grown to love her, how beautiful she seemed to me, how sweet, how divine.

"If I am so," she said softly, "it is you that make me so. Love can make us fulfill all our best and highest possibilities."

"Where did you get such ideas of love?"

"Why, it is our religion here. But you have not even told me your first name," she continued, "or about your life before you came here."

I told her that my parents had died when I was yet a boy, leaving me an ample, though not unusual property. I went over my school and college experiences, and my first ventures and small successes in literature. I even revealed to her my one unhappy love affair, explaining how the woman, although professing herself in love with me, and knowing fully my infatuation with her, preferred a man she despised, but who had thousands of dollars to my hundreds.

"Are you sure you do not love her still?" Kate raised her head and looked me in the face. "I do not mind it if you have loved others. I do not care how many. But I should not be happy, nor able to make you so, if you still loved another woman."

"Love Isabel Blakesley?　No, I hate her."

Kate let her head drop to my shoulder again, and put her hand in mine. But I was for an instant so full of indignation for the woman who preferred wealth to love that Kate's gentle reminder passed unnoticed. "I had rather," she said, when I carried her hand at last to my lips, "that you had satisfied yourself by experience that she could not make you happy. Then you would have been indifferent to this Isabel."

But it did not take me long to convince Kate or myself that there was no woman to me in the world but her. It would be a poor lover, indeed, who, on the very afternoon of his acceptance, could not forget the woman who had more of a passion for wealth and power than for the man she professed to love.

"But it is now your turn to tell me about yourself," I said, when complete accord seemed restored. "Just think of it," I added with a laugh, as Kate had not replied, "I only know your first name. How do you come to live in this house alone? Have you no father, no mother, nor sisters? Does every woman of Grape Valley have a house of her own?"

"I will answer your questions," began Kate, with a slight change of voice, "but I can talk better—if I sit erect. There, let me go for now. By and by you can have me again if you wish."

So Kate seated herself by my side, and folded her hands in her lap. I thought it well not to insist on further endearments just now. Women are capricious creatures, and it is a wise lover who respects the moods and whims of his mistress.

"In Grape Valley," she continued, "the land, and the houses built upon it, belong to the State, and are allotted to women who set up homes. Our young people remain at the schools until twenty-two, and their homes are in the dormitories attached. Our men and women, until married, live in the larger buildings, which we call phalansteries, where all have the pleasure of privacy in their own rooms, when desired, but meet each other and the householders as well at the common evening meal, and at the social gatherings and entertainments which take place in the central halls every evening.''

"But why," I asked, as she seemed wandering from my question, "do you have a house by yourself? I should think you would prefer to live in a phalanstery."

Kate gave me a startled look. Then she answered hurriedly : "I took for granted you knew I had been married."

A dull pain settled about my heart. Some other man had once been loved by this woman whom I had thought all my own. She had thrown her arms about some other man's neck as gracefully as about mine. She had looked into some other passionate eyes as fondly as into mine. She had learned that clinging kiss of hers from some previous lover. I felt a chill creep over me at the thought that at every stage of my courtship, at every advance in our intimacy, she had doubtless compared me with my predecessor. Perhaps I did not embrace her as gracefully, but held her hand more tenderly. It was too hard to bear. I could not look at her, but sat staring fiercely at the opposite wall where hung the clock whose hands pointed to twenty minutes past three. I could feel her sad, reproachful eyes upon me, and knew she understood what feelings of impotent wrath possessed me. Then I heard her voice coming as from a distance, faint and low, but pleading.

"You are sorry that I married. But how could I know you were coming?"

"How long have you been a widow?" I asked, in a constrained voice, but without meeting her eyes.

"A widow?" she exclaimed. "I am not a widow, my husband is away on a business trip."

I could feel the blood forsake my face, and knew my cheeks must be as white as death, from which she had saved me. I sprang to my feet and turned on the frightened woman as stern a countenance as ever avenging angel could assume.

"And you are the wife of another man? Still you have won my heart and accepted my love. What have I done to deserve such punishment?"

In my desperation I turned my back to her and walked toward the door. I forgot I was sick, and longed as only a man overwhelmingly in love can ever long to escape from the presence of the woman I loved. Then she sprang to her feet, remembering that I was ill, and followed me, her womanliness overcoming her shame. But I felt only a desire to scathe her with new and terrible rebukes before I should go, to tear her fond heart with agonizing reproaches and bitter taunts. She had wounded me. I would give her scar for scar. So before I reached the door I turned to face her again. My lips opened for words but they would not come. A strange dizziness affected my brain. I felt that I was dying, and was glad if it would but break the heart of this most cruel of women. I felt my knees shaking and then I knew no more.

When I began to come to myself, I was lying on the bed, and I opened my eyes to see the pale, tear-stained face of the woman I loved bending over me in that most winning of all her attitudes. My arms obeyed my heart, and throwing them about her neck I drew her to my face. Her cheeks were cold, even her lips, as they pressed mine, were like ice, while my heart was beating high with renewed life and love.

"Then you forgive me?" she murmured.

"Forgive you," I repeated in astonishment. "For what?" Then the memory of her terrible confession came back to me. Joy was not for me. I fairly moaned in my misery, and my arms unwound from about the woman's neck, and fell inert to my side.

Then came a knock at the door, and in response to

Kate's "come in" the young man from the hospital entered. He would have been somewhat else than human if he had not experienced a slight sense of satis·faction at seeing me lie pale and haggard on the bed. And, when Kate explained that I had fainted while trying to cross the room, a look very near akin to ecstacy passed over his face. The absurdity of the second mistake in diagnosis the young man was making appealed to my sense of the ludicrous, stricken as I was. But he merely said with a satisfied air:

"I told the doctor that Mr. Vinton was not as well as he thought."

# CHAPTER X.

The next morning the young man came from the hospital provided with a new sort of medicine from my physician. But when he found me dressed and in my easy chair, he looked at me as if he could not believe his eyes.

"Surely you did not dress yourself?" he ejaculated.

"But I did just that," I insisted, "and what is more, I shall try my legs a little in the outer air to-day."

"Then this is of no use," he exclaimed in disgust, as he threw the bottle of medicine far out of the window.

I was not at all in a merry mood, but his complete discomfiture was almost enough to bring a smile to the stone face of a statue.

"Don't be angry with me for getting better," I urged.

"But why can't you live up to your symptoms? That is what I want to know."

"I always was an eccentric man," I said. "Let that fact explain the other. But sit down here, my dear boy. I want to ask you a few questions."

His face brightened, true philanthropist that he really was, at the opportunity of making himself useful. He drew up his chair and assumed an attentive expression.

"In the first place," I began, "whose house is this I am in?"

"Why, Mrs. Vegas' of course."

"You mean Mr. Vegas', I presume?"

"Oh no, I don't. It is the wives to whom the

houses are allotted in Grape Valley. The husband is her guest. As for Mr. Vegas, he is one of our buying agents, and is at San Francisco now."

"Who supports me here?" I continued.

"The State, which takes care of all the sick and disabled people in Grape Valley. You will have a chance to go to work later, never fear."

"Now, my dear boy?—By the way what is your name? George? Well, George, I want to get away from this house as soon as possible. I have been a burden on Mrs. Vegas too long already."

"I don't think she regards it in that way," said George. But I insisted.

"Of course she couldn't say so, but, if I am able, I want to go from here to-morrow. Now where am I to go?"

"Why, there is the phalanstery, No. 1, that is where your friend is."

"Just the place," I cried eagerly. "Now will you make the proper arrangements for me to go to that phalanstery?"

"Certainly I will. It is a very simple matter."

"And then come back for me to-morrow morning. I think I shall be able to go by then? But George, be careful of one thing. Don't let a word of my plan get to Kate — I mean to Mrs. Vegas' ears. We can go in the forenoon, when she is at work, you know."

"Just as you say. But wouldn't that be a little rude to her? However, that is your affair, not mine."

When the young man had gone, I put on my hat and ventured to open the door, and slowly make my way across the hall. In a moment more I had passed down the steps and was on the street. I was much stronger than yesterday. I almost wished I had made my plans to go to the phalanstery this very morning. The prospect of Kate's return, and of the tortures her presence would cause me, made me dread the afternoon. I glanced up and down the street on which I stood, and up the intersecting street, lined with little houses like the one I had suddenly grown to hate. I saw no large building such as the phalanstery must be.

Indeed, if I had seen it, and had been strong enough to walk there unassisted, I had no credentials such as I supposed would be necessary to show, entitling me to be received. I leaned against a lamp-post and tried to reconcile myself to the unavoidable return to Kate's home.

I laid out a scheme of demeanor. When she first returned from her work, and knocked at the door, I would call to her that I was just taking a nap. This would, perhaps, preserve my solitude for an hour or more. When she should at last sit down with me, and wait for my first word of reproach, I would surprise her by uttering none. I would proceed precisely as if no word of love had ever been spoken between us. I would talk of impersonal matters, and meet all approaches toward sentiment with silence, or with affected misunderstanding.

Did I still love her? My whole nature was aflame with a passion which even the thought that she was another's wife could not abate. But my passion was not of the baser sort which would be satisfied at the cost of honor or decency. No stolen delights could indeed satisfy such passion as mine. I wanted her for mine and mine alone, mine to make happy and proud, mine to cherish early and late. The more I loved her the less was I disposed to dishonor her, the more determined was I to endure the agony of living sacrifice before I should tempt her by word or look, or even by unguarded tone of voice, to lend to me what she had given to another. I would go away to-morrow because I was afraid that the tense fibres of my resolutions might relax after too long a strain. But it would prove me a weak and unworthy creature indeed, if I could not stand the trial of one afternoon.

Suddenly my heart gave a bound as a familiar woman's figure appeared at some distance up the street which intersected the one on which I stood. It was Kate, and she was running toward me as if in great excitement. Could she have met with some accident? It seemed an eternity before she reached my side. Her face was flushed, her eyes were shining as if in high fever, her bosom rose and fell tumultuously with her distressed breathing. She caught my arm.

"Where—were—you going?" she cried, catching her scant breath. "Were you going to leave me?" Then she drew me toward the house, "Oh, come back," she said. "Only come back."

In vain I assured her that I had merely come out for a walk. She did not release my arm until she had helped me into what had been my sick room. Then she threw herself into the nearest chair, and leaning her head upon the table, began sobbing as if her heart would break. Her thick coils of hair became loosened, and fell like sheets of burnished gold to the very floor beneath. Then in sudden shame—a woman looks on unbound hair as one sort of nudity—she straightened herself, and with trembling hands tried to fasten up her hair. But in an overwhelming spasm of abandon, as if she cast all thoughts but of her own misery to the winds, she released her hair again and dropping her head upon her hands gave way to weeping.

Now, as the reader will remember, I had made no plan or laid out no procedure for a case like this. The interview for which I had prepared myself was to have in it no sudden outburst of pitiful weeping. Indeed I had been taken off my guard by her very appearance in so excited a condition, when I had believed she was still at her work, and could not return for hours. Now followed this mute agony and ravishing picture of womanly beauty in distress. Was it a wonder that I forgot my scheme of behavior, and sought to meet the emergency as man has met similar ones since men and women first gave each other rapture and misery? I laid my hand upon her head. I stroked her wonderful hair, taking its shining lengths between my fingers and wondering at its softness, all the while murmuring some soft words of pity, and I am afraid, in spite of all my high resolutions, of endearment. I could only remember that she was a woman who loved me, as she sobbed there, trembling like a child. It would be time enough by and by to remind myself that she was another man's wife.

Little by little her grief seemed assuaged. Her sobs grew less frequent, and she tried twice to speak before she could catch her breath.

"I grew so worried about you, I could not work," she said at last, without lifting her head. "I felt something might be happening. And oh," she suddenly lifted her face wet with tears from her hands, " Oh, when I saw you on the street, I thought I had just come in time —— you know I couldn't live if you left me," she cried in hurried excitement. " Promise you will not leave me."

Then it was that I did something else quite out of my plan, and quite out of keeping with my sober sense of right. I bent down and kissed her, just as if the fact that we loved each other gave me any such privilege. But after this I got my bearings again. I left her side, and crossing to my own easy chair, sat down.

" Kate," I said with an air of calmness, which I found easier to assume at this distance, " sentiment is very beautiful, but we must look this matter fairly in the face. Come and sit by me, and let us talk for a few minutes."

Without a word she rose and went to the mirror, where she carefully bound up her hair. She dried her face and eyes, and afterward came, and placing her chair where she could see my face, seated herself.

" We have fallen in love with each other," I began.

" Then you love me still? " she said, and a radiant

smile overspread her face, at which I became so transported and confused that the clear delimitations of right and wrong, of honor and dishonor which had been so apparent a moment before, seemed vague and fugitive.

"Yes, I love you still," I struggled on, "and I believe I always shall love you. But that is so much the worse for me, I could not be satisfied with a part of a woman's life, even if I were base enough to be willing to cheat her husband."

"I didn't suppose you could," she assented.

So my duty became easier for me. The woman agreed with me. I did not, indeed, see how so noble a creature could be otherwise than pure.

"We ought to see each other no more," I went on. "These mutual confessions and embraces, these kisses of passion, make the ultimate parting more difficult. We should part at once."

"Don't say it," she exclaimed, putting her hands to her ears, "it is impossible."

"But," I insisted, in astonishment, "you yourself said only a moment since, that you thought as I did."

"Oh, no," she answered. "I said I didn't suppose you could be satisfied with part of the woman you loved, or be willing to deceive her husband."

"Well," I cried, "isn't that the same thing?"

She looked puzzled for an instant, and then a slight smile passed over her face, and she uttered words which were like a new and startling revelation to me.

"You forget we are in Grape Valley. Here we marry for love, and when we find we love another than our husband we can close a marriage relation — which has then become unnatural, as quickly as we created it."

To be sure. This was what Gillette had meant by free divorce. This other man's wife could cancel her marriage at will. Apparently, according to the laws and customs of Grape Valley there was nothing to shut me away from the happiness which I was so con-

12

fident this woman could give me. I had come hither
to study the workings of this institution. Before I
had so much as walked through the settlement, or had
the first conversation with the leaders of this new society, I was offered that lesson which comes from experience.

A moment ago I would have believed that I should
welcome as a special dispensation of fate the opportunity to marry this woman. But now the information
that I could marry her in accordance with the laws and
customs of Grape Valley, instead of ravishing me, affected me with a shock. Instead of bringing her nearer
to me, it seemed as if we were more divided than ever.
The prejudices of six generations of Puritan ancestors
were deeply imbedded in my nature.

But the situation was becoming very trying. I had
told this beautiful creature that I loved her. She had informed me that under the laws of the State I had entered, she could cease to become another man's wife
when she chose, and become mine. She is expecting
me to give some sign of relief and joy, but I sit there
in gloomy thought. It is at this fortunate juncture
that there comes a ring at the outer door. · With a
pretty move of impatience Kate leaves the room, and
in a moment more ushers in no other than my friend
**Ward.**

# CHAPTER XI.

He bore not a very close resemblance to the elegant Mr. Ward as he was known, and as he is doubtless remembered, at the most fashionable New York clubs. Not having shaved since we left St. Louis, his cheeks, chin and upper lip were covered with a stiff, scrubby growth of beard. He had lost the clean cut, Grecian style which he used to affect. He had doubtless expected to see me as much changed for the worse as himself. So the first remark as he limped across the room to my side was:

"I can't see that your appearance has been injured at all by your sickness, my dear boy."

I rose and we clasped hands with an heartiness which was almost an embrace. I believe, indeed, if there had been no one else in the room, we should have exchanged a genuine hug. I had not appreciated before how much my old friend really was to me.

"All you need is to use your razor," I said. "Haven't our trunks come yet? Gillette promised, you know, that they should be here soon after we were." Then I noticed my friend's inquiring glance at Kate, who was busying herself with her charming air of ingenuousness, about the room.

"Kate," I called, and Kate came to where we stood. "Kate, I want to present you to my oldest and best friend, Mr. Ward. Ward, this is the woman who has saved my life."

Then I remembered that I had been using her first name, and my voice changed in spite of my effort to control it, and a warm flush of consciousness rose to her cheeks too as I added : "This is Mrs. Vegas."

Ward, trained man of the world and accomplished gentleman as he was, could not keep the surprised look from his face. But he bowed as gracefully as if such a thing as a sprained ankle were unknown in his experience, and responded in his most courtly tones :

"Mrs. Vegas is entitled to my sincerest thanks."

"I will leave you for a little while," she said; "such devoted friends must have much to say to each other. Only do not make him too tired, Mr. Ward."

But just before she opened the door to go out she glanced anxiously, I thought appealingly, at me. I think she felt, with what we sometimes call woman's intuition, that she was leaving me exposed, at a most critical moment, to an influence very hostile to her and to her heart's desire. If so, she left in the remembrance of that appealing look a powerful shield against whatever my friend might say. I was conscious, too, that Ward saw the smile I sent to her at parting, and that his face grew more serious still. Then I set my teeth and morally braced myself to resist an attack.

What stupid mistakes our friends make. They put us upon the defensive, when we are about to surrender our position. They stir us up, by opposition, to invent excuses for doing something which in fact we were quite undecided about. So Ward, who I had instantly concluded was anxious lest I might marry Kate, took the very course most adapted to determine me to marry her.

"I have any amount of things I want to talk over with you," he began somewhat constrainedly, as is the manner of those who feel impelled to discuss our love affairs with us. "But I feel as if there is one particular matter which it is my duty to speak about, first of all."

"I concluded so."

"Ah," he continued with more freedom, "you expected it. So it is 'conscience makes cowards of us all.' I need not mince matters then?"

"Not at all," I replied with a somewhat cheerless smile. "Avail yourself of the ancient privilege of friendship, and proceed without delay to make yourself disagreeable."

We had both seated ourselves, he taking the chair recently occupied by the woman whose fate we were about to settle.

"I think I noticed the familiar signs of a quite good understanding between you and the—— I must acknowledge —— the exceedingly handsome young woman who just went out."

"With your usual acumen," I assented, calmly.

"I think also you spoke of her as Mrs. Vegas," he continued. "May I inquire is there a Mr. Vegas, or shall I use the past tense?"

"From the present outlook," I answered, "the past tense will apply to Mr. Vegas very soon."

"Great heavens," ejaculated Ward, forsaking the interrogative for the imperative mood under stress of excitement: "You don't mean to say my boy that you have already decided to marry another man's wife?"

In fact as the reader knows, I had not so decided, but my friend had driven me past the possibility of so ignominious a confession, and I replied coolly:

"You have it."

He leaped to his feet with the idea of walking to and fro across the room, a very exasperating habit of his. But he had, in his excitement, forgotten the sprained ankle, and after hobbling a few feet away, he came back and seated himself once more.

"The woman is not yet divorced, I conclude?"

"A just conclusion," I assented. "Kate is now legally married to Mr. Vegas. But I believe it does not take long in Grape Valley —— to ——"

"To make her free to marry you," interrupted Ward impatiently. "You are right. I have been studying the laws and institutions of this settlement while confined by my sprains and bruises to my bed, and can give you all the particulars. It is only necessary for her to go to the record office, make a declaration of her wish to be divorced, serve a notice on her husband; he comes to the house no more, but returns to the phalanstery, and she is free to marry again."

"Then there need certainly be no uncongenial marriages in Grape Valley," I remarked unflinchingly.

"But, Vinton, my dear boy," and Ward exchanged his sarcastic for his persuasive tone, "just stop and think what this is that you are doing. Do you really want to marry a woman who has been as fond of another man as she can be of you? Love and marriage ought to be things of eternity."

"And when true love finds its fruition in true marriage it must be for eternity," I said, a flood of new ideas touching the peculiar institution of Grape Valley rushing in upon me. "But that a woman is tied forever to a man whom she does not like, or, for that matter loves, but not to the full capacity of her nature, does not make true marriage. That is simply bondage, humiliating, brutalizing, stupefying bondage."

"But perhaps her husband loves her," urged Ward.

"Suppose he does," I retorted. "Does that entitle him to make her an unwilling victim? Is she not entitled to her experience in love as well as he? But for my part I do not believe in the reality of a love which inspires no return in its object. Love is a harmony of the male and female nature. One alone cannot make it."

"But how do you know you and she are ideal lovers?" objected Ward. "Her present husband and she made a mistake, you believe. Why may it not be that you and she may make alike error? The romantic circumstances under which she first saw you, the pity and interest any handsome invalid has for a woman, may have captivated simply her imagination. As for you, the proximity of a fond and beautiful woman when your senses were in a weak and tremulous condition, gratitude and complacency in the enjoyment of the evident admiration you excite, may well have made even a less fanciful man than you believe himself possessed by a love which is enduring. How do you know that you may not, both of you, awake at no distant date to find your marriage too a failure, or at least a failure to one of you ? "

" Let me see," I remarked with an air of testing my memory. "That would resemble the case of a widow who makes a second poor marriage. There would be this difference, however; in civilization a mis-mated husband and wife only have opportunity to marry again under happier auspices through the death or disgrace of one or the other ; in Grape Valley a mistake is no sooner discovered than it can be rectified. As you shrewdly suggest, a mistake is possible even in the instance now under discussion. It is always possible that infatuated men and women may not discover, until after the intimacy which marriage only can bring, that they are inharmonious. But, while in civilization such mistakes result in life-long misery, in mutual unkindness, in hunger for the sympathy and inspiration only a true marriage gives, in Grape Valley they can be corrected as soon as discovered. Here the man and woman who cannot answer to each other's needs are permitted to find their way to other hearts, ready and waiting for them."

" Then the idea of marrying and remarrying *ad libitum* does not shock you ! " demanded Ward. " After a woman has had several husbands how must a sane and unprejudiced man regard her ? "

This question was, to be sure, a searching one, and I did not answer it as readily as most of my friend's challenges. It appealed to my prejudices, and not wholly in vain. I recollected the not always undeserved slurs cast upon the women in civilization who

had been through the divorce court, the common reflections, too, on widows and widowers who ventured
again and still again into new bonds of matrimony.
But not content with his advantage, Ward proceeded
to follow it up.

"Think of the disgrace to a woman of being repeat-
edly divorced."

But my friend had himself suggested a point of view
taking which the aspect of matters seemed to me changed.
"The conditions in civilization and here are entirely
different," I answered. "In New York a divorced
woman is counted disgraced because the causes for
which divorces are issued are disgraceful. In Grape
Valley you tell me the desire of either party to be free
is sufficient. In civilization, the cause of a divorce
must be bad conduct of at least one party, implying
most commonly some fault in the other. Here incompatibility is the all-sufficient occasion for divorces, and
since it is a matter of common sense to see that the
man and woman who are not suited to each other are
no less likely to be entirely suited to some other natures, so both man and woman are freed here from all
possible stigma or reproach. It is the very frequency
of divorce here which must make the fact as touching
this or that woman insignificant as a measure of worth,
amiability or virtue. As to your comparison of widows
and widowers, whose too often repeated marital experiences serve to point so many ghastly jokes and se-
pulchral witticisms——"

"Well, as for them, what?" interjected Ward.

"Why there is no analogy, my dear Ward," I continued; "a husband or wife in Grape Valley does not
have to wait until the other's death for freedom when
desired. It is because rapid remarriages by widows
and widowers indicate that they have been hoping for
the death of their partners that we look upon them
with such disfavor. It must be considered one of the
advantages of society in Grape Valley that, under no

circumstances, could a husband or wife here be suspected of wishing the other under the ground."

Ward arose. "Not going?" I exclaimed. "Why there are a thousand things I want to ask you about — when is Gillette coming back? How long before——"

"Not to-day," he said shortly. "I am out of all patience with you, and am going back to the phalanstery. Where did Mrs. Vegas put my hat? Oh, here it is." And taking his hat from the table and pulling it low on his forehead, as I had known him often to do when out of temper, he walked slowly toward the door. Just before reaching it, however, he turned and said:

"I presume nothing will keep you from doing this very foolish thing. You forget all your previous beliefs and faiths; you forget that by taking this step you are binding yourself to this system of society, and to the sacrifice of a civilization for which you are particularly fitted. You forget every thing but the overmastering passion which you would be the first to despise in another."

"Excuse me," I began.

"No," he interrupted; "I am not going to stay to hear any more foolishness. I just want to urge you, in the name of the good sense you once possessed, do not offer yourself to her to-day. Think over all I have said in cool blood through the watches of another night. I can't think that you will be as foolish to-morrow. I will see you, then. Good-bye."

And he opened the door and shut himself out so quickly that I had no time to answer even his good-bye.

Did I intend to follow his discreet advice and postpone further love-making until to-morrow? Why, when he had come I was very far from being ready to offer myself in marriage to this woman, who was another man's wife. But after an hour's discussion of the subject, after hearing all his objections, which were, indeed, my own, and forcing myself to answer

13

them, I felt that my mind was made up. I was only glad my friend Ward had not insisted on my making him a promise to postpone a proposal of marriage until to-morrow. I should have been very sorry to be discourteous and refuse so small a favor to so old a friend, and very probably would have given him the promise. I always dislike lying, too, and despise a liar, such as I know I should have proved myself, if I had promised what he desired. Before his footsteps had ceased to be audible, as he limped angrily up the street — what is more vehemently expressive than the limp of a man out of temper — I was already listening for the other step I knew so well, and which never failed to make my heart beat faster. Before I saw her I knew I was going to say, and to-day, just what Ward had asked me not to say. The longed-for knock came, but it was more timid than ever before, instinct with a dread of that loving heart for what my visitor might have urged against her cause.

I crossed the room and opened the door myself. As Kate turned up to me her doubting, questioning face, as if she were almost certain my friend was not hers, and had made my heart cold to her, yet still ventured a sweet little hope that I had resisted him, she was, indeed, quite adorable.

I led her into the room, with my arm lightly about her, and waited to hear her speak. Man is a cruel being. He delights in the tender tortures of the woman he loves.

"Your friend is gone," she said faintly, and then, in a moment, as if yielding to irresistible impulse: "Did he urge you not to —— not to ——" But her lips quivered and she did not complete her sentence.

"Yes, Kate," I answered calmly, for all the loud beating of my heart. "He told me that what I wanted to do would be the most foolish act of my life."

"And you?" She raised her eyes to mine, as if she could not wait for the dreaded answer from my lips.

How sweet is the spectacle of the agonies of love, when one knows he can turn them to raptures with a word.

"In spite of all, I have decided to ask you to be my wife." Then my voice trembled too.

She threw her arms about my neck in that sweet fashion I wonder no other woman ever learned, and drew my face to hers, pale no more, but flushed with the glad crimson of satisfied love.

"You know my answer," she murmured.

# CHAPTER XII.

The next day Kate Vegas filed her record of divorce, and I removed to the phalanstery.

The evening that I went down to the main hall for the first time I was met at the door by Kate. She drew me into a retired corner and whispered:

"Mr. Vegas has returned. I have notified him of my divorce."

The thought of the man who had lately stood to my sweetheart in the relation of husband was a pain to me.

"How did he take it?" I asked, in a rather perfunctory manner.

"I don't think he was displeased. I almost suspect he has met some one in San Francisco whom he thinks he can love better than he has loved me."

"I hope I shall never see him," I exclaimed vehemently, "I cannot bear the thought that a living man besides me ever gathered you to his heart."

Kate gave me a reproachful look. Her lips parted for an eloquent protest, but she closed them again, and turned away from me. Her womanhood had suffered insult, and from the man whom she had expected would be the first to cherish it.

"There comes Mr. Gillette," she said, as a figure separated itself from the groups in the center of the hall, and moved in our direction. "He will want to talk with you, and I will go."

Like a coward, I let her go without a word to heal the wound I had given her. A convalescent is, perhaps, entitled to some excuse for the faults which grow out of low vitality and enfeebled tone. I crave all the allowance due me.

"Raised from the dead!" exclaimed Gillette, as he took my hand in his hearty grasp. "Now you can seriously begin to study the institutions of Grape Valley. By the way," he continued, looking around, "who was the woman whom my approach seemed to drive away."

"It was Mrs. Vegas. She nursed me to renewed life and health, and I am going to marry her in a fortnight."

"Bless me,' ejaculated Gillette. "Let me congratulate you. You are going to study our institutions from the inside, I see."

He laughed, but, noticing that my face did not relax, he suddenly grew serious in turn. "Excuse me. I am, perhaps, too frivolous. By the way, Vinton, this is no place for us to talk confidentially, and I know we must have a great deal to say to each other. Suppose you take me to your room. You look too pale to be in such a crowd to-night, anyhow."

Within a few minutes more he was seated in my room. Having accepted a cigar from my guest, I was enjoying my first smoke for several weeks. As the genial influence of the tobacco began to diffuse itself over me, my heart began to expand, so that when Gillette said, "Tell me all about it," I rehearsed the short story of my courtship and acceptance. Perhaps my manner lacked the enthusiasm and my tone the fervor to be expected of one of my temperament who describes what should be the happiest experience of his life. Gillette, however, had far too much tact to inform me that I betrayed an unloverlike feeling. If he had been a more intimate friend, he might have committed the indiscretion of cross-examining me. As it was he sought refuge in abstractions, and betook himself to generalities.

"It is one of the most striking features of our system," he said, "that it puts to death so many of the artificial sentimentalities, and false conceits which have flourished through centuries of courtship and marriage, under the old regime. That a woman has ever been engaged to a predecessor is always a most painful revelation to your lover of civilization. It takes the fine edge from his sentiment. He would have his sweetheart come to him without ever having known that men were handsome and fascinating. He craves the privilege of teaching her heart to beat full and strong, her breath to come in sighs, she knows not why. All that is a remnant of the ages during which women were the slaves of their lords and masters, men, and unworthy a time when women proudly claim to be our equals. Men in Grape Valley ask no more of the women they love than the women in civilization ask of the men. As the women of the old order of society usually prefer men who have had their affairs of the heart, and received the expansion and education such experiences give, so the men of this settlement for the most part prefer women who understand enough of themselves to know what qualities in a man are to their taste, and enough of men to escape the error of being too exacting, on the one side, or too careless, on the other. The rest of the world appreciates what experience does to develop and to proportion a man, to make him agreeable, considerate, sympathetic, to make him wholly himself. We in Grape Valley appreciate that experience does the same for a woman as for a man. If she has grown to be adapted to our taste we have only thanks for the lovers or husbands who have made her all that she is. We care not whom she loved when her nature was only partly formed, and has outgrown. We care not who it was to whom she was attracted for certain qualities which she afterward found insufficient to hold her love. We care not whom she thought she loved, so long as she loves him no more, and, we believe, offers us the cream of her life's experience, so long as we believe she finds in us that spiritual and physical completion that her fully-developed nature requires."

Thus Gillette seemed to take for granted that I agreed with all he said, and it was only long afterward that I suspected that he was really reading me a lecture of which he saw I stood greatly in need. What he said, indeed, came like balm to my heart, torn and bruised as it was by the reawakening prejudices imbibed through the commonplaces to which I had listened since boyhood, and which in fact fill the pages of all the sentimental literature of the world. There are times when the nature is as hungry for counsel, as eager for correction as the sick man for his medicine. But to be accepted, that counsel or correction must come without exciting our combativeness or our distrust. Human nature is always most willing to be led, but it always dislikes to be reminded that the process is threatened or going on. Finally, however, the discussion of this subject, even in generalities, was more than I felt as if I could longer endure, and after a few silent puffs at my cigar, I changed the current of the talk.

"You have told me that this settlement of a thousand men, besides the women and children, is but seven years old. Surely you did not all emigrate here at once?"

"No," answered Gillette, calmly accepting the dismissal of the other theme, "there were but two hundred of us, and all men, who first set up here new industrial and social institutions. We were from different cities, but all belonged to societies and clubs organized to discuss and promulgate advanced or radical ideas of some sort. The scheme of a colony originated in a New York club, and the full number of two hundred for the original colony was made up by sending one of our number to other societies of like scope, and proselyting. Only those with plenty of money could be taken at first, for there must be no hindrances to success founded on a lack of money." ˙

"How did you decide upon the place?" asked I, intensely interested in the remarkable story.

"Oh, a committee was sent out, first of all, to find a location where we would be likely to have no interference while we should carry out our plans. The committee was unrestricted in its choice by nation, continent or hemisphere. The general feeling seemed to be, however, that we had better seek out some small island in Australasia or Polynesia. It was by accident that the committee, while lost in the desert lying south of us, came upon this valley. There were no signs that it had ever seen the face of human being before. It had every advantage and convenience as to market and of climate, indeed, the conveniences of every climate. It was large enough at least to congregate our colony, and enable us to pass through our provisional and experimental period. From this center we could gather new converts with the greatest ease; then if, or rather when, we were discovered, and the wiseacres should proceed to adjudge us mischievous, and interfere with our social institutions, it would be time enough to sell our possessions and emigrate with our acquired strength and numbers, to some country where we might make and keep our own laws."

"There were but two hundred men of you, you say; where did your women afterward come from?"

"It is simple enough. There is every thing in our scheme of equality of the sexes and of the removal of old restrictions which operate so much more to the injury of women than of men, to commend it to the imagination and judgment of intelligent women. But you ask for details. Many of the two hundred had wives of intelligence as enthusiastic for the colony as their husbands, others had sweethearts. Some had female relatives dependent upon them and most eager for this opportunity to emancipate themselves. But

far the greater portion of the first female colonists
were bright and beautiful women who were known as
having advanced ideas, and who threw in their lot with
us full of a faith and devotion which fairly shamed
certain fearful ones of the men. When the committee
reported, the first delegation of two hundred went out
to put up such buildings as we should need, plant the
first crops and prepare the site of what was afterward
to be the happy home of the colony, which when it
finally arrived and set up the new State, numbered
four hundred and fifty in all, including a few
children."

" And what is your total number now ? "

"Something over three thousand," answered Gillette. Then he continued with a smile for the excitement
which I could not but display at his narration : "I suppose
that you want me to tell you how we have more than
sextupled our numbers in seven years. Well, every
year we have added nearly as many to our settlement
as constituted our first colony. Propagandism we consider one of our first duties ; for a few hundred of us
to rest happy in the enjoyment of institutions, which,
if adopted, would cure all the diseases of the old
social order, would seem unpardonable selfishness to us.
We seek, therefore, for new converts, and seek for
them on an organized system, which, if our success
continues, will soon overcrowd the valley. Then we
plan to equip a new band of pioneers, who shall seek
out some other unknown spot, and make another city
as happy as this. It may be by that time there will
have been changes in the outside world, however,
which will open to us far greater possibilities of
proselyting, and a field for illustration of our principles
on a more open and progressive scale than we now can
calculate on. Our agents, of whom there are none
more persuasive than Mr. Vegas, whose wife you have
won, move in the most cultivated society of our large
cities. When they meet a progressive spirit, a hint

14

is first dropped, and if properly received, then a partial description of our ideal State is given. Sometimes men and women are prepared by their own ideas to be converted, but more often they are the scholars of bitter experience. You have no idea how radical the cultivated mind of to-day has become. It fears nothing, dares every thing. Nothing is too high for it to doubt, or too low for it to study. There are innumerable men and women of culture in the United States alone, who would gladly join us to-morrow if we could reach them. And as for the millions of the poor and suffering to whom any change would be welcome, such a state of society as ours would seem like paradise itself to them. Universal as is the disgust of men for nineteenth century civilization, society and morals, almost as great is their faith in the possibility of something better."

My cigar burned my moustache and I threw it away. Gillette had suffered his to go out while he talked, and now meditatively chewed it. I was filled with a thrilling desire to become a positive part of this marvelous State, but I was in a dense condition of ignorance as to its industrial and economical organization.

"I must not be looked upon as a guest here," I said after a short pause. "I shall be able to go to work in another week. Just tell me how I can pull an oar."

"Our system is very simple. Of course you know what socialism is so far as employment and livelihood go. If not, read up on the subject. We practice it in Grape Valley, as it is only under proper and natural economical conditions that even the most shocking failures of civilization can be corrected. You can choose the line in which you would be active, as long as you choose something you are capable of doing reasonably well. You need to work but four hours a day. You will receive a card entitling you to receive your share of all the good things brought to Grape Valley or produced here. Everybody shares alike here." Then Gillette glanced at his watch and exclaimed: "Ah, it is high time a convalescent like you were in bed. I have talked to you too long. But one thing more," he said as he rose: "Every time I look at this watch, I think of that awful experience of ours in the cañon. Now as to that gold mine. I have not forgotten it, though you may have done so, amid your more delightful meditations. As soon as you are entirely well, and Mr. Ward's ankle is strong again, we must make up a party and explore. It will be a great boon to our colony, and make you new comers very popular, as bestowing it. Good-night."

The next week I felt able to begin my activities, and being urged on account of my literary experience to take a position on the weekly publication which entertained and sought to instruct the valley, I acceded. My first work was to review a novel which had made the hit of the season in the outside world by exposing its vices, and the editor was pleased to compliment me on my effort.

In another week Kate Vegas became Kate Vinton, and I went to live with her at her pretty home where I had already experienced so much happiness and such keen distress.

# CHAPTER XIII.

I have no space in this record to describe in detail the economical system of Grape Valley, except so far as necessary to give a correct impression of the peculiar social institutions. It was simply an example of practical socialism. The State regulated and directed labor, and divided among the laborers all the profits thereof. Each adult man and woman worked four hours of six days in the week at the tasks assigned, and each man and woman received an equal share of the profits of that labor. Thus no one had more than he needed while all had enough, with leisure and cultivation to enjoy it. It was a state of society where selfishness tended to die out, and the principles of religion, hard to follow elsewhere, became the natural impulse. The tendency was to develop the higher faculties and enlarge the spiritual capacities. The viler passions and grosser impulses, from lack of field or occasion, fell into disuse.

But it is with regard to the effect of this new economical system on the emancipation of women, and in bringing into being a fuller and higher sexual relation, that I want to write more particularly here. The religious revival in this society is of very great importance, but I must leave even that for the present. If I can give the outside world a true sense of the meaning and full scope of the altered relations of the sexes as exhibited in this new colony, I shall, perhaps, have done all that my duty now lays upon me.

As soon as my friend Ward had recovered from his lameness sufficiently to be assigned to some activity, he selected a position on the newspaper, more I think to be near me than from any inclination for what he rather contemptuously styled "everlasting scribbling." His leisure time he devoted most assiduously to studying the social and economic conditions of the settlement. He was as fond as ever of discussion, and with the single exception of the peculiar marriage laws in Grape Valley, a subject which was tabooed between us for a long time, we used to analyze, philosophize, correct and revise every thing said or done in this most interesting State.

He did not care to talk about the peculiar relations of the sexes here because he saw me irrevocably committed to them, and to attack and score them, as I knew he wanted to do, would be intolerable to his only friend. For the first few weeks after my marriage I was naturally in no mood to hear profane criticisms. I was as happy a husband as the certainty of eternal possession of the woman I called my wife could have made me. I was, to be sure, thankful that free divorce had been a possibility in Grape Valley, because it was owing to this institution that so happy a union as mine with Kate became a fact. If it had been in New York that I had met her, although her husband might be the object of profoundest aversion to her, and I the sole object of her tender thoughts when awake, and of her dreams when asleep, we could not have become what we longed to be to each other. We might have caused open scandal and made ourselves notorious, regardless of the customs of decent people. We might have met each other by stealth, and sacrificed our honor and self-respect for the sake of stolen hours which would have had more of agony than of rapture. But the free divorce law of Grape Valley gave us to each other fully and ungrudgingly, so I could not take offense at the institution.

To be sure I did not forget that Kate was free, if I showed myself surly or unloving, to put a limit to our intimacy to-morrow. Nor did I forget that if I saw a woman whose beauty thrilled or whose intellect attracted me more, I could leave my new-made bride forever. But Kate and I would prefer each other always I was sure. No law was required to keep us always close to each other's hearts. We would continue to love each other forever, because we were each what best supplied the wants of the other.

I had lost the sense of outrage that scourged me when I first knew that she had had another marital experience. She was mine now and I believed mine forever. So, when one evening she dropped a casual word which implied that she had been married more than once before, and then gave me a frightened look, as if expecting an indignant outburst, I bore the test without a change of color. I even asked her to tell me her whole history, and felt prepared to listen to it calmly. It was at dusk and we sat on a secluded piazza in the rear of the house, when the conversation took this turn. I drew her head to my shoulder while she talked, so she should be spared the discomfort of meeting my eyes.

"I was one of the first four hundred and fifty who came to Grape Valley," she began. "It did not look much as it does now. But you don't care about that. I came with my father who was a famous radical, and who gladly put all his own property into this experiment. Those who were already married lived as we are living now in separate houses. Most of us, however, were unmarried then, and occupied rooms in the phalanstery. There was but one phalanstery at that time. There are six now. Forenoons we were at work. Afternoons we usually gave to reading or study, while the evenings went for amusement and social intercourse in our large hall. I was called pretty then."

Of course I kissed the beautiful up-turned face, and gave the proper rebuke to her false modesty. Then she continued with a laugh:

"But not as pretty as you call me now. Love and courtship were in the air. I was wooed to my heart's content. But I did not know what love was, much less what marriage ought to be. I thought if I liked and respected a man, and if there was nothing in his person which offended me, that was reason enough for marrying him if he asked me. I laughed at what I considered the wild words of passionate lovers. I thought they must be constituted very differently from me, or else language meant very little to them. You must remember it was not because I was rebellious against the restrictions which civilization puts about the passion of men and women that I came hither. I was here simply because my father was a convert, and brought me. So when I married it was a friend of my father's, an elderly man who had as little sentiment about the relations of the sexes as myself. He was an enthusiast over the solution of the labor problem, and was a firm believer in the emancipation of women through pecuniary independence and free divorce. Toward me he was always polite, and used to talk a great deal about the principles of the new order, but not at all of love or sentiment."

Kate sighed and was silent for a moment.

"It can't be," I broke in sharply, "that you regret a man whom you do not think loved you even for one minute?"

"Oh, no, it was not for him I sighed just now. I was thinking of my father."

"Why have I not seen your father?"

She pressed my hand. "He died when I had been married two years. Upon him I had lavished all the tenderness a woman must give somewhere. When he died I suffered intensely, but my poor husband could not give me the smallest consolation. Yet I so longed for love then. For weeks I did little else than moan and weep, and the obvious discomfort I caused my unsympathetic husband was almost absurd. I grew to despise him, and so the first young man after that who breathed a word of ordinary human sympathy into my ear won my heart. It was a month from the death of my father that I had become unmarried again. As for my first husband, he has not ventured a second time into matrimony. Hundreds of thousands of tender impulsive girls marry such men in the outside world, and beat their very life out against such cold, unresponsive natures. There is no release except in death. In six months I had married the young man who had first comforted me. His affectation of pity had won fondness from me which was as near love as my nature was ripe for then."

She released my hand for a moment, and turned her face a little more away from me. "My life with this young man was an experience I do not like to call to mind. I do not doubt that even Ralph —— but never mind his name, I don't doubt that even he, sensual as was his nature, purely physical as was his whole attraction toward our sex, served to develop me. Yet he had no conception of intellectual or spiritual attraction. His love was nothing but animalism, and in my ignorance I believed him to be what lovers always were. To be sure my first husband was not of his sort, but my first husband, I remembered, had no idea of love of any kind. I believed I had now married a representative man, the sort of creature women die for, the hero of love sonnets, the ideal of sentimental girlhood which does not, in its purity, suspect the brute under the thin disguise. If my first marriage failed to teach me the real meaning of the sexual relation, I certainly learned to despise it as exemplified in my second. I pitied every wife in Grape Valley. I hated every man in Christendom. But speedy as was my conviction that marriage was too great a degradation for me, this second husband of mine was before me with his application for divorce. He had wearied of me already, and had passed on to educate some other woman. I could but think of the shame worse than death of being bound, as countless women are to such husbands for life, as completely gross in their nature as the beasts of the field, selfish, cruel creatures of flesh, to whom women are simply victims."

She gave a shudder of repugnance and continued : " I lived at the phalanstery for two years after this. A woman once married has the choice between her allotted house and the phalanstery. I became a satirist on marriage, even as it is in Grape Valley. If indeed all men were as my second husband, love was a mockery, and women would only be really emancipated when they ceased to marry at all. I was quite a favorite in the theatricals we had at the hall, and the object of the attentions of many suitors. But it was only after being convinced that all men were not beasts that I married Henry Vegas. I was not infatuated with him, I was not oblivious to his faults, which, however, I will not rehearse. But until I met you, I thought I loved him and that he loved me." Then she raised her head from my shoulder and throwing her arms about my neck, turned her eyes to mine. " Now I know not only that I did not love him but that he did not truly love me."

I kissed her, but an uncomfortable thought was troubling me. " May I ask you one more question ? "

" Any thing you like," she answered, without removing her arms from my neck.

" Have you had no children ? "

" None," she answered. " But if I had been a mother, you know, the children would not be with me."

" I know," I answered, " the nursery and schools take the little ones." I hesitated a moment and then I added softly: " I do not believe this part of the system would suit me. Would you leave Grape Valley if I asked you ? "

She had dropped her eyes, although her arms still clasped my neck. Her face flushed with emotion as she answered: "I will go where you ask me to go. I believe in you so."

The next afternoon I suggested to Kate that we visit the nursery together. I felt that there was no detail of the whole system more important than this matter of the disposition of the children. She readily assented, but just as we were setting out who should appear at our door-step but Mr. Gillette, come to pay us his first call since our marriage? Gillette was always charming and full of tact, genial in his manner, apparently enjoying our society, and eager that we should enjoy his. He congratulated me on the good work Ward and I were doing in the "Fraternity" office, and said it was exciting general interest. He spoke of the plans for a new sort of evening entertainment at the phalanstery halls. Finally he announced that he should start on another trip East, during the next week, and remarked:

"Before I go we must organize an expedition to the gold mines." Then he added: "I take it for granted that the temporary insanity which made us want to keep the treasure for ourselves has left us all long ago."

"Of course," I answered. "But how can we reach the mines?" I asked. "Must Rapid river be drawn off again, and so every time when the miners set out for the mine, or return from it?"

"You doubtless remember," answered Gillette, "that the gold mine was found at the head of a second gorge, perhaps a former bed for Rapid river, or certainly for some stream. "Well, I think I have found a spot where that gorge opens into this valley."

"Then all we shall have to do," I exclaimed eagerly, "will be to follow up the ravine to the placer mine." A sudden thought struck me. "But what object can be so much gold to this community?"

"It would be of little good, except for its purchasing power outside, as we all appreciate, but through that purchasing power it will be of inestimable value to us. Our gold mine, if it is as rich as we believe, will make a great change in Grape Valley. We are comfortable now ; we may be luxurious. We live in simple homes ; we may be able to convert them into mansions."

" Shall we start on our exploring expedition to-morrow ? " I asked.

" Why not ? " Then he rose to his feet. " But I see Mrs. Vinton is dressed for the street. I am detaining you."

" We are going to the nursery," answered Kate, rising. " It would be pleasant to have you go with us. You could explain to Mr. Vinton better than I. Besides, he always stares when he hears me talk half reasonably about the principles of our life here."

So Gillette went with us.

" This is the nursery proper," said Gillette, when after a short walk, he stopped us in front of a large building, in general appearance resembling the phalansteries. " Here our little ones are kept and cared for until about six years old. Sometimes they stay for a shorter, and sometimes for a longer period, depending, of course, on the greater or less precocity of the child. When old enough for school, the children are transferred to the building in the rear, with the white pillars, which you see. Still another building takes them at eleven, and keeps them until seventeen, after which they are ready for advanced training, industrial and intellectual, until twenty-two."

"Are they separated from their parents all these years ? " I inquired, and I know I looked any thing but satisfied with this feature of Grape Valley life.

"Separated from their parents ? " repeated Gillette. " Why, there is no separation at all. In infancy, in youth, in early manhood and womanhood, the children meet, know and love their fathers and mothers to the heart's content of all concerned. All the features of the relation of parent and child which give unselfish

joy are gratified through our system. The family, as
an alliance, offensive and defensive, against the world,
however, has no occasion in a state of society where
the feeling of good-will and fraternity is universal.
Fathers and mothers are no longer the stern mentors,
the masters and mistresses of their children, forced to
discipline more often than to pet, and in case of the
death of a child, having usually more words of irritation to repent than memories of caresses to cherish.
Under our system parents seem to their children love
and tenderness personified. The natural emotions
have full scope unmixed with the vocation of teacher
or disciplinarian. Why, my dear Vinton, our system
of nurture and education of children is as satisfactory
in its results as the altered relations of the sexes here.
But let us go inside the nursery."

There was not the slightest restriction upon our
coming and going as we wished. Indeed, many men
and women entered while we were there, some in
pairs, but others alone. Each seemed to know just
where the little one he or she sought was to be found,
and the joy shining in baby eyes and the smiles dimp-
ling baby cheeks were sweet to see. If the visitor
were a man a short call usually sufficed. The nurse
put the little one on its points and the father admired
and kissed his baby for the usual length of time babies
are wont to amuse their fathers the world over. Then the
men were wont to saunter out. But most of the mothers
came to spend hours, and no nurses were needed then,
you may be sure.

In other rooms were children who could play and
talk, and there, too, were fathers and mothers listening in delight to the prattle of infancy and joining in
the games. A happier sight I had not seen in Grape
Valley.

"How long can the parents stay with their little
ones?" I asked.

"All day and all night, too," answered Kate, "if

they choose, always provided they do not interfere with the sanitary rules of the nursery."

"What more could a parent's heart desire?" demanded Gillette. "During his working and his sleeping hours his babies are well tended and carefully nursed. Their food is the most healthful than can be provided, and every device of science and invention is exhausted to insure health, growth and entertainment. Whatever leisure the parent may have can be spent with the children, if desired. To be sure the parents of Grape Valley are not deprived of needed sleep by the demands of the baby; to be sure the mothers are not worried out of their health and defrauded of their youth by the tasks of doing housework, attending to a husband's necessities, and nursing crying and unhappy children. I know that you are a little prejudiced against this one of our institutions. Admit now, don't you begin to think we do these things better here?"

"But some mothers would, I should think, want to be with their babies, and care for them more than during what you call their leisure," I objected.

"Our system is elastic enough to suit such cases," replied Gillette. "If you will notice, my dear Vinton, I think you will see that such mothers have every right or privilege they could desire. A mother, who chooses, can have nursing assigned to her for her labor, and so can stay with her little one as long as in this building. In such cases she is taken from the rolls of her previous employment and entered here. It is from such women, indeed, that the force of nurses is kept supplied, their hours of labor, however, being made as light as those of other workers. In such cases the husband rooms here with his wife as long as she remains. As a matter of experience we have found, however, that while, of course, most mothers remain here for about a year, after that period they usually prefer to resume their regular avocations and live in a home by themselves."

Before talking any further we began a tour of the building. There was perfect cleanliness everywhere, and the sweet-faced babies in every stage of growth, from that of a few weeks and long dresses, to the toddlers, just taking their first steps, and the rompers, with bright eyes, rosy cheeks and curling locks, made an enchanting spectacle.

"Behind these portals are the very little ones," smiled Gillette, as we passed a row of chamber doors, "and their mothers."

"Then this is a lying-in hospital, as well as a nursery?" I inquired.

"Yes," he answered, "the women of Grape Valley in coming here are assured the best of care and medical attendance, and the little one from the moment of its arrival in the world is subjected to only the best advised sanitary influences. The first few weeks of a baby's life should have the wisest of nursing and most judicious management. Nothing should be left to accident or to indiscreet if affectionate attendants. We have prevented that careless nurture of very little children which in the outside world results so commonly in the slaughter of the innocents."

Then Gillette took us to the room where the larger children were at play, watched and assisted by their nurses, and the numerous visitors, and having most royal fun. The door into the playground was wide open, and each child took its own choice of indoor or outdoor delights.

"Even the plays of the children," said Gillette, "we make the means of their education, moral, intellectual and physical. All plays which really interest children do so because they develop certain faculties or muscles, employ, and hence educate certain moral qualities. It is because manufacturers do not remember this fact that children in the outside world throw away so many of the toys brought them by fond, but not discriminating parents and friends, and prefer some rude inventions of their own. In Grape Valley we make use of our knowledge of this principle in our scheme of education, beginning at infancy and lasting through all our school period. We make the plays and the sports educate, and in turn we make education entertaining."

Then we glanced into the dining-room with its rows of high chairs and dainty trays. The bed-rooms next came in for our attention, and a more sweetly suggestive sight than the hundreds of little cribs, in each of which nestled at night some little one fresh from the clouds, I do not expect ever to see. Then we glanced into the hospital, happily unoccupied.

"No children are sick, I am glad to see."

"Sickness is a very rare thing with our little ones," answered Gillette. "Their nurture as you have seen is not a matter of accident. Each one is always under the eyes of the nurses, whose entire duty it is to look out for the health and entertainment of their charges. Such a thing as an exposure to chill, or too great heat of the sun, or as over-excitement, injudicious eating, serious falls, or accidents of any sort, are well-nigh impossible. So they grow up strong and robust, and will make healthy men and women, with every advantage for after life which perfect physical condition can give. So, too, they will be more likely in turn to have healthy offspring. Calisthenics are also provided to form and develop the children's muscles, and promote complete circulation of the blood. A few generations of such physical training as the children and youth of Grape Valley receive will produce a new athletic race of both sexes."

"It is a most charming place," I said as we made our way slowly to the street. "I would not have believed it possible you could have solved the difficulty so well."

"Yes," remarked Gillette. "You see that we had a great difficulty to overcome. There were three reasons why children and parents could not live in one

family under our system. First, it would have inter
fered with the attention of husbands and wives to each
other, have shut the women out from social pleasures, and
have made impossible the financial independence which
alone can emancipate them. Second, without the labor
of the women in general industry, we could not reduce the hours as much as was advisable. Third, the
presence of children in a home would be insurmount-
able obstacles to free divorce. But while we solved
those difficulties and without antagonizing nature in
her smallest promptings, without flying in the face of
any instinct, we have accomplished most excellent results in other directions. The children are the future
members of the social State. They should be fitted for
their duties and enjoyments by the State herself, for
whose well-being and for the gradual uplifting of
human nature it is vital that the children im-
bibe no mischievous individualizing ideas such as tend
to disintegrate society, which should be organized on
universal relations of fraternity. Under our system,
too, the parents need be put to no anxiety as to the support or education of their child. All this is taken from
their shoulders by the State. The intense desire of
parents that their offspring should have every possible
advantage in their start in life is at once a cause of
harrowing anxiety and a constant spur to overwork.
Yet in civilization that longing is seldom gratified.
Here, on the other hand, every child is assured a complete and symmetrical education, and is started in life
with all the natural powers in the most-perfect possible
development. What consummation could be more de-
voutly wished for by any father or mother? Moreover
the life and activity, hopes and fears of men and women,
when just entering upon what should be their most
pleasant and useful period, need not be entirely absorbed in providing for the present or future of their
children. The mother may retain here her fresh-
ness of mind and body. Her vigor and vitality are

not sapped by the constant care of children at a time when she should be in her glory. She can continue to be ornamental and useful to society. She is able also to continue to make herself pleasing to her husband, to hold fast his attachment if there is the proper relation between them, and if on the other hand, he proves not to be her ideal, she has kept her attractiveness, and is likely to make a new and more happy connection."

"But," I suggested, "this nurture of the children by the State would naturally tend to destroy individuality, I should think, and make the man and woman of the future less interesting and less useful."

Kate made haste to reply: "If we have, through our system, prevented the perpetuation of some of the eccentricities which make people different, I think it a general advantage."

Gillette listened to Kate's remark with interest, but apparently he concluded she had not disposed of the whole question. "Our system," he said, "gives to all the benefits of the best conditions for nurture and education, so that no victim of circumstances can ever grow up in Grape Valley to curse early associations or lack of training. I think the breadth of our scheme of education will provide, too, against distorted or perverted growths, which are commonly due to narrow influences and limited knowledge. Our graduates, too, will be certain to have the personal habits and manners of what are called in your civilization gentlemen and ladies. But as the same sunlight, the same showers, the same variety of soil develop different seeds into entirely different fruits and flowers, so the infinite diversities of inherited traits and capacities must develop into diversified maturity in human beings. Just as different fruits and flowers intensify their diversity under the highest cultivation, so it will be with our nurture and education of the human slips committed to the broad and universal care of the State. The variations caused by comparative ignorance or

16

knowledge, by unnatural perversions of disposition or of taste, from scant or defective education will, I hope, disappear. But the men and women of the future, the graduates of our State nurseries and schools, will show far more variety of excellence, far more diversity in genius than has ever been dreamed of in the past.''

"You think the education of the children is the reasonable service of the State?" I remarked, as we turned into our own street.

"Yes, for two reasons," answered Gillette. "First, because the State can do it so much better, as I have been showing; second, because the burden is too great for the individual. The father, freed from such responsibilities, can give his energies to perfecting himself, extending the scope of his usefulness to his fellows as well as enjoying the fulness of the lover relation with his wife. The burden which weighs down the father usually crushes the mother, and by its removal she leaps at once into the glory of complete womanhood, the source of infinite improvement and inspiration to society. Thus our species will make rapid progress as much through the continued education of the parent as through the better education of the children.''

By this time we had arrived at our home, and Gillette was raising his hat at parting, but I detained him.

"By the way, why don't you invite me to your house? Where do you live, anyhow?"

"At the phalanstery, No. 1," he answered with a laugh. "Come up and see me." And he hurried off as if to shut off further questioning.

"Poor fellow," I said as I put my arm about the shoulders of my sweet wife. "You don't mean to say he is not married? That is very strange."

"Charming as he is," answered Kate, as soon as her lips were free again, "he has failed to commend himself to the only woman in Grape Valley he has ever seemed to care for. Oh no, I don't mean myself," she laughed. " But they now say that he has found con- solation in a rich widow of New York, and is likely soon to bring her to Grape Valley."

# CHAPTER XIV.

The next day the proposed exploring party was organized and we set out for the Rapid river placer mine, *via* what was known as White Gorge. The party was composed of Gillette, Ward and me as leaders and guides, the mining expert of the settlement, Harvey by name, and a half dozen able-bodied men, whose names are of no importance in this history. We had two pack mules loaded with implements for washing out the "pay dirt" in a more modern fashion than before, axes to clear away the path when necessary, and provisions for two days.

The trip thither was without accident, but involved a considerable amount of hardship and unpoetic labor. The theory of Gillette as to the location of the mine proved to be correct. For many hours before we reached our destination we could hear the dull roar of Rapid river, which grew louder and fiercer every rod we cut our way through the thickets, until we reached the head of White Gorge and saw the stream rush boiling and seething on its course down the cañon. For the first few seconds, Gillette, Ward and I stood a little apart and looked down the cañon where we had fled only a few weeks ago from the madly pursuing river. It was as if the river had been a dire monster set to guard the treasure of gold, as if he had been bound hand and foot for awhile, but when our profane eyes had searched out the secret he protected, he had burst from all restraint and rushed upon us with awful fury. Even now he was cursing us in impotent wrath, and when some spray from the foaming stream leaped higher than the rest, it almost seemed as if we should yet be overwhelmed.

"Show us your mine," demanded the practical Harvey. " We have no time to waste."

" I see nothing that looks like a gold deposit," said another. " Perhaps you dreamed it."

It took but a moment, however, to lead them to the knoll where Ward had taken up the first handful of soil, and then our seven companions became as excited as we had been that other afternoon. As we watched them the memory of the baseness which had been in our hearts that shameful day came back to us. Three faces turned askance toward each other, and three pairs of eyes sank in self-contempt to the ground. Then Gillette laid his hand on the arm of one of the new-comers, as he said in a brisk voice: " Come boys, this isn't business. Let's set our sluices and wash out the 'pay dirt' to some purpose."

Every thing was soon made ready for the test. The sluice was arranged so that it took its supply of running water just where the river made a sharp descent. In the bottom of the sluice were the " riffles " to catch the gold as it sank of its own weight freed from the dissolving earth. Then we all threw off our coats for the work of washing for gold. Shovelful after shovelful was taken from the knoll and thrown into the sluice, and it was not until nearly a cart-load of soil had been washed away that we prepared for examination. As the ten men bent low to see how much, if any, of the precious metal had been gleaned from that mass of earth, a sight met our eyes which was fairly dazzling. The places between the riffles were packed with gold dust. There was at least five hundred dollars' worth of gold still on the boards, and it seemed more than probable that in our recklessness we had suffered as much more to be washed away into Rapid river.

"It is one of the richest placer mines ever known," exclaimed Harvey. "If the yield continues at this rate the streets of our settlement can soon be paved with gold."

For a few minutes we all stood there fairly dazed, and it was only the fast deepening shadows which reminded us that it was time to make ready for the night. While some of us were pitching the tent, others lighted a fire and prepared supper. As for myself, I could hardly swallow a mouthful. The circumstances and their suggestions impressed my mind and fancy overwhelmingly. As it became quite dark, and the fitful gleam from the camp-fire reflected from the river was the only relief from the blackness of the night, the thoughts bred of the situation came faster yet upon me. I felt I could not endure the dull commonplaces of the company, and made my way to a flat rock overhanging the foaming torrent. There I threw myself down, intending to enjoy the sweetness of revery, without so much as making one demand upon my will. In a few minutes, however, I heard steps approaching, and then Ward's voice came out of the darkness close beside me :

"Where are you, Vinton?" followed by a suggestion from Gillette:

"If he doesn't speak we are likely to stumble against him and jostle him into Rapid river."

I had had quite enough experience of the scant mercies of that wicked stream, and so I responded somewhat ungraciously to the salutations of my friends, and grudgingly made place for them on the rock.

"We felt like talking," remarked Gillette.

"I did not feel so," I retorted.

"Well," said Ward, "we will do the talking and you need not so much as open your mouth. I say, Gillette," he continued, "this enormous find of gold is a strange thing. Why, if so much as the vaguest rumor of what we have done to-day was spread through the country, a hundred thousand greedy men would start for Grape Valley to-morrow. No mountain would be high enough to stop them; no desert arid enough. Starvation, savage Indians, outlaws and desperadoes more savage still, could not hold them back. The unquenchable desire for gold would burn fiercer than ever did the delirium of fever."

"And millions of gold lie buried here — enough to buy all the pleasures of life for thousands now suffering hunger of body, and more intolerable a hundred times, hunger of soul, of taste, of intellect." And Gillette sighed.

My impatience at the intrusion upon my solitude had vanished. These friends of mine were voicing my revery, making my thought articulate. I was very willing they should continue.

"I don't wonder at the agonizing struggles of men for wealth," said Ward. "Although the moral philosophers reprove it, the satirists ridicule it, and the poets decry it, isn't it true that an abundance of money is necessary to obtain every thing of value in life? Without a large share of it we have cares and anxieties which torment the soul as in a hell. Without it our bodies lack the nutriment, the clothing, the shelter they require, and the comforts, the luxuries they crave, without which latter even we are little better off than the beasts of the field. The poor man cannot cultivate his mind or his fancy, indulge his tastes or gratify his aspirations. The world has only wounds and bruises for those who have no gold in store. No wonder men covet riches with all their souls, no wonder that for them they will commit all imaginable wrongs, crawl in the mire of moral degradation, offend all laws of honor or justice. No wonder that the dawning possibility of acquiring wealth will make nine out of ten human beings ready to commit murder if necessary to make the possibility a certainty."

"Ah, Mr. Ward," exclaimed Gillette, "how well you have described the evils and the monstrous inhumani-

ties of the old civilization.  It was to cure the terrible
ravages of the disease you have just diagnosed that this
settlement was founded.  In civilization one of the
maxims is:  'Each man for himself.'  Another, more
rudely phrased, says:  'Root hog or die,' as if all mankind were indeed swine, brutal, selfish, merciless, greedy.
In Grape Valley, by putting men in the relation of
brothers to each other all of whom work for the common good, covetousness, envy, hate, treachery, all the
vile and hideous progeny of your system of individualism
are no more known."

The faces of my two friends as they sat at opposite
ends of the rock were completely shrouded in darkness,
and it was with difficulty I could make out vague and
broken outlines of what might be human shapes.  It
was as if their voices came out of the night, as if invisi-
ble creatures of space were debating, over my head, the
great problems of life.  The weird effect touched my
imagination intensely.

It was a few seconds before Ward spoke again.  It
seemed as if he had been fairly silenced by Gillette's
unexpected retort.  Then he took a somewhat different
line:

"But have you yet stopped to calculate," he inquired,
"what will be the effect of the discovery of this mine,
and of the harvesting here of tens of millions of dollars'
worth of gold every year?"

"Why," exclaimed Gillette, "I have no objection
to wealth.  It is only its unfair distribution of which
I complain.  The gold we expect to find here will be
of the utmost advantage to us.  We can have libraries
which would be the envy of the old universities; art
galleries worthy of Rome or Florence, Paris or Dres-
den, and architecture, such as never earthly city knew
yet.  We can surround ourselves with every elegance
and with every convenience.  What wealth can only
begin to do in civilization for its few possessors it will
accomplish for our whole settlement.  Suppose every

citizen of some town in civilization a millionaire; imagine, then, the grandeur of their buildings; the perfection of their streets, the beauties of their parks. There would then be no squallor to shock the senses, no ugliness to hurt the eye, no rude sounds to violate the ear, no misery to distress the heart. But that picture would be but a poor thing compared with the effects of the same amount of wealth in a socialistic settlement like ours. The rule of all for one, and one for all, would still prevail, and the effect of the universal wealth be multiplied almost in geometrical progression. We should have an earthly paradise indeed."

" But who would do your work ? " demanded Ward. " Who would be disposed to do the hard labor necessary to provide your happy valley with all the wonders of architecture, the marvels of convenience you describe ? "

" It would be clear enough to all," continued Gillette, " that without continued labor, all our wealth would be of little value to us. It would only be by improvement of the means which nature had provided, that the means would effect the desired end. It would plainly enough be as necessary for all to continue to work in order to enjoy the luxuries and amenities great wealth can give, as it now is, in order to satisfy the ordinary requirements for food, shelter, clothing and education. Besides, we do not regard labor here as an evil, as a humiliation, or even as a disagreeable necessity. Under the old system labor is a badge of poverty, of weakness, and of subjection, and on that account is hateful. Then your laborers work twice as long as they should, and have merely their food for their labor, the same as any beast of burden."

Ward this time made no reply, but rose to his feet as if about to return to the camp. I rose, too, but Gillette laid his hand on Ward's shoulder to detain him, and continued:

" Think, too, how this sudden discovery of enor-

17

mous wealth will extend the possibility of spreading
our great truths, and making converts to find happiness in Grape Valley and other settlements colonized
from here. Our additions then would be numbered by
thousands, while now they come by scores. To Grape
Valley we might not bring many of them. It is
doubtful whether we have room for more than double
our present number. But there are countless other
spots on the earth, where truth can be taught and its
principles practiced without interference from legis-
latures, kings, or emperors. So we can have our full
course, until we carry the whole of civilization with us."

Next morning we were early at work, scraping the
gold from the riffles and collecting it carefully in a ves-
sel. Then the sluice was set once more in position,
and Rapid river poured ferociously down its length,
as if doubly enraged to be forced to do our service.
Eagerly we began to shovel the earth into the sluice.
This time, however, it was when less than half as
much earth had been washed out as the night before,
that we made our examination. We did not want again
to run the risk of having a considerable portion of
our treasure washed down the stream because the
riffles were too full to hold it.

But it appeared that we need not have been so cautious. In some of the riffles there was no gold sedi-
ment at all, in others but very little. Our total harvest
was not one-twentieth part as much as that of the night
before. Nobody ventured a word of discouragement.
Not one of us was willing to admit to himself that
there was a possibility of failure. The sluice was
cleaned and restored to its place, and, with a new
feverishness, we set to work to wash out a new lot of
earth.

Before my mind as I dug, floated visions of the beautiful city of the blessed, to be made possible by the
gold for which we were delving. Such a city no poet
ever ventured to describe, no artist to paint, no phil-

osopher to foreshadow. It was to be through us that the glorious dream would become a fact; that a city which it would be happiness to look upon would be built; and people walk its streets to whose every want there would be a full response, for whom it would only be necessary to ask and it would be given. Through our discovery, too, it would be that the work of proselyting the world at large were undertaken on a grand scale, and the ultimate fulfillment of the millennium prophecy hastened perhaps hundreds of years. My heart swelled with pride and triumph. How glorious that to me should be granted the privilege of helping to bring about these marvelous results.

Then Harvey's voice broke upon my revery, with its hard practical tones.

" Shall we try again ? We have thrown in at least a cart-load of earth this time."

" Not yet," said one of the workers. " Let's double it and then try."

The man voiced a common feeling. We all dreaded another disappointment. When, a few minutes later, Harvey told us that we had now washed out the two cart-loads, I think most of us were more irritated than pleased. But the sluice was removed, and the instant the water ceased to flow, all bent over it in hope of a glad sight, all except one. I drew back and leaned upon my shovel, and listened for the announcement. I did not even look at the eager company. But my ears were all the keener for the first sound that should betray the truth. As they looked there was not so much as a single exclamation, not a word, and the silence told me more forcibly than words could have done, that it must be there was even less gold than before on the riffles. As I stood there with wandering eyes and pale face, while my sense of hearing was strained for the merest syllable, my dreams took flight, my ecstasy of triumph turned to the anguish of disappointment and humiliation.

All day long we shoveled and washed, and went to sleep with bitterness in our hearts. Another day until noon we kept to our task, taking soil for washing from all parts of the knoll by turn, but each time we examined the riffles there was less of gold among them than the time previous. But it was two o'clock in the afternoon that the final washing was completed. Soil had been scraped from the whole surface of the knoll so that this test should be unerring, and when we all examined for the result, we found absolutely not one grain of gold.

The great placer mine had been completely exhausted, and in almost perfect silence we packed our tent and utensils, and started homeward, Ward and Gillette keeping far apart from each other and from me.

# CHAPTER XV

Married life in Grape Valley was very different from married life in civilization. The wife was not here expected to devote her whole life to serve and please her husband, any more than the husband was expected to limit all his friendly relations with women to his wife. It was not the theory in Grape Valley that when a woman married, she resigned all active interests except those of her husband, and henceforth it should be enough for her to make herself agreeable to him; that the opinion of other men was henceforth to be of no account to her. Nor was it the unwritten law here that the husband should confine his interest to his wife. They were both believed to be fitting themselves to be worthy companions, by making the most of the social intimacy with both sexes encouraged in Grape Valley. In civilization each wife watches her husband in his relation with those of the opposite sex with jealousy, and the husband reciprocates in kind. In civilization, too, there are weighty reasons for this distrust. Feeling sure that his wife is his, bound and fettered by law, the husband usually takes little pains to keep the admiration she cherished for him in the courtship which she never ceases to regret. He does little to entertain her. He no longer treats her with his earlier tenderness, or makes her happy with praises as of old. With other women he is quite a different creature, seeing which it is small wonder she distrusts him. But she, too, is a very much changed woman from the sweetheart he used to think so dainty in her pretty clothes, so winning in her manner, so irresistibly gentle, so thrillingly responsive. If another man pays her some little attention, she is something like her old self again. But to her husband in his own home she is usually as indifferent in her manner as if his opinion had ceased to concern her. She keeps in the closet her bright dresses when he alone is to see her, and even arranges her hair in the most unattractive fashion when he only is with her, as if he had ceased to have eyes after marriage, as if the qualities and graces which made her seem beautiful and charming to him when they were lovers, were now of no account. The married man and woman in civilization are quite too sure of each other, legally, to give them motive enough to keep themselves attractive. Thus they leave each other exposed without armor to the charms of others, and may well be fearful of results, though they seldom think of causes.

In Grape Valley, however, as much is expected by society of the man and woman after marriage as before. It is not believed here that marriage is a ban, condemning the husband and wife to seclusion, and society to the deprivation of their activity. If a husband and wife are properly mated, they will love each other not the less, but rather the more if they continue to meet others in the unrestrained social intercourse by which development and education are continued after marriage. While aiding the whole community with whatever good judgment, inspired thought, poetical ideas, witty satire, keen criticism, they may be especially able to give, they are also rendered better companions to each other.

The fact that there are no home cares upon them makes this stimulation and useful outside life possible. The acceptance of the principle that no marriage should be a lasting one which does not completely satisfy, also requires free and continual social activity, as an essential element of the system; such social activity as opens each one's eyes to the demands of his nature, and makes recognition of harmonious qualities in others possible.

The light repast which served for a morning meal was the only one prepared at home, and even this was very often ordered from the general caterer. The midday lunch was taken wherever the forenoon's work was done, while the principal meal of the day took place at evening, in the dining-room of the phalansteries, to some one of which all the families were attached; dinners which were more of the nature of banquets. Husbands were assigned as escorts to other women than their wives. These meals were quite elaborate, and were always followed by short speeches. It was a sluggish nature indeed which was not stimulated on these occasions, a poverty-stricken man or woman, whose intellect, when inspired by the influences of the hour, could not yield some treasure to enrich the mind and experiences of others. Then came the evenings in the general phalanstery halls. There were sometimes concerts, vocal and instrumental, sometimes theatrical entertainments. At other times there were dances or games; still again we would have an essay on some social question or some significant epoch in history. Then there were debates, exhibitions of psychological feats, and at other times purely social gatherings, at which the assembled men and women had no entertainment provided except what they found in each other.

There was of course no restraint laid upon any one to insure attendance at these gatherings, but the conditions of existence here were such that it was only very exceptionally that we absented ourselves from them. Our labor was all done in four hours of the day, so there was no duty to detain us, and the whole of the afternoon was full time enough for leisure or reading. To meet together and to understand each other, to grasp each other's feelings, sound each other's strength and weakness, to exchange ideas and criticisms, was at once delightful and necessary to achieve the full results of the social institutions of Grape Valley. It was in a line, too, with the principles of the system, to draw men together as into a common soul, overcoming the individualizing influences which are the fathers and mothers of what is called original sin.

The happiest year I had ever known passed away. The transport of my relation to my wife was replaced by a spirit of genial comradeship, on my side at least. I no longer felt as if the place from which she was absent lacked something as necessary to my comfort as sunlight. I no longer felt a glow come over my heart at her approach. Yet I did not doubt that I loved her as much as ever. I liked to be with her. I enjoyed her conversation, I respected her opinions, I admired and enjoyed her beauty. Surely, I told myself, it was unnecessary that I should always keep the ardent disposition of the new lover. The lover before marriage, and for a short time afterward, is laboring under a stress of emotion which custom naturally mitigates. As he becomes wonted to intimacy with the woman whose very presence was at first like a strong draught of wine to him, it is reasonable that he should cease to be so overwhelmingly affected. It was not owing, I thought, to abating love that I was growing into a cool, comfortable, but not at all exciting relation with Kate. I was very much at peace, completely satisfied with Grape Valley socialistic life, and filled with great hopes for the coming conversion to this system of the world at large. I believed I was as much in love as ever, but my wife Kate did not entirely agree with me on this point, as will soon become manifest.

It was one evening something over a year after my marriage that Kate and I were putting a few finishing touches to our toilets before going to dinner at the phalanstery hall. It was the universal habit to appear at all public gatherings in full dress. I tied my cravat and threw myself into an easy chair to wait for Kate.

Noticing that she seemed an unusually long time adjusting her breast-pin, I at last cast a quick look at the mirror to see what could be detaining her. I saw to my astonishment that she was weeping. Her beautiful eyes were dimmed with tears, and great drops flowed down her cheeks.

"Why, Kate, darling," I exclaimed, leaping to my feet and crossing to her side, "what is the matter? Are you sick, dear?" And I put my arm about her round waist.

"If you did that more often," she sobbed, "you would not have seen me cry." Then she turned and looking eagerly in my face, threw both arms about my neck in that old impulsive way of hers, and putting her head on my shoulder cried harder than ever.

To say that I was bewildered and non-plussed would be coming as near to describing my feelings as perhaps words can do. I did not understand at all what she meant, and tried to tell her so in the gentlest way I could.

"It is simply because I know you do not love me as you did," she cried. "Don't tell me that you do. Oh, I don't mean that. Tell me that you do. Keep saying you love me. I have wanted you to say it for so long."

"Don't my actions show that I love you, Kate? Am I not kind to you? Am I not happy with you?"

"You are kind simply because you like me," she answered, "or because you are sorry for me, or because you are so good you could not be any thing but kind to any one. Yes, you are somewhat happy with me. Are you as happy as you could be?"

"Happy?" I echoed. "Indeed I am happy as I never was before."

She gently released herself from my embrace, and taking a handkerchief from the bureau dried her cheeks. "You do not say as much as you once did about how dear I am to you. You do not always think to say some tender word for me to remember when I go out.

18

Sometimes I come where you are, and you do not even notice me." She hurriedly completed her toilet. "Then you do not seem to like to talk with me as you once did. I notice you vivacious and full of ideas when with others, but I seem to have ceased to call out your best, as I should do if you loved me. Then I miss the glad light of welcome in your eyes which I used always to see there when I came to you." She put on her hat. "Come, I am ready now."

"But Kate," I insisted, "it is not to be expected that we shall be just as we were while lovers — I mean, before our marriage."

"No," she said quickly, "we should not be just as we were before marriage, but if we truly love each other we should be a hundred times fonder, since we know each other so much better than then. But come, my dear," and she moved toward the door, "it is of no use to talk of these matters. All the reproaches in the world cannot make a husband's heart beat one pulse faster."

As we entered the reception-room of our phalanstery, as was the custom before dinner, I was surprised and delighted to be met by Gillette, who had been absent in the East on a very long trip. I noticed at once that he was under considerable excitement. He listened with ill-disguised impatience to my expressions of pleasure at his return, and to Kate's greetings.

"Come with me," he said. "I want to present you to my wife."

"So you have charmed the Eastern beauty at last," I laughed. "We shall be delighted to know her." As we started with him he met Ward, whom he took by the arm, and in a moment more had crossed the room and touched a queenly woman lightly on the shoulder. She turned, revealed a dark, richly-tinted face, lips of vermilion and eyes the most bewildering, I thought, man had ever looked into.

"My wife," said Gillette, and as he spoke Mr.

Ward's name that gentleman bowed, and then stole a quick glance at me where I stood a little back as if in a dream.

" I have met Mr. Ward before," she said, extending her shapely hand to him and then to me. " And Mr. Vinton is one of my oldest friends."

Yes, it was certainly unnecessary to introduce me to the woman who had been the idol of my heart and who had so basely jilted me two years before.

" Mrs. Blakesley," I exclaimed, stupidly, "and here?"

" Not Mrs. Blakesley at all, my dear sir," answered Gillette, rather sharply, " but Mrs. Gillette for two months now, and right here is the place for her."

Then she turned in that queenly fashion of hers I used to think so perfect. " But, my dear husband," she said, in half-caressing rebuke, " why did you not tell me my old friend was here? I suppose you did not know he was my friend." By this time I had recovered my senses sufficiently to resume the manners of a man of society, and my wife coming up was also duly presented to Mrs. Gillette. Perhaps only two of us noticed the peculiar look Mrs. Gillette gave the woman I had married ; a measuring look, as if to see how far beneath herself, my old idol, I had chosen. Both Kate and I saw it. Then the chamberlain came toward us, and on Gillette's suggestion, to me was assigned the honor of taking his wife into dinner, and to him the care of Kate. As Gillette drew Kate away she cast one anxious look back at me, as if fearful of the fascinations of my old idol, a look which I was extremely provoked to see was observed by Mrs. Gillette.

Our seats at table were far removed from those of Mr. Gillette and Kate, and my companion was not slow to avail herself of the opportunity to talk very freely.

" You must wonder at my being Mrs. Gillette," she said. " But I had been a widow a year. It is strange you did not know of it."

"I had taught myself that what Isabel Blakesley did was no concern of mine," I answered.

"You blamed me too much for marrying Mr. Blakesley," she said softly. "Women of my complexion are more fond of wealth and power than of love. The former are usually more lasting, but not always."

"What do you mean? Did your husband lose his money?"

"When he died I found there was nothing of any account left for me after paying his debts. That is," she explained satirically, "all his other debts had to be paid before the great debt he owed me, who married him for his money, was reached."

"You would have done better if——" But I bit my lip and stopped.

"If I had married you? So I have often thought. And I would have had such a royal lover, too," she added, with a sudden uplifting of her eyelids which unveiled an expression in her eyes of bewildering passion. A wild rush of feeling overcame me. I saw the others as through a mist. She only seemed really present. Once more I felt, as I did in the old days, that my whole life was in this woman, that I would be willing to die to-morrow if I could possess her to-day. It was not a spiritual yearning, it was absolutely physical, but physical emotion to an intensity which made ordinary feeling seem tamenesss itself.

"Be careful," she murmured, dropping her eyes again, "people are observing us. I will see you alone before I go home."

Then the tumult in my veins turned to rapture. I was sure now that she saw my passion and returned it. I seemed to float on air. In vain I made a pretense of eating. I was unable to swallow a mouthful. I had supped on ecstasy. I was surfeited with joy. If earth had pleasures greater than our happiness in anticipating them, what a heaven this would be! I dared not trust myself to look at Isabel again, but without turning my face I saw the gleam of her glowing neck, the polished glories of her matchless arms, and my passionate heart kept saying: "She is mine." Her every motion sent its different thrill of delight through me. I listened for her breathing, and when I caught a soft sigh, it was as if my whole being was lifted on a mighty wave, and swept onward whither I knew not and cared not.

"You did not talk much after all," remarked Gillette, as he came to where we were standing, speechless, in the reception-room."

"No. It is such bad form, you know," answered Isabel lightly, "to engage in absorbing conversation at meals."

I was so ashamed of the injury I was planning to do my friend that I could not look him in the face.

"It is a lovely moonlight night," continued Gillette. "Why don't you step out upon the piazza and have it out?"

"Since you suggest it," I muttered between my teeth.

"Yes, that will be better," she smiled gaily, as she rested her hand on my arm. As we crossed the room I tried to think. What was I doing? Reviving an old love affair with my friend's wife? How then would it end? How but in misery to him and to Kate? Yet, if I loved Isabel and she loved me, better than we could either of us love any other human being, it was only right we should be brought together, whoever else suffered. But then, I asked myself, was this indeed love, which burned my whole nature until my head swam and my brain refused to do any thing but dream? Or was it mere animal passion, mastering to be sure, such as few women can excite, but only physical in its nature, in its life, in its death? Mere passion is fleshly and dies. It is mortal, while love is of the spirit also, the attraction of harmonious souls to each other, and is eternal as is the spirit.

But it was as if my destiny compelled me onward, and left me no choice. Memories of the purer joys I

had known with Kate flitted across my mind, pictures
of her anxious, despairing face were painted by my better
spirit upon the tablets of my fancy, but the touch of
this woman's burning hand upon my arm, her thrilling,
perfumed breath upon my face, made me incapable of
resistance to her influence. I led her apart from the
others, to a spot secluded by a trellis, where indeed
Kate and I had often come for something between
solitude and society. I seated Isabel here on the very
spot where Kate had sat, and seated myself by her
side.

For a moment we looked into each other's eyes, and
such perfect sensual beauty I had never seen. The
languorous softness of her face, the drooping bow of her
red lips, parting a little, denoted the very incarnation
of physical passion. Then, as it seemed, unconsciously,
our faces drew nearer, until her breath mingled with
mine, and her eyes shot their liquid fire into mine,
almost touching them. All the world beside passed
from my mind. It was as if I were dying. Then our
lips met and I lived again in a bliss which was agony.
I put my arm about her, and drew her to my bosom,
and kissed her as she palpitated against my heart, until
my whole being was intoxicated with hers.

Then came a sound of rustling skirts, but neither of
us heard it; then a footstep on the walk outside, but it
did not arouse us. Our senses were drugged with bliss.
Then there came a voice, familiar, but almost as from
another world; it pierced my heart like a dagger.

"Harry," it said, "Harry, this sight is killing me."

We sprang from each other's arms, as if impelled
by a shock of electricity. Isabel tried to draw back to
some kindly sheltering shadow. I leaped to my feet,
now wide awake to every thing. It was my wife who
stood before us, and the look of agony on her face was
more than I could bear.

"Kate," I cried, "I have been mad. I have been
mad. I love you and will always love you." And in

the presence of the very woman who had so deeply infatuated me, I tried to take my wife's hand. " Forgive me, Kate."

But she drew back as if a wasp had stung her where my hand touched hers.

" Forgive you? There is nothing to forgive. You are not to blame simply because you do not love me."

" But listen to me. I do love you. I was beside myself to-night."

" I have seen you changing," she said with desperate calmness. " I warned you of it before we came here this evening. I knew then that you were no longer my lover. Love me, indeed! If you did such, madness as this should be for my kisses, not for hers." And she turned to cast a look of scorn and hate at the beautiful woman who had made me forget every thing but herself. The place where Isabel had sat was vacant. She had escaped from the painful scene.

" Sit down," I urged, " and let us talk a few minutes. I promise you by all that is holy——"

" What use to promise?" she asked, wearily.

" Sit here, Kate," I persisted. But she suddenly flamed out for the first time.

" Dare you place me where that woman just sat? Now I am sure you never loved me." Then she turned on her heel, " I am going home. Good-bye."

I stepped to her side. " I will go now, too," I said. But once more she turned a stern face toward me.

" Never again," she exclaimed. " Did you for a moment suppose I could ever live with you after this ? "

The woman who had so captivated me a few moments before was entirely forgotten now. The fever she had stirred in my blood was cooled. I thought only of what I was about to lose. Kate once more seemed as lovely as when I had first offered her my heart. As the sun sometimes sends a brilliant gleam of light and radiance from behind a cloud, just as he sinks below the horizon, so sometimes love gives forth all its forgotten splendors, for the moment before it goes out forever.

"Kate," I cried, "it would kill me to lose you."

But she shook her head. "You do not know yourself as I know you. To-morrow I will apply for a divorce, and you will be free to seek once more for the woman — she must live somewhere — whom you can truly and wholly love."

"But you are that woman," I said.

She let me take her hand, but I felt, in gathering despair, that it was merely in token of parting. She then spoke more softly. "No, you had ceased to love me before you again met this Isabel and I was forced to endure to-night's shame. But you will find some one who will be all in all to you; that will be love indeed. But it is not this woman; do not believe it for an instant. I cannot bear that you should go down to her level. But good-bye?"

She released my hand and drew a step or two away. Then suddenly she turned and rushed up to me, and for the last time twined her arms around my neck.

"No, do not kiss me, I could not bear it after what I saw. This must be our good-bye. You were so dear to me, Harry. Good-bye." And she was gone.

# CHAPTER XVI.

The next six months was a most wretched period for me.  I had taken a room at phalanstery No. 1, and my friend Ward was so much pleased at my companionship, that he failed to show any sort of sympathy for me in my bereavement.  But during those months I could have been of little more satisfaction to him than a lay figure.

Ward, as the reader has seen, had not by any means been the convert to the institutions of Grape Valley that I was.  He approved the economical relations established here.  He gave in his adhesion to the principles which in practice made all men and women work, and gave them all equal shares in the fruits of labor.  He was even enthusiastic over the short hours of labor, which left the afternoons free for leisure or study ; and admitted that the stimulating social life here was the most delightful he had ever imagined possible, and, as a means to the culture of all the intellectual and moral qualities, was perfection itself.  He had nothing but praise, either, for the spirit of brotherly love which seemed to find its full scope here, driving out the selfishness, with its attendant miseries, induced by the competitive system on which outside civilization is based.

But the scheme of marriage and divorce as carried into practice here did not please him at all.  The subject had been too delicate a one for him to discuss with me while I was married, but now that I was divorced, and plunged into bitterness and general displeasure with the institution from which I thought I

19

had so unfairly suffered, Ward felt free to say any thing he chose concerning the marriage relations of Grape Valley, and I was not unwilling to listen.

As for Mrs. Gillette, whose advent had been the signal for my discomfiture, I fairly hated her, and I think the feeling was reciprocated, for it is usually safe to conclude that if one feels a strong repugnance to any particular person, the feeling is returned in degree. From absorbing infatuation to intense dislike seems like a very long step, but in fact it is a most natural transition. We dislike a woman because she is very different from others of her sex. She affects our sensibilities very keenly. We are far more likely to be infatuated with just such a person than any other. We hate her or we are bewitched by her, as the case may be. Very often we first are bewitched by her and then hate her, and as often we first hate and then are bewitched by her. But the infatuation was over, the charm was forever broken, and if Isabelle Gillette and I had been cast on a lonely island together, I could never have felt toward her again as I did that terrible night when I lost Kate. So much for the difference between infatuation and love. But Ward, to whom I had told the whole affair, thought differently.

" You apparently must either hate or go crazy over this woman ; one state indicates the imminence of the other. Only when you become indifferent to her shall I consider you safe."

This is one of the instances where my friend Ward has been mistaken. But my unhappiness over the loss of Kate continued unabated. To see her familiar form across the reception-room, and give a sudden start to go to her, and then to remember that she was mine no more, was like a twinge of physical pain to me. To hear her voice in conversation with others, and feel that I should never listen to its gentler accents in words of endearment again, intensified my melancholy almost to the point of despair. But one day I met her face to face, on one of the city streets, and she extended her hand to me as sweetly as if we were brother and sister. Her voice was calm, and to my astonishment I found mine became so.

"We need not cease to care for each other," she said sweetly, "merely because we do not love each other."

"May I feel that you always think kindly of me?" I asked, eagerly.

"Yes, and wish you the best of fate." And so we parted, and I did not feel as inconsolable afterward. It seemed clear enough that Kate was not a martyr, so I had nothing to reproach myself with in that respect. Then I gradually took more interest in the marvelously active social life of the valley and grew to be more like myself again.

One evening as Ward and I stepped into the phalanstery hall after dinner, Gillette joined us and said:

"It is a social evening and we can have an old-fashioned talk."

"Isn't Mrs. Gillette here?" inquired Ward, with his ever present courtliness.

I thought a peculiar expression passed over Gillette's face. Could it be his dream of bliss was so soon over? How indeed could a woman who had so much to give to others make her husband happy?

"Oh, yes, she is here. She is entertaining Harvey, the mining expert; you remember him." Then he added plainly willing to change the subject: "You are not looking as well as usual, Vinton."

"I have been a good deal out of temper. Kate's leaving me was a terrible blow." I was thankful Gillette did not know the occasion of the rupture between my wife and me.

"I tell him," said Ward, "that the peculiar institution of Grape Valley is to blame for his sufferings. The only way to keep a man and woman together is to tie them."

"That would be bondage in the full sense of the word," exclaimed Gillette, "bondage of mind, body and soul, brutalizing to the body, degrading to the soul, and stunting to the mind. It is only when both man and woman love to the full capacity of their natures that they should live together. Such love as that should be the only bond."

"But all men and women are not capable of sustained feeling," said I. "Some of us can be very intensely affected for a time, and then become almost indifferent."

"That is," said Ward, "they can be infatuated with one woman to-day, and with another to-morrow. Such men and women will spoil the workings of your institution."

Suddenly a light feminine voice broke into our conversation.

"Who is it speaks of spoiling our institution? Avaunt, profane one."

Turning, I saw a woman of perhaps thirty, with a high broad forehead, exquisitely chiseled features, and wonderfully expressive eyes. Her smile was so full of brightness that I was attracted to her at once. Mr. Gillette introduced me to her as Miss Barden. Ward appeared to be already an acquaintance, for he retorted:

"I am the profane one. I was saying that there are many men and women unfitted for lasting love."

"Like yourself, Miss Barden," laughed Gillette, giving her a significant look.

"Perhaps you mistake me," she answered. "The fault may be with the manhood of Grape Valley, unable to supply me with a counterpart."

"Describe to me your ideal," said Gillette, "and I will put the whole world under contribution. It would be payment sufficient for all my trouble to see you once in love. Experience shows it is women of the intellectual type who make the most perfect lovers. Describe now the man you could adore."

"How can I?" asked Miss Barden, with a cool

smile. "It is not given to us mortals to know ourselves. The Socratic injunction sounded like very wise advice, but like most such, is impracticable. I can only tell whether any particular man is my counterpart when I meet him."

"Then, you are not an infidel as to the possibility of true love?" I asked.

"Far from it. But I think, too, that there is a great deal of love founded on the condition of natures at certain periods which they outgrow as they outgrow those conditions. Hence, true love is not always lasting. There are numerous imitations of pure love, however, most deceptive of all of which is the excitement a novel intimacy always induces. Most of the mistaken marriages in Christendom are founded on this delusion, which, of course, disappears as the intimacy becomes an old story."

"You must believe, then," I said, "that the social freedom of Grape Valley tends to reduce the frequency of mistaken marriages."

Her face lighted up with appreciation, and she turned for an instant to Gillette. "Why haven't you introduced Mr. Vinton to me before? He is worth talking to."

"Perhaps I need not scour the world for you after all?" suggested Gillette, maliciously, and then he added: "Come, Ward, these four-handed conversations are somewhat difficult. Suppose you and I find some place where we can have it all our own way."

No sooner were Miss Barden and I left together than she gave me an arch glance. "If you are afraid of me you may go, too."

"I fear nothing in petticoats," I asserted boldly. "But let us take seats in the window while you answer me."

We found two chairs which overlooked the well-lighted street below. We could see in the distance Rapid river winding its shining length in the moonlight; while if we chose to look within, there were hundreds of beautiful women and attractive men with faces which expressed every grade of satisfaction, interest and delight. Compared with any social gathering I had ever seen in the outside world, it was as light to darkness. I have met friends and intimates, with whom I had no sense of restraint, whose conversation was as free and stimulating as that which generally prevailed here. Here all were friends and intimates, so there was a total absence of the restraint which destroys the meaning, the pleasure and the profit of society. Woman was really emancipated here in mind and soul, as well as in her physical relations. She was no longer a constraint upon man, but a stimulus to constant intellectual and spiritual excitement. The most brilliant salons in the history of the world have been those of women who had emancipated themselves from the restraints of tradition and at the same time from those of good morals. Here all were emancipated, the married as well as the unmarried, but the moral nature was never in a higher state of refinement. All wanted the best that others had to give, and sought it without regard to existing marriage relations. If a love fuller and more satisfying than a marriage yielded was awakened, so much the better, for that was progress. No ill consequences, according to the theories of this community, could result from the most unrestricted social relations. If husband and wife were well mated their married harmony would not be disturbed; if not, the sooner each met some one who could inspire a complete love the better. All this wonderful liberty of the sexes in their relations with each other put the men and women always on their mettle. The interchange of wit and wisdom, of repartee and epigram, was constant, and the faces in the company before me were alert and flushed as if with champagne.

After a moment's pause Miss Barden said:

" The idea you have just suggested interests me. In

the outside world so many artificial restraints are placed on the acquaintance of the sexes, that intimacy of any kind between a man and woman, however unsuited for each other, is likely to cause an excitement which is mistaken for love. Hence rich heiresses elope with their father's coachmen, and heads of families marry their servant girls. If a man and woman are thrown together on an intimate relation for a considerable length of time, it is almost a foregone conclusion that they fall in love, as they call it, with each other, and marry if they can; if not, disgrace themselves.

"If, on the other hand," I continued, "the sexes freely meet and become familiarized, this mistake of a novel intimacy for love would not occur. Intimacy would cease to be novel. Men would not be completely bewitched when a glimpse of peculiarly feminine qualities was revealed to them. Women would not lose their heads when they saw in this or that man the strength or energy of our sex. To look into each other's eyes without palpitation of the heart, to touch each other's hands without a tumult of feeling, would be the result for both sexes except in cases of true love. Your freedom of restraint and untrammeled relations of the sexes will clarify the air in time, so that a man and woman will not be likely to think they fall in love unless they have a peculiar fitness for each other."

"There is another idea that occurs to me." As she turned her face toward me it was fairly illumined with intelligence and vivacity. "In the old civilization a man is expected to find everything in his wife, to see, or at least to enjoy no charms of manner, no suggestiveness of thought in other women. The result is he is either deprived of social delights and educating influences, or his wife considers herself abused and society looks on her as deserted. But if a husband or wife in the outside world had free social intercouse with those of the opposite sex, were permitted and en-

couraged to make the most of every attractive and interesting personality, love might invade hearts that
hitherto had not known it. And the old civilization
makes no provision for such cases. This is another
respect in which Grape Valley presents the ideal civilization. Here we all associate with whom we like,
gather sweetness from every flower, broaden every
faculty of our mind, as well as expand the sympathies,
which are the best proofs of immortality, and by culti-
vating which we best cultivate the soul and strengthen
its divine attributes."

I was fairly carried away by the eloquence of my new
acquaintance. I had not met a woman before with
such perceptive and analytical powers. She paused for
me to speak, but I preferred to listen.

She resumed after a moment. "That you love one
woman is no reason why she should be required to
please your every taste, satisfy your every demand.
Every human being is a specialist. Some quality, some
attribute, some insight, is more developed in some one
of us than in any other. Each person has some experience, has learned some lesson out of life which
others do not know. From acquaintance and intellectual intimacy with men other men have always
learned most that they know, acquired the chief part
of their education. Women have their exclusive
personal experiences too, their intuitive powers, their
sexual clairvoyance, their peculiar religious and sympathetic inspirations. Men should be as free to exchange
their intellectual and spiritual treasures with women as
with each other. Thus only can women share in the
strength of mind, breadth of generalization, the fullness
of knowledge of the sterner sex, and thus only men
become more the equals of women in the delicacy of
understanding, the quickness of perception, and the
gentleness of heart peculiarly feminine."

"That would be a glorious consummation, indeed," I
said. "But can one man and woman love each other

as completely where they have so much to give and to take from others?"

"Why not!" she demanded. "Does a man in the old world love his wife less because he has free intercourse with other men? No more would the husband of Grape Valley be incapable of perfect lover relations with his wife because he enjoyed and profited by what cultivation of mind and soul other women in the world could give him. It might rather be expected that, by what he could learn from these other women, he might be brought into a still more harmonious relation with his wife. She is, or ought to be, the only woman in the world he can love. If she is not that woman he should lose no time in finding the one who is, and in releasing the mistaken object of his first choice to accomplish her own destiny. But it does not follow that she should be the only woman to him in the world simply because she is the only woman he can love."

I hesitated a moment and then taking courage from her remarkable frankness, I asked:

"What is the difference between the interest which a man may take in other women without love, and the feeling you call love which he should have for his wife?"

Miss Barden laughed somewhat oddly and seemed at a loss what reply to make. I was afraid I had pressed her too far. But while I was meditating some excuse for my question, she began to speak.

"Now you force me to make an honest but awkward confession. I know nothing of this love from experience. I was never in love. I have met many men who interested me and entertained me, many whom I wanted to see again, as you for instance, but all I know of love is through my study of others and of my imagination. If an opinion founded on such poor data is good for any thing you are welcome to it."

"Perhaps," I answered, pleased at what I thought an opportunity to make a good point, "perhaps your

20

definition is likely to be broader and less biased than if offered by a person who thinks he has experienced to the full the grand passion. Definitions may be offered by those who are in error in supposing they were ever in love, and hence define the false for the true, the delusion for love itself; or even if the person has known, in his own experience, true love, he may be all the more likely to describe accidents as essentials, to color his definition with the individuality of that experience."

"You are very ingenious," she said, giving me a very appreciative look. "I will take courage and offer my definition since you think it is quite as likely to be near the truth as those of men and women who boast of having run the whole gamut of passion. A man loves a woman and is a fit husband for her, if their natures, physical, intellectual and spiritual, are suited to each other. They should mutually stimulate each other in every direction, mutually soothe each other, mutually satisfy each other. The stimulus each supplies to the other keeps every faculty and perception alive and progressive, and is the strongest force for improvement to which a human being can be subjected. The world at large, through its imperfect social institutions, has made very little of this force for good. It is almost accidental when the full relation of lovers exists between married people in civilized countries. As a possible force for mischief, for outbreak of violence, it is sufficiently recognized. The sexual influence is the greatest enginery for the development of our whole natures which this world supplies. Our bodies, minds, and souls, are educated and uplifted, perfected and purified by true love. If sexual selection is rightly practiced, each man and woman will marry where the stimulus most adapted for the development of the triple nature is best supplied."

As she finished speaking she rose to her feet. "I must leave you now. I was to meet a friend to-night

for an historical lesson. You have made me very late."
Then she gave me her brilliant smile, a sort of greeting
more vivid than words. "Shall you be here to-morrow
night?"

"Yes," I answered eagerly, "but it is theatrical
night, and we cannot talk. Can't I come to see you
in the afternoon?"

"Why, yes, if you do not think I am talked out. I
feel something as an exhausted reservoir looks." And
she moved a step or two away.

"A reservoir often fills up over night, you know," I
threw after her, and then she left the room.

The foundations of my intellectual life had been
stirred, as never before, and by a woman. I was glad
to go to my room, and locking the door, to abandon
myself to reverie.

# CHAPTER XVII.

I do not think, however, that I had been a half hour alone, when a knock came at the door, and, as with considerable reluctance I opened it, Mr. Harvey, the mining expert, entered.

"I want a little talk with you," he said. "Lock the door so we shall not be interrupted, please. Gillette might blunder in any minute."

I locked the door not without some manifest surprise. "And if he did come in, wouldn't he be a desirable addition?"

"Not to-night," answered Harvey, seating himself, "for it is about Mrs. Gillette I want to talk."

I was fairly amazed. "About Mrs. Gillette?"

"Yes, I am infatuated with her. I am as crazy over her as a mad inventor over perpetual motion. Why, Vinton, when I think of her going home with Gillette as her husband, it makes me quite frantic. Wild ideas of attacking him and taking his wife away this very night, overwhelm me."

"Beware of the woman," I exclaimed, startled and humiliated at the thought that she, who took such pains to charm my senses so recently, should already have set her snares for another man.

"Why do you tell me to beware of her?" he demanded, angrily. "If she loves me better than her husband, is there any reason why I should not marry her?" Then doubtless remembering that he had opened the subject to me, not I to him, he saw that too much sensitiveness on his part was absurd. So he mollified a little.

"She has spoken of you, and somewhat unpleasantly by the way. So I thought, perhaps, you could give me some advice. I do not feel, myself, that her influence over me is good. Perhaps I ought to shun it if I have the strength."

"Oh certainly you ought," I answered, determined to do my duty by Harvey, if I could without revealing too much of my recent experience with her. "It is not true love you feel for her or that she feels for you. She is too sensual in her nature to be capable of any passion save of the senses. She would enslave you to-day, and be enslaved herself, and to-morrow or next week or next month, perhaps, be as ready for a new lover or husband as she was for you. Such women as she would, I believe, be impossible after a few generations in Grape Valley. They are the offspring of those relations of the sexes in civilization which were so distorted that there followed the most monstrous perversions of instincts. Men most commonly exhibit these perversions, which are often merely over development of the purely physical aspect of sex. The more brutal an indulgence, the more coarse its surroundings and associations, the more degrading its suggestions, the better satisfied are such perverted men in their relations with women. Sometimes decent and accomplished gentlemen in other directions, they are simply beasts and glory in their degradation, in their sexual relations. Women are naturally more fitted for the true functions of love than man; the physical relation is seldom foremost in their minds, very often hardly recognized until the mental and spiritual harmonies are fully established. When we find a sensual woman, however, she is capable of spreading more poison through the social State than a dozen preachers of anarchy and assassination. Such women have done much to destroy faith in the reality of the complete triple attraction of the sexes which is love, to make beasts of all who come beneath their influence, and to make gross all who know of their history. They are instances of atavism, retrogression toward a former type, toward the brute without intellect or soul and which only responds to physical instinct."

"But how did such a refined man as Gillette come to marry her?" demanded Harvey, apparently amazed and shocked at what I said.

"He married her for the same reason that you want to marry her, and will do so unless what I say opens your eyes. You are maddened by the physical attraction which she puts forth with a boldness and abandon well nigh irresistible. The display of sensual passion on the part of a woman is usually absolutely intoxicating to a man. This woman displays it so alluringly, so seductively, that your senses are enthralled and your judgment suspended. You do not stop to see that the basis for your attraction is absolutely of the flesh, and, however rapturous to-day, will to-morrow turn to dust and ashes. But the triumphs of such women are only limited by their opportunities. Kings and potentates, conquerors of kingdoms, prophets and philosophers have fallen beneath the lightnings in their eyes since history began to keep its records. Perhaps, after all, they are not wholly without use in the world. They help to show at least what love is not."

Harvey rose to his feet and took my hand. "I believe you speak the truth, Vinton, and I thank you from my heart for your warning. The thought of her fills me with no good aspirations, with no exaltation of soul. It is merely the apotheosis of flesh, a profanity and a mockery. Good night. I thank you for what you have done for me."

After he went out I dismissed the queens of sensual passion from my mind, and went to bed to dream of Miss Barden.

The next forenoon, however, when I entered my editorial room, I found the whole force in great excitement over the announcement that Gillette's wife had that morning filed her notice of divorce. In a week more Isabel was married to Mr. Harvey, and doubtless he confided to her all that I had said about her and her kind. At any rate she did not ever recognize me again. But it must have been a secret humiliation for her to feel that, in spite of herself, she irresistibly fulfilled my prophecy and justified my description of her nature by procuring a divorce from Harvey, in turn, before six months were gone. Her future history is of no particular importance to detail here, and she was not after all a very mischievous element in Grape Valley social life. The men whom she beguiled became aware of their delusion in good time, and were all the wiser for their lesson. She served as a healthy corrective of sensual tendencies, and if she did not seek for her freedom as soon as the eyes of her successive husbands were opened and their lessons learned, they had, of course, the blessed privilege of taking the initiative themselves.

Under the old order of society, the years of Isabel Blakesley, almost her months, could be counted by the number of homes she destroyed, of honored men she disgraced, of careers she wrecked and victims she drove to despair, crime and death. Gillette had certainly done civilization a good turn in bringing the woman here, where her influence over no man's life could be any thing but temporary.

Of course I could not for a moment forget that Miss Barden had given me the privilege of calling upon her, but I felt that I owed a first duty to my friend Gillette, and finding that he had returned to his own room at our phalanstery, I went up to see him.

"Poor fellow," I bega grasping his hand. But Gillette apparently did not regard himself as a proper object of sympathy.

"Congratulate me rather," he exclaimed. "Why, Vinton, you cannot conceive of the miser , that I was suffering with Isabel. But since I had brought her so far, I felt a certain embarrassment in divorcing her."

" I have a confession to make," I began with considerable embarrassment as I seated myself. " The first evening I met her here I was completely enslaved. She was an old sweetheart of mine, the woman I told you about that night on the Brooklyn bridge, you will remember. It was she who threw me over for a rich husband. I was in despair at the idea of taking your wife from you, even at the moment when I was most infatuated with her. But I was saved only by Kate. It cost me my wife, so I received my punishment."

" You surprise me ; I understand now why it was that she was so bitter against you after that first night. When I presented you to her I thought she showed an interest somewhat unbecoming in so recent a bride. But later in the evening she spoke of you very disdainfully. Even your features, which I know you regard, not inexcusably, with some complacency, she criticised. Your figure, too, was too slight, or too tall, I forget which, now. As for your manner, it was too assured, insolent she thought. In vain I tried to defend you, Vinton, but I assure you I did try. So it was all because your wife discovered you making love to Isabel ?"

I was a good deal taken back by Gillette's unconcern, but managed to say : " I presume it seemed ungallant of me that I should forget her presence while I pleaded for my wife's forgiveness."

" She ought to have been more reasonable," mocked Gillette ; "she should have appreciated the extreme awkwardness of your position. If it had been a choice between the sacrifice of a man or of Isabel, you would of course have trampled upon the man without remorse. But when it was a question which woman of the two you should honor, it seems to me even Isabel ought to have had reason enough to see Kate was entitled to the preference."

I was quite at a loss to know just what to say, and while hesitating, Gillette continued more gravely :

" Thus endeth the first chapter of my passionate experience, and the last, I think. I always thought women too cold, but in Isabel I found a volcano. The first week of my married life was pleasure in perfection, I thought. I was blind to evidences of selfishness and of grossness. I would not entertain my dawning suspicions of ignorance, of laziness or of cruelty in my wife. I fancied I had found a woman who would be everything to me that woman could be, more than ever woman was to man before; the same old story you know. Our life should be one ecstasy. But I shall not marry again, Vinton."

" How long before you go East ? " I asked.

" I had planned to stay here a month, but I now am anxious to get away to-morrow. There are quite a number of converts of both sexes on the point of joining us. When I return in a month or so, I shall bring a very interesting company with me. Must you be going ? Well, good-bye."

At his door I met Ward just coming to make a call. I was for a hurried salutation and departure, since I was eager to see Miss Barden. But Ward absolutely declined to remark my haste, and taking me by the shoulder, said :

" I want to speak with you a minute."

" But I have an appointment," I protested, looking at my watch.

" You have your whole afternoon for your appointment ; you must give me a minute or two."

" Well, what is it ? "

" Not particularly pleasant news, at least not flattering," answered Ward, laughing.

" I might have known it," I retorted. " You are so anxious to give it to me."

But Ward continued imperturbably : " Your former wife is receiving attentions from a new lover. He is

21

the superintendent of the shipping department, I believe."

"I don't blame him," I answered, indifferently, yet I could not subdue the disagreeable sensation in my throat.

"And I may add," continued Ward, maliciously, "that I think she appears to like it."

"What do you judge by?" I asked hotly, forgetting my role of nonchalance. "What does a confirmed old bachelor like you know of the signs and tokens of love?"

He winced, somewhat unnecessarily I thought, at this fling, but answered:

"They have been walking since lunch, and I think if you sauntered up 'A' street, and assumed your most unconscious air, you could meet them without seeming to intend it. Thus you could judge for yourself, since you distrust my advantages. By the way, his name is Sawtelle."

"I am sure it is not my affair whom she likes or dislikes," I exclaimed, as I broke away from him.

"Nor mine either, I suppose you think," he laughed as he knocked at Gillette's door.

Of course I had no intention of following Ward's suggestion. If Mr. Sawtelle chose to make love to Kate, and she to listen to him, it was outside of my jurisdiction entirely. Yet instead of entering the phalanstery reception-room, and sending up my card to Miss Barden, as I should have done, I passed out of the main door and went down the steps. I had no excuse for walking up "A" street, unless it were to meet Kate and Mr. Sawtelle, in accordance with Ward's recommendation, which I had scornfully rejected. Yet I turned up that very street, and when I saw a woman leaning on her escort's arm and coming toward me, I took a last week's copy of my newspaper out of my pocket, and affected to study a paragraph in it, most intently. Still I managed to see every turn of Kate's head, every movement of her graceful figure, and as, with her companion, she came nearer, I could even catch a word or two of their conversation. They doubtless saw a man on the sidewalk near them. But so absorbed were they in each other that the existence of other specimens of their race was of no moment to them.

Why was I in haste to conclude so? Because when he spoke she turned her face toward him as a rose opens its rarest beauties to the sun, denying them to the moon or to the brightest stars of night. Because when she addressed him every atom of his body seemed to lean toward her, to respond to her, to listen to her. The words I heard were in disjointed sentences, which they, perhaps, thought, with the usual fatuousness of lovers, were meaningless to outsiders.

I heard him say: "I have always felt so, too, when the wind blew." He was confessing some wonderful affinity between them, extending even to their common experiences of nature.

Then I heard her say : " It seems to me that I did not half see the beauties of the world until now." Thus she showed him how his influence had stimulated all her senses into a new activity.

When they passed me I put up my newspaper so they could not see my face. I was filled with indignation at Kate, who had once lain in my arms, for now believing herself in love with another. I was doubly angry because I was sure that I saw signs of an intensity of love, and a perfection of sympathy such as she had not offered for me. For a few moments I stood where they had passed me, but neither of them looked behind. In my wrath I concluded to follow them until they should separate, then I would overtake her, and upbraid her with her unfaithfulness. I did not wait to meditate what I should say. My breast was almost bursting with a sense of the outrage I felt had been put upon me. I was only eager for an oppor tunity to plead my wrongs. No woman could stand against my reproaches.

At the corner of the street they paused. Apparently, the man had business calling him away, and here they must part. I, of course, paused, too, supposing their adieux would be over in a moment. Why should they delay? Had they not been together during a long walk, with opportunity to say every thing which was of the slightest importance? If he wanted to tell her that he loved her, he surely had had time sufficient. If she wanted to let him know that she returned his passion, she certainly had had opportunity. But yet they seemed to find it hard to separate. He would start as if to go, and some unuttered sentiment would occur to him, and he would speak it, as if it were a matter of life and death to share it with her, and straightway forget that he had been about to leave her. Or she would take his hand in hers for a last caress, the sight of which naturally increased my impatience, and they would immediately become oblivious to the passage of time. If I had doubted before that they were in love, the sight of their lingering parting would have convinced me of it. None but lovers ever part so reluctantly, each movement toward separation stimulating more intensely their longing and ability to please each other.

Finally he went his way and I followed Kate. But as long as they were in sight of each other they still kept turning about hoping to see each other's faces. At every one of these tell-tale signs of love my indignation at the fickleness of woman grew deeper, until Kate went into her little house, once my home, too. Almost immediately afterward I stood at the door with my face set like a flint.

# CHAPTER XVIII.

It was apparent enough to me, from the first glance at Kate's countenance as she opened the door, that she had hoped to see quite another form than mine. She had been with her new lover for hours, and yet her face was illumined with joy at the thought that she should so soon see him again. But in an instant the beautiful light had faded, and in its face was a disappointment she tried in vain to conceal.

"Good afternoon, Mr. Vinton," she said, as she held out her hand. "I am glad to see you." And she led the way into what she used as her sitting-room.

As I entered the house where I had been so happy my old life seemed to rush back upon me irresistibly. In this very room how many hours of sweet interchange of love's secrets I had passed with this woman. Why was it she sat aloof from me now, with only an expression of cold curiosity on the face where I had so often seen tenderness chase away shame? It was the very room where I had been sick and so sweetly nursed by her. The bed was removed now, but I knew so well where it had stood. Every square of paper on the wall had been etched on my memory in the hours of semi-consciousness I had lain there. I now sat by the window in the very spot, in the very chair, where, with her fair head upon my shoulder, I had sat the afternoon of our betrothal. The memory of all the kisses which she had given me in this room, clinging, burning kisses, of all the eager confessions of passion I had heard from her lips, was with me. She had never looked more beautiful than at this moment, when there was a wall of ice between us.

"Kate," I began, "once more we are together in this room. It seems impossible to believe that we are no longer anything to each other."

But she visibly shrank into herself. This movement, unconscious as it was, was one more proof that she was in love with another man. Words of passion except from the object of her devotion seemed profanation to her.

"Why," she exclaimed, "all that is as far away as if it had been in another world."

"But," I insisted, "when I think how we learned the easy lesson of love in this very room, how in this very chair I——"

"Don't say it," she exclaimed, as a warm flush mounted to her forehead. "It is blasphemy to call to mind such scenes when their higher meaning is lost. We thought we loved each other then, and everything we did was glorified. But why refer to it now?"

I felt as if a spray of ice water had been thrown in my face. "Did you never love me then?"

Then her eyes took an expression of reproach into them.

"Why don't you ask, too, if you never loved me? For both questions one answer will suffice. We thought we loved each other. That belief of ours made sacred all we felt and said and did. Since we have learned that we made a mistake to rehearse now our experiences as lovers becomes intolerable."

"But I love you now," I cried. "Love is eternal."

"No, I do not think that even all love is eternal," she answered, coolly. "I believe that human natures very often make progress in different directions, unfitting for each other those who were at one time well mated. At a certain stage in their lives a man and woman answer perfectly to each other's demands and sympathies. They are truly in love then, although one or the other may soon develop faculties which destroy that affinity. I think that our relation, however, was only a partial attraction. Yet it was nearer love than anything either of us had ever known before."

"Or will ever know again," I urged. She hesitated a moment before replying. I began to hope she was convinced and would consent to take me to her life again. How beautiful she was, her complexion like a flower, her red gold hair like a crown which was never laid aside, her lips perfect food for kisses. But even while she paused a different train of thought made its rapid transit through my brain. Always prone to analysis and comparison, I tried to compare my feelings toward Kate now and as they were at our first betrothal. I was able to discern that it was more regret at what was gone than hope of renewing our past relations, that was disturbing me. It was not that I was so much affected now by her physical loveliness, as that I was full of vivid recollection of how it had once moved me. It was not that I was in love with her now, but that I was in love with the vision of our past. But she was speaking again.

"I do not like to have to remind you of your infatuation for Mrs. Gillette."

"I did not love —— "

"No, I do not believe that you had any love for her, but I believe she had an overpowering physical attraction for you. If my physical attraction for you had been complete there would have been no place for her. I am sure you will find true love sometime. As for me, I have found it."

"It is the man you were walking with?"

"How did you know it?" she demanded, quickly. "I did not suppose any one guessed it."

I smiled grimly. "Why the very birds of the air can see it," I answered, satirically, "can see, at least, that you think yourself in love."

"Think myself in love?" she smiled. "Ah, but I

know it. You are about to remind me that I have been mistaken before. But for that very reason I am less liable to error now. If I were a young maiden listening to the tender nothings of a youth as untried as she, as ignorant of himself, as undiscerning of others, you might well say that I was liable to mistake for love what were perhaps the flutterings of vanity, or was perhaps the first feverish sense of physical response." Then she gave me a look of half apology as she continued: " You will forgive me for saying it, but it is by comparison with my feelings for you, who came so near to being my true lover, that I am assured he has come at last. Of course I cannot be as sure that he loves me as I love him, and in Grape Valley we do not trust in those one-sided love affairs which are so much in vogue in the outside world. If a man does not love a woman as much as she loves him it is so much the worse for both of them. It proves they are not meant for each other. He cannot give or enjoy as he should, and soon her love will fade. Yet I feel that such fulness of feeling as I have can result only from a perfection of harmony between us."

"I suppose your new lover is as brilliant as a two-edged sword," I said, bitterly, "as learned as an encyclopedia, as handsome as a new Apollo."

A look of surprise crossed her face. "I should not have expected such a tone from you, but I suppose the feeling of the old world, that a woman is the perpetual slave of the man whom she once loved, clings very strongly. No, my lover is not an Apollo. I suppose he would not be called nearly as handsome as you. But in my eyes he is beautiful. He is not a scholar nor a literary man. You could overwhelm him with knowledge in a fifteen minutes' conversation. But he knows quite enough to make his way to my heart. He is not even as ready a talker as I. He is not quick with his answers nor is he at all witty. But I am interested in every word he drops. Everything he says arouses in me some current of thought and sentiment. I love him, that is all, except that he loves me too."

The sweetness of this woman's disposition was marvelous. I was conscious I had deserved no such magnanimous treatment as I had received, but yet did not soften under it. It humiliated me beyond endurance that a woman who had been mine could now confess herself so wholly another's. As long as she had lived unmarried, I could think of her as still missing me, still longing for me, in spite of her dismissal of me. But that my place not only should be taken by another, but so much more than made good, was very bitter to me. In a few days it would be this interloper who should sit where I sat now, and on his shoulder would be pillowed her head, which had once lain on mine. For him would she whisper her tender emotions, from him hear the same old words which the lovers of unnumbered centuries have used, and their descendants can find nothing to improve upon. I rose to my feet and my head grew hot and dizzy.

"So he will kiss your lips as I have done," I cried. "He will stroke your hair, and you will twine your soft arms about his neck as you have done about mine, and give kiss for kiss, caress for caress. Oh, it is shameful."

Her face grew so white that I was frightened into my senses. How vilely I was insulting her.

"Oh, forgive me," I stammered. "I did not know what I was saying."

She had risen to her feet too, and as I murmured my broken excuses, a little of the lost color returned to her cheeks. Her lips moved for a reply, but she she stood with downcast eyes.

"Yes, I am ashamed," she said, in low even tones. "You make me ashamed that I was ever so much to you, who have the heart to taunt me with giving the best a woman has to the man she thinks worthy. But you must remember that then I believed we were true lovers. I believed you were the desire and satisfaction of my life. It is for that reason I had not thought it a shame to give the best I had. It made me no poorer. It ought to have made you happier and purer. But that I am ashamed to have given my kisses and embraces to one who remembers them only to despise me, does not make me ashamed to offer them where they will be a real sacrament."

"I did not know what I was saying," I repeated, in my confusion. "I know you are the purest woman in the world."

She raised her eyes at last and gave me a sad smile. "If anything was lacking to break the last tie between us, you have supplied it. Yes, I forgive you. Good-bye." I took my hat and went out without once looking back.

# CHAPTER XIX.

As I walked up the street I met Ward and Gillette. The latter tried to avoid meeting my eye. With a delicacy peculiarly his own, he wished to avoid seeing signs of emotion which I might not care to betray. Ward, on the other hand, was intent on his lesson in vivisection, and scrutinized my tell-tale face very narrowly.

"I see you have convinced yourself that Kate is in love again."

"Yes, I have," I answered defiantly. "And she loves this time far more deeply than she ever loved me. I can see that too."

Gillette took my arm and said in that very winning way of his:

"Come, my boy, there is an hour yet before dinner. Let us talk it over."

Ward stalked along on the other side and only gave me a few seconds' respite.

"I hope this will be a lesson to you, Vinton, to keep out of further entanglements."

"For my part," said Gillette, "I hope he will learn quite a different lesson — a lesson of gratitude, that when he makes a mistake he is in a place where it can be rectified without ruining two lives directly, and causing, God knows, how much outside mischief."

"But how can you expect a man of sensibility to tolerate it," urged Ward, "when his wife informs him that she loves him no more, and is going to marry some other man? Of course never having been in love myself, I am not able to go into details as either

of you could do.    But it would seem to be like snap-
ping heart bands and breaking tender associations
enough to make a whole life miserable. '

"So it would be," answered Gillette, leaving me,
very considerately, a silent listener, "so it would be in
the old world.   But our whole idea of the relation of
the sexes is different, and our institutions, manners and
customs permit our idea to be carried out without
these heartrending effects you mention.   There are no
children in the home here, to make a division of
parents also a division of children.   The affectionate
parents can always be assured that their children have
the best of care, and that they can be with the little
ones as much as desired under any circumstances.   Then
the Grape Valley wife is not a dependent on her husband for support, nor he on her for the comforts and
conveniences of a home.   They are not shut up to
each other during their marriage, nor shut out from
the conditions essential to comfort after divorce.   Under
our system a husband and wife are simply companions,
whose continued intimacy depends on their love for
each other.   When that love ceases or is discovered to
be imperfect, there is nothing to keep them together."

"Why, look at it a minute, Gillette.   What kind of
a thing is this marriage of yours?   It is not deserving
the name.   I don't see any reason why a man might
not marry a different woman every year, or more often
still if he chose."

"What we seek," explained Gillette, "is the perfect
freedom in the marriage relation, which in the old
order of society is impossible.   The absolute dependence of the woman on the man for support, the absolute dependence of the children on their father for
means of support, and on their mother for care, made
it necessary that marriage ties there should be as near
indissoluble as possible.   A husband and wife might
hate and despise each other; they must still be united.
The very existence of your whole organization of

society depends upon it.  Thousands of years of such customs bred a secondary morality, a system of artificial virtues.  Hence has come the sentimentality that a woman is sullied by experience of passion, that ignorance is virtue, that inexperience is innocence, that simplicity is honor.  The superstition went so far that it was as if the very kisses of a man's lips left physical stains upon the woman he did not marry.  If a girl, yielding to the force of what seemed to her a sacred passion, granted a lover her greatest favor, she was regarded as physically impure, as having irretrievably lost her honor, henceforth only to be pointed at as an object of scorn."

"And how would you regard such a woman in Grape Valley?" demanded Ward.

"Why, my dear friend," answered Gillette, "three-quarters of our women have been married to different men for short periods, and divorced for no cause except that they believe they could love some other men more, or that their husbands have been attracted elsewhere.  They would be regarded as women lost to shame in your old society.  Here we have only respect for their devotion to love itself, which we regard as a great influence for good in human life, if given its full course.  We do not believe it defiles a woman's lips to have given the kiss of love to more than one man.  We believe she is better fitted from her experience to make the man who is her final choice perfectly happy."

"And if she does not find her perfect mate?" asked Ward.

"Then she takes to each successive lover some new mental accomplishment, some richer spiritual experience.  For that matter there are many of us, of both sexes, who are not fortunate enough to find a perfect marriage.  Probably this failure is owing to the limited numbers in the colony.  We do not meet the person of the opposite sex fitted to make us happy.  To such of us is denied the great joy and culmination of life.

But still, under our system, the experiences of even those perpetually mismated are varied, and their progress in education rapid. This year one of us marries for pure sensualism; it is at a period which comes in most lives, when the physical seems of disproportionate account. Perhaps one short experience is enough to teach him that there must be a higher sensibility than that of the flesh. His first marriage being to a woman of coarse, animal traits, and thus bringing speedy discontent, he, perhaps, marries next a more refined epicurean. These two experiences passed, the man is likely to marry, the third time, a highly rarified spiritual nature. As long as his curiosity is piqued and his interest unappeased, she holds him, but if she cannot attract his whole nature, one of them soon wearies of the other, and he is free to try again. Now, perhaps, he is attracted by the romantic woman, and this marriage only endures until he has learned also somewhat to understand her nature. The education of our example has been nobly carried on, and different faculties and tastes have been pleased and stimulated by these different women. To each one he has carried capacities to improve, which he would not have had without his previous experiences. As he leaves each one he has achieved some new advance for himself."

"But you do not tell me whether you have no sexual frailty here?" insisted Ward.

"Yes, there have been cases of men who did not wait for divorce or marriage to pursue their experiences. But such irregularities have so little occasion or excuse here that they are growing to be of rare occurrence. In your society they come when wives love other men than their husbands, husbands other women than their wives, a very common condition. They occur also among those shut out by poverty from the privileges of marriage. Very frequently, too, they occur when women are forced by want to barter for bread what should be given only for love. But here marriage exists no longer than both parties desire. Here there is no poverty to hinder marriage, and marriage does not increase the responsibilities or burdens of either husband or wife. Here there is no want to drive suffering womanhood to shame and humiliation. You might expect danger in the perfect freedom of the social intercourse of the sexes, married and unmarried, and in the removal of all the restraints to intimacy, to which men and women have been subjected for so many thousand years. But women have with their independence gained a new dignity. They do not regard it as a compliment that a man should profess to be in love with them unless he offers marriage, since marriage is free of burden here, and divorce so easy. Men become ashamed to propose an illicit relation to a woman when the public and reputable one is so open to them. Still there are some cases where women give favors to men whom they would not want to marry, some instances when men seek and obtain privileges from women whom they would object to marrying. Divorces usually follow exposure in such cases. But no disgrace or dishonor is visited on either of the indiscreet parties, much less are they punished. They are regarded simply as not having been wise, as not having shown a proper appreciation of what the relation of the sexes should be. The woman, too, is as likely to have another lover and one who will desire marriage as is the man."

" But you are letting down the gates to vice," exclaimed Ward, sternly.

We had reached the phalanstery door, and I stood waiting to hear Gillette's reply before going to my room and preparing for dinner.

" You should rather say that we are removing the motive for vice," said Gillette. " The sexual instinct is one of the most destructive forces in your society. We are making it not only the means to an ideally happy state, but the most elevating and educating influence

ever known. Every man must acknowledge how pure,
how strong for right, how wholly unselfish he feels
when in love. We are utilizing that force to uplift
society and clarify and glorify the character of the individual. Your society has treated men and women
as if they were beasts whose appetites must be legis-
lated against, and whose passions must be provided
against, or society would fall to pieces. We have for-
mulated our society on the basis of immunity from
physical want and from social restraints. The brute,
when restraint is removed, satisfies his animal instinct
as he has the opportunity. Man, with his triple nature,
seeks a three-fold satisfaction. Mind and spirit have
sex as well as has the body, so if under proper conditions we only free man from checks and restraints,
he will seek the fittest object for love. He may not
find it at first, but he will be actuated by the worthiest
desire to perfect his nature, and he may be trusted."

"But —— " began the indomitable Ward.

I, however, tarried to hear no more, but drawing
my arms from those of my friends, hastened to my
rooms and prepared for dinner. I was surprised to
find I did not continue miserable over Kate's new betrothal. A slight sense of humiliation at the ease with
which she seemed to have transferred her affections
still rankled in me, but I was able now to regard her
and her future doings with considerable tranquillity.
Perhaps Gillette's talk, while not addressed to me, had
in some degree softened my prejudices. Possibly it was
only that he had kindly distracted my attention from
my bereavement, and, meanwhile, my unreasonable
fever of jealousy had had time to cool. I remembered
now the appointment with Miss Barden which I had
completely forgotten, and while I selected a particularly becoming necktie, I racked my brain for some excuse beside the true one for my failure to call upon her.

I was early in the reception-room, and getting the
ear of the chamberlain, suggested that he assign me as

Miss Barden's escort to dinner. This arrangement having been consummated to my satisfaction, and the dining-room doors being just then thrown open, we walked along without exchanging other than the merest commonplaces. As we passed through the doors, however, Miss Barden glanced behind us, and then murmured to me in an undertone:

"I see your old sweetheart and her new lover behind us. How can you endure it?"

I was very well satisfied with my behavior at this moment, since I did not even change color, but responded with ready gallantry:

"Miss Barden reconciles me to it."

Before she could speak again we were at our places at table. But once seated she turned her bright face toward me:

"Now, you musn't spoil all my fun by falling in love with me."

"And why not?" I demanded, not at all displeased at the obvious admission that she entertained the possibility.

"I told you that love and I were strangers," she replied, with a smile.

"Let me make you acquainted, then," I answered, quickly. At this the lady laughed outright.

"I acknowledge I like you," she said, "but I want to give you warning in advance that I do not believe I shall ever love any one. An intellectual union would be perfectly to my taste; but these kisses and embraces, bah!" And she shrugged her shoulders. "I don't see how any one can be so gross."

"But how glorious a thing it is to learn something new," I suggested, as we began our dinner.

"If you ever urge me to marry you I know I shall hate you," she insisted, with a frankness which had a very piquant effect. "It would simply distress and exasperate me to be asked to do anything more than talk with you."

23

When the dinner was cleared away the toast-master rose from his chair and looking hard in our direction, said:

"I have warned a certain lady who graces our table that I should call upon her to-night to defend her position. She has been among us four years, but none of our best favored men has yet found favor in her eyes. She lives in an atmosphere of love and marriage, but will have neither — Miss Barden."

My companion rose after only a moment's hesitation, and her clear voice thrilled me with a new power.

"I presume our brilliant toast-master expected me to reply with light repartee and pungent epigram. But I shall disappoint him by taking his question seriously, and answering him logically. However callous I may have seemed to the urgency of ardent lovers, I have never yet been accused of avoiding the society of men. I prefer, infinitely prefer, to talk with a man above all the women in Christendom. I listen to his ideas with eagerness and feel mine stimulated. Every word he utters suggests new lines of thought to me. I am intensely happy as I reply to him. I am thrilled with a peculiar delight as I notice his quick response, his full appreciation. I do not feel this stimulus in talking with women. I do not experience this suggestiveness from woman's conversation. Neither am I conscious of pleasing them as I have been vain enough to imagine I have pleased men in what I say. But do not speak of marriage to me. I am, Mr. Toast-master, an intellectual free lover. The sex in mind and spirit I recognize and enjoy to its full. Do not ask me to do more."

As Miss Barden sat down, I bent toward her and whispered under my breath:

"You will sometime know what the other love means."

She gave me an almost insulted look. It was as if her Diana-like instinct was aroused and put upon the defensive.

"I defy you to teach me," she answered. The toast-master rose again, as I whispered to her in sudden new excitement:

"I accept your challenge." And as her ear caught my words I saw a delicate flush as of frightened maiden-hood rise from her neck and diffuse itself over her cheeks and brow. But her face was resolutely turned toward the toast-master, who was just speaking again.

"A year since two students of social phenomena, as we were informed they were, came here. One of them has so far accepted our institutions as to give us to be-lieve he approves of them. The other makes no secret of his criticism. It may be instructive, and it will certainly be pleasant for us to hear from both of these gentlemen before we return to the hall for our evening of dancing. We can take the bitter with the sweet. Let us begin with the bitter. Mr. Ward will you tell us what you think of us?"

I was very glad it was Ward who was called upon first, as this gave me some opportunity to get my own thoughts in order. I was anxious to make a favorable impression on Miss Barden, whose cool, piercing in-tellect almost terrified me. I have usually been pos-sessed of a more than ordinary degree of self-confi-dence, but I dreaded this girl's judgment as a patient must dread the surgeon's knife. I saw Ward rise and heard him begin by saying:

"To criticise those whom I esteem so highly, and who have treated me so kindly is a most ungracious task."

Then I forgot all about Ward in a feverish attempt to arrange in some sort of order what I had to say.

"Your friend is a very pleasant speaker" said Miss Barden, giving me a quick glance which disturbed my train of thought and decided me to abandon all anxiety as to what I should say, and depend on my usual guide, temporary inspiration. Apparently my friend had overcome his very commendable disinclination to criti-

cise. Probably he had explained it away in his usual
courtly fashion, for certainly when I next began to listen to him he was handling Grape Valley institutions
in anything but a gentle manner.

"You are destroying those feminine qualities which
have been most admired. The woman of Grape Valley cannot long remain timid, shrinking, ingenuous.
She must lose the quality of self-effacement for the
sake of her dear ones. She must become self-assertive,
forward; shall I say immodest? In our old world, which
you so despise, the maiden is shy, innocent, unsuspect-
ing the wickedness of the world. The wife feels
that her hopes, her dreams, her possibilities, are
limited to her own home. She thinks, struggles and
suffers only for her husband, and thus shows the
full glory of womanhood. Under your system the
distinctive feminine qualities will soon disappear.
Our system intensifies and perpetuates them. As I
close let me say that your industrial system I wholly
approve. By it you insure to each individual satisfaction of his necessities and a certain modicum of pleasure. Men fight no longer for the privilege of doing a
piece of work, but are all working together peacefully
to perform it for the common benefit. If you had
but preserved what seems to me the natural relations
of the sexes, making marriage a permanent bond, and
restoring the home, I should only have words of ap-
proval and good speed for you."

Then Ward sat down amid general applause and the
toast-master rose again, and in well-modulated phrase
called upon me. All my diffidence had vanished.
Ward had shown himself my friend on many occasions, but never more than in his speech this evening.
He had supplied me a text for all I cared to say. After
paying the customary compliment to the toast-master,
I spoke as follows:

"The gentleman who has just addressed you has
been my particular friend for many years, yet we have

never agreed except on very insignificant questions. Every subject ever mooted between men has been discussed by us. We differed when we began, we differed at every stage of the discussion, we seemed to differ when we finished. Still, I have often been convinced that my friend's logic had been mortally wounded, although he would not lower his sword. I was the more sure of this because I know how often I have hurled back defiance at him when I felt that I was entirely overcome. Once more we differ, and once more we oppose each other, but I shall not despair of converting my friend to what I have learned to regard as the truth. He will hold out to the last, but I have no doubt I shall yet carry his scalp at my belt."

Just here a little stir ran over the company, and a rustle, that sweetest sound to the ear of the public speaker. I had made a point, and in a second more I heard two hands applauding me at my side. Then a wave of applause swept around the table. The company was wholly in sympathy with me, and was eager to see me demolish my friend.

"I am the more encouraged to expect his confession because without assistance from me he has reached the point that he wholly approves the industrial system of Grape Valley. He approves the system which makes all adults equal sharers in the product of their joint labor. He admits that he approves of a system which makes women as materially independent as men. Now, it is this very system which permits and calls for new institutions of marriage. Women may naturally decline to be subject to men unless the men have a material basis for the authority they wish to exert. For countless years women have been dependent for their fate on attracting some man's favor, and thus securing a marriage which would relieve fathers or more remote relatives of the burden of their support, or in lack of relatives, would alone secure them against positive want. So, after marriage, came the necessity of clinging to that husband through good and ill report, of enduring everything at his hands, even although he might be morally repulsive or physically disgusting. If she parted from him there came the blasting of the lives of children, the loss of home and comforts, the deprivation of the very food her poor body required, and the raiment to protect her from the cold. The whole legal and moral force of society was accordingly exerted to make perpetual the marriage tie, to protect the home as it was called. Poets, novelists, preachers innumerable, have built up a mighty wall of tradition about this marriage. All other considerations are as nothing in the eye of the moral teacher of civilization compared to the maintenance of the inviolability of the marriage bond. That most marriages take place on insufficient acquaintance, and the young and ardent are far more likely to make a mistake than a judicious choice, is of no account; that accident and not suitability are the causes of most marriages, and hence that love wanes with the honeymoon, and the marriage relation becomes, very commonly, a union for convenience, a mere friendly companionship, or a daily scourge. Marriage was the very foundation of the old order, and must be preserved as nominally perpetual long after every good or true element in the relation might have disappeared. At last we are shown a system of society where marriage can be regarded as a means for the intimacy of the sexes, as a relation which can double each soul's life and joy. Friendship does not enable us to overleap the bars which seclude the individual life. It is only through sex that perfect sympathy becomes possible, only through sex that one being can enter into the life and share the experiences and profit by the knowlege of another. But the forced intimacy of the sexes where the fullest form of love does not exist is the real offense against honor and chastity. The Grape Valley institutions make it possible for a man and woman to meet and know each other without fear or favor, without diffidence on her side for she has no cause to be ashamed, without patronage on his side, for he has no more to bestow than she. She is no longer a timid creature first to be captured like a shy bird and then held forever in the toils. Her sex is rehabilitated. Its place in progress and civilization, as a power for the spiritual development and intellectual culture of the world, is assured. The time has forever passed when shyness and shamefacedness must be considered her crowning attributes. Her longings for a union capable of perfecting her nature need no longer be concealed."

Then I took my seat and was rewarded with more applause than I merited. My friend Ward joined as heartily as the others in the tribute to me, as was always his magnanimous fashion, but I could see no signs in his face of the yielding which I had prophesied.

"You spoke beautifully," said Miss Barden, turning her steel-blue eyes upon me. Then I remembered again that she sat by me, and my interest in her revived as she added: "It was just as I would have spoken if I could."

Then I called to mind her challenge and my acceptance. What worthier woman indeed would I be likely to find in the world than she?

# CHAPTER XX.

Miss Barden of course accepted my invitation to waltz. With my arm about her waist, and her hand in mine, I tried to hope that she was beginning to feel as a woman does when her nature awakes and recognizes all compelling love. She danced gracefully enough, but when we had once made the tour of the hall, she said :

"This is tiresome. Why waste time in athletics, when we can please each other so much better by talking."

Without a word of remonstrance I offered her my arm, and we left the floor. She drew me to one side where a winding staircase led to the balcony overlooking the hall.

"Come up here," she said. "We can see everybody, and I will tell you about some of the people. I am not ripe for love myself, but I can analyze the love affairs of others so as to interest you. Try me."

I did not care to confess my disappointment at the preponderating activity of the intellectual side of my companion, but in fact I was almost discouraged with her, and so nearly out of temper that I was disinclined to talk. I was more than willing that she should take upon herself the chief burden of the conversation. Perhaps she would reveal some weak point in the armor which now appeared invulnerable.

"Do you notice the young man with black moustache and imperial? He stands in the further corner near the musicians' platform," she began.

"He is talking very earnestly to the girl in black

lace," I assented. "What a dazzling white complexion she has."

"Yes. Now I think I can make a shrewd guess as to what the young man is saying at this moment. Do you see how eagerly he bends over her? He has drawn her a little apart from possible listeners, you see."

"A love affair, I suppose."

"A one-sided one. He is now saying something like this: 'Listen to me, Annie, I want you to leave Mr. Bissell. He cannot love you as I do. He is too old for you, too conservative. You married him before you knew me. You admired him, I suppose, but that isn't love.' So much for what he is saying. Now she is answering him."

I laughed. "She seems to have a reply ready. She must have known what he was going to say. Are you wizzard enough to guess that too?"

She smiled gaily. "This is what she is saying: 'It is of no use, Mr. Rollins, for you to tell me this. It isn't true that Mr. Bissell is merely kind and good to me. I am sure I love him, though I am not delirious over him as you would probably insist I should be over you. I am not of the extreme demonstrative sort. You are mistaken in thinking you want me, that I could make you or that you could make me happy. Now let us finish the waltz.' See how disappointed he looks as he offers her his arm, but I think she is right and has married the man best suited to her."

"This is very instructive," I said. "Can't you give me some more of these modern 'imaginary conversations?'"

Miss Barden gave me a sharp glance. "Please understand that I know the relations of these people, and although they may not use just the words I quote, yet the sentiment is exact. Do you believe me or not? I do not prophecy for sceptics."

"I believe," I assented with an attempt at an humble expression

24

"Do you observe the unamiable countenance of the young woman sitting on the rear row just opposite us? She is next to a middle-aged gentleman, but they are not in conversation. She has been married twice since she came here, but both marriages were of very short duration. I doubt if she will have another opportunity. That very man who sits next to her has had a similar experience in matrimony. She is ill-tempered and narrow-minded. He is stupid and greedy. Under the marriage institutions of civilization each of them would have been able to make some body miserable for life, and, worse still, would have transmitted to future generations the bad qualities which here will die with them."

"You give sexual selection a fair field here, to be sure," I assented, more seriously.

"Yes. That great force for human progress and for the development of the species works with us in two ways. The constant necessity is upon every husband and wife here to keep on good behavior and make the best of natural graces or talents in order to hold each other's affection, or, losing them, to win the love of another. Thus the race is improved and a good heritage of character and attainment for the children is assured. The freedom of divorce here also enlarges the scope of sexual selection since it shuts out from the lists of fathers and mothers the ill-favored of both sexes, whose defects of body, mind or character are thus confined to their own generation."

"You are very interesting," I said, after waiting a few moments for her to continue. Her keen eyes flashed hither and thither in search of more material for sketches.

"Do you see your friend, Mr. Ward?" she asked suddenly, as she leaned over the edge of the balcony. "He stands by the pillar at the other side of the room He is just inviting a woman in black to dance with him. See! She accepts. I have noticed your friend devoting himself to her quite frequently of late. You do not suppose his heart is at all touched, do you? She is Lydia Trenk, the wife of one of our board of directors, one of those phlegmatic blondes, cold, slow and stupid I should say. But see how her eyes brighten as Mr. Ward talks to her. He must talk well. Do you notice a new sprightliness in her face and figure? Perhaps he is the one man in Grape Valley who can stir her nature. His face changes, too. It has lost its mask of impassiveness. A new color comes into it. The very movements of his hands show a new vivacity. Do you know I almost suspect that your friend is in love in spite of himself, and with another man's wife."

"It is impossible," I exclaimed, while following with my eye every detail she had called to my attention. "Ward hates the very thought of your peculiar institution."

"Oh," she answered, "I do not claim to be infallible. Your eyes are as good as mine, and you know the character and peculiarities of your friend far better than I. But see, Mrs. Trenk accepts his invitation. How proudly he bears her away. He is happy to possess her even for so short a time as a dance. Now he puts his arm around her, so tenderly. All he worships on the earth is within that woman's form. I am sure of it now."

"But," I said, "my friend Ward has never cared for women. He has regarded them as petty in their thoughts and narrow in their souls. I have known him intimately for many years, and I have never heard him yet speak ardently of any woman."

"Because," answered Miss Barden, "he has not seen woman under proper conditions. I almost wonder that men of character and intellect even fall in love under the old state of affairs. The physical attraction of sex, however, exists under all conditions and circumstances. If all women were deaf-mutes it would still exist. But what a poor apology for love is that.

The whole brute creation is subject to that sort of attraction, but love is not the word to describe it."

"Men of intellect and character," I suggested, "are famous for their marital infelicity. Perhaps Ward has taken warning."

"Do you blame them? They differ from others in that they know what they want. When, having risked everything to secure it, they find they have it not, and that they are forever shut out from the opportunity to seek for it elsewhere without disgrace, is it a wonder they are out of temper? But, speaking of Mr. Ward, I am not at all surprised that his first experience of woman in the free exercise of her faculties and accomplishments, interests him. In your old world young women are forbidden by your laws of propriety to be free and unrestrained in their demeanor toward men. They are expected to pretend to be what they are not, or what, if they are, offers attraction to only the most mediocre of men. To show as little individuality as possible is one of their unwritten rules; so, I suppose, they will be likely to offend no possible suitor. They may not have but a single opportunity to obtain that great end, the necessity of their existence — marriage, and any striking characteristic might not harmonize with that possible suitor's taste. They must not show any passion, either. They must behave as if the whole idea of sex was an unknown world to which the husband's expert hand should lead them. All this is a part of the tradition of centuries that marriage is the sole end for woman, and that indissoluble, that she should have no thoughts save for her future home, no feelings except for that man whom, perhaps, nothing but chance association has made her husband. In the old state of society the fascinating young woman is that exceptional and shocking creature who thinks her own thoughts, feels as she likes and acts as she feels. All the young women of Grape Valley are fascinating, except me."

She gave me an arch glance as she corrected herself, which seemed like an invitation to me to say something lover-like. But, judging it best not to make any digression at this moment, I affected not to have noticed her little ruse, and objected seriously:

"You have explained why your young women are irresistible here, but not why my friend Ward should be fascinated by a married woman."

Her eyes flashed as I had so often observed them to do when a bright idea occurred to her.

"Except in the ultra-fashionable or literary society of the leading cities of the outside world, a woman ceases to be of any account after marriage, except to her husband and children. And even in the fashionable circles of society her limitations are comparatively strict. She is hedged in from all directions. To be sure, she enjoys something which might almost be called liberty as compared with the condition of her humbler sisters. Her education, her cultivation, her progress do not entirely stop at marriage. The attractiveness of the married woman in the old society, who by virtue of outside employment profits by constant attrition with man, and increases in the power to charm by the use and cultivation of her charms, shows what even a small degree of freedom in the relations of married women with man will do for our sex. Here we have perfect freedom, not only of the intellect, but of the feelings. Body and soul we are our own mistresses. The result is that our women, charming as they are before marriage, improve with every year, become more interesting with every experience. Her whole nature progresses together, and a man must have a brain of wood and a body of stone who can be indifferent to the married woman of Grape Valley."

"You are very enthusiastic over the married woman," I said. "I should think you would join her ranks."

"So I would," she answered, lowering her voice, "if

I could only have the good fortune to fall in love, or
even to imagine myself in love. If I understand myself aright there is a barrier of reserve about me which
curbs my spirit and limits my intellectual advancement.
I know it, but nothing except the enthusiasm of love
can break down that barrier. Intimacy without love
would not do it."

"Are there many unmarried women in the hall to-
night?" I asked.

Her bright eyes swept the room. "I think I am the
only one here. You will remember our young girls
are still at school. It is only at twenty-two that their
education is ended and they are introduced into the
full light and liberty of Grape Valley. Each one of
them is sure to have some admirer almost at once, and
a year from her *debut* it is hard to find one unmarried.
The old maid is, I think, an improbability at Grape
Valley, which is not the least of our advantages. That
victim of circumstance is, so far at least, unknown
here. Every woman is constantly thrown into such
free relations with the other sex that it is only a matter
of time when she must meet a man who thinks to find
what his nature wants in her."

Miss Barden's conversation kept my brain fairly
aglow with excitement. Every sentence she uttered
suggested new and tempting lines of thought. She did
not stir my blood nor quicken my pulses. I experienced none of those great waves of longing I had
known with Kate. But was not this a better and
more perfect love? She was beautiful and graceful.
There would certainly be nothing to desire in the way
of physical attraction. We were alone in the balcony
so I could touch her hand without attracting notice.
She did not draw away and I clasped it in mine. It
lay cool and nerveless in my grasp, and she turned her
eyes, a little more wide open than usual, upon my face.

"I believe you must be making love to me," she
said, with a little smile.

"I would like the privilege," I said, in a voice as cool as her own. "Will you be my wife?"

"Why should I?" she asked, looking down in a half-quizzical fashion at her hand as it lay in mine. "I like you as one man, I suppose, may like another. But that is not love. And for that matter, if you love me, then all signs fail." Then she drew her hand away. "This is growing tiresome," she said. "I am sure I can amuse you in better fashion. You see that tall, thin gentleman standing just at the corner of the stage?"

"He seems to be watching the dancers very intently," I suggested, trying to fall in with her humor.

"Nay, not seems, he is. It is his wife he looks at. You see the woman in brown, with the wavy black hair, dancing with a portly gentleman in a white waistcoat? There they are now, just under the chandelier. She smiles back at her husband. See the wonderful light come into his face. If you could look at me like that, just once, I might believe you loved me. Let me tell you something about that man and woman. They are both considerably past middle life. Both have been married more than once before, and have been the parents of children. Now, for the first time, they are happy. They are all in all to each other."

"What was their attraction for each other, do you suppose?" I asked.

"It would take an unerring psychologist to say why any man and woman should or should not love one another," answered Miss Barden. "Certain qualities are in themselves attractive — beauty and grace, sweetness of temper; and first marriages are contracted most commonly in consequence of these qualities. Awkwardness, inharmonious features, obstinate or sullen tempers are in themselves repelling. Still, love stays or goes without reference to outward attractions. The plainest women often, most often it seems to me, are the objects of the most passionate devotion. Men with unattractive features are among the most irresistible with our sex. Perhaps it is a matter of magnetic currents. Perhaps it is a matter of spiritual insight, the groping of the soul for that other nature which will enable it to complete itself. Perhaps each nature is dual, as in so many plants, male and female. Its halves are separated, and ever reaching out for the union which is their perfection, a union, spiritual, intellectual and physical. This reaching out for completion is called desire. This perfect union, when attained, is perfect love. The more or less perfect, and more or less lasting unions, give us tastes of love. Love, in perfection, comes only with the perfect union." Then she rose. "It is growing late," she said, "I must bid you good night."

I rose, too, and we passed through the hall into the corridor. "Will you step out and enjoy the moonlight for a moment?" I asked. And without a word she rested her hand on my arm.

We had passed up the street for a few rods before I spoke. By this time I was sufficiently excited to assure myself that I was in love. I did not know, after repeated failures, how to phrase my declaration so she should listen to me. She liked me, she was interested in me. But her physical nature had not as yet awoke to the existence of mine. I paused and as she turned toward me, I passed my arm about her waist and drew her toward me.

"Are you going to waltz out here?" she murmured in some confusion.

"No," I said, and my voice trembled, "I am going to kiss you." I bent my face toward hers until I felt her breath come faster and warmer on my cheek. My lips touched hers, as soft and sweet as the petals of some rare rose. There was an instant of resistance, then she returned my kiss, and gave a beautiful movement toward me, while her eyes sank before mine.

It was surrender.

"Is this love?" she whispered at last, as she lifted her eyes toward mine with a new expression in them.

How could I answer her, but with another kiss?

"Then it is very beautiful," she said. "I only hope it is forever. I think I have only lived since you kissed me."

The next month we were married.

25

# CHAPTER XXI.

It was a very short honeymoon for Gertrude and me. As I look back upon it now, I can see that I was at no time more than a little in love with her. There was a great deal in common between us. She was interested in the same sort of subjects that interested me, and her mind worked by much the same method as mine. We agreed in our judgment of men and things as I have never agreed with man or woman before or since. I would, of course, have been a very unappreciative man if the possession of such a beautiful woman was not very pleasing to me; and the imitation of love I offered her I believe I could have kept up for an indefinite period if she had continued as ardent and enthusiastic as during the first few weeks of our married life. As I think of it now I am inclined to believe that it was her very fear lest her passion should not last that made her at first so breathless in her devotion. She could not bear to awake from her dream of love and find it a delusion, and, so to speak, willfully drugged herself.

It was before our brief honeymoon was far advanced that I discovered my friend Ward was avoiding me. I determined to have an explanation with him at once, and seeing him start, one afternoon, on what I thought one of his long walks, I excused myself to my wife and started in pursuit. I kept at such a distance as to make his immediate discovery of me improbable, as I did not want him to see me until well up the valley. When Ward was very obstinate it sometimes required considerable time to bring him to reason, and I was anxious to overtake him where he could not get away from me until I had said all I had to say. I followed him up one street and down another in what I was sure was not the direct course to either the mountains or the country. Could it be he had discovered I was following him and was bent on giving me a wild goose chase? When he finally turned up a short street that had no opening at the other end I became sure he was tricking me. So instead of plunging blindly on I waited at some distance from the corner for him to come back.

In vain I waited. Seconds had become minutes, when it suddenly occurred to me that there might be some path, unknown to me, leading from the other end of what I had thought a blind street. If so, he had escaped me, unless I made up in speed what I had lacked in brains. So I walked rapidly up to the corner, and when, glancing up the street, I saw no one, I exchanged my walk for a run. Suddenly the door in one of the houses just beyond me opened, and a man and woman came out. The woman was Mrs. Trenk, and the man no other than Ward himself. He had a light wrap of hers over his arm, and she carried a sort of alpinstock in her hand. It was apparent enough they were just setting out for a mountain ramble. All that Gertrude had said about Ward and this woman recurred to my mind. There could be no doubt of the correctness of my wife's conclusion. He was in love, and expounder and upholder of old world traditions that he was, in love with another man's wife.

My position had now become a very embarrassing one. Looking ahead I could see no outlet from the street, and even if there had been one I could not have escaped through it without passing Ward and his companion, which would, of course, strike them as a very suspicious performance. It only remained for me to turn about and hurry back the way I had come, trusting, through my friend's absorption in his sweetheart, to be unnoticed. I heard their steps behind me and would have given a great deal if I could have known their eyes were not fixed on my back, as I seemed to feel they were. I think that length of sidewalk to the corner was the most uncomfortable stretch I ever traveled. Every instant I expected to hear Ward's voice hailing me, and when it came at last I actually think it gave me a certain sensation of relief. My suspense was over at all events.

"Is that you, Vinton?"

Of course, all I could do was to stop, turn and affect as much surprise as I could reconcile with my dread of appearing ridiculous.

"Isn't this an unusual direction for your walk?" he asked, in a very satirical tone. "Or were you looking for something? Mrs. Trenk, permit me to present my friend and well-wisher, Mr. Vinton."

It was, of course, as I had feared. He believed I was prying into his love affairs. Between my surprise at what I had discovered and my anxiety to have it known that I had not come in search of that knowledge, I was taken completely at a disadvantage. My confusion seemed like confession, which of course heightened my discomfort, and to cap the climax, the lady began to blush furiously, which intensified Ward's indignation.

"I will tell you this evening all which you appear to want to know," he exclaimed, nearer hating me, I could see, than ever before in his life. They passed me without another word.

Of course I confided my misery to my wife, but I have doubted whether one ever gets consolation by confiding his humiliating experiences to any one. He is conscious of having humiliated himself once more, and unnecessarily, and he is inclined to believe that his confidant either pities or despises him. But Gertrude carried it off very well. She laughed heartily at my predicament, thus relieving me of the more trying suspicion that she wanted to laugh at me, but restrained her merriment out of regard for my feelings. Then she told me that Mr. Ward had no cause for such sensitiveness, except it was supplied by his own conscience. A hundred people could and must have seen him take Mrs. Trenk on the mountain walk, and there was nothing startling in the affair according to Grape Valley ideas, either, except that he seemed to look on it as such himself. She was inclined to think that my friend was on the eve of yielding his traditions, and conforming to the customs of the colony. She told me that she could hardly wait until evening to learn the truth.

Although Ward entered the general hall after dinner, looking very stern, Gertrude urged me to go to him at once. He received me very stiffly, and proposed that I come to his room. Once there he even so far forgot himself as to neglect to take or offer a cigar. No sooner were we seated than he exclaimed :

" I suppose you imagine I am going to break the law of the land and the traditions of civilization, because you do it so easily. But you are as absolutely wrong in what you imagine I am about to do, as in what you are doing yourself."

" What do you think I imagine about you ? " I demanded.

" You imagine that because I take pleasure in the society of one woman in Grape Valley that I am in love with her. It is false," he fairly shouted. " I don't know what the word love means."

" Before we go any farther, Ward," I began, anxious to show him I had not been spying upon him, " let me assure you —— "

" I want you to hear me now," he said, almost fiercely, " and I only wish all Grape Valley had one ear that all could hear it at once. I would sooner cut off my right hand than fall in with the practices of these people. Can't I talk to a woman without scheming to

win her heart? Can't a woman enjoy the conversation
of a man who has thought and studied and traveled,
without being anxious to leave her husband for
him?"

"I don't know that any one suspects you of being
in love," I answered, mendaciously. But I was beginning to become indignant at his manner and corrected
myself rather significantly, "or at least that anybody
would suspect you of being in love if you did not do
so much protesting."

He gave me an indignant look and then rose and
paced the floor without replying. I made use of the
opportunity to offer the true explanation of my pursuit
of him, and he said, more mildly:

"Well, well, I did not think you meant anything
cowardly or underhanded, my boy. I only thought
you were trying to make sure of my being a fool so you
could try to advise me. Everybody advises a man in
love. I have, as you remember, attempted to advise
you. But I am not in love. Don't you suppose I
know myself? Do you suppose I have lived to be
forty-eight and have met the most beautiful and fascinating women of America without a heart pang, now to
fall a victim to the tender passion here? Here of all
places I should most avoid it."

"She is a pretty woman," I remarked, rather incon-
sequently.

"Pretty?" he repeated, stopping in his walk just
opposite me. "That is a cheap word to apply to such
a woman as that. I am ashamed of you. Why the
woman has a face an artist would go wild over. That
divine calm, that serenity, that expression of assured
power. Pretty, indeed! Did you ever see such eyes,
black, brown, almost bronze, by turns? But her beauty
is the least of her charms. She seems to understand
what one means almost by intuition, all that one means,
not a tithe of it, as most of the sex do. And her
answers show how much more deeply she feels one's

thoughts than he can do himself. Any man might well love her."

"Does her husband?" I asked, significantly.

"Her husband? Don't mention him," exclaimed Ward, throwing himself into his chair. "How such a woman came to marry such a man is one of the mysteries. To him she is, apparently, nothing more than other women. He sees her beauty; none but a blind man could help doing so much; her gentle spirit, her sweetness of disposition give him no cause of offense. But her marvelous sympathies, her rare responsiveness, he cannot appreciate."

"Perhaps," I suggested, "she does not have them for him."

"Sometimes I think so," continued my friend, unconscious how his manner was giving the lie to his assertion that he did not love Lydia Trenk. "It has often occurred to me that it might be because I called out these qualities that I see them; that they were not there for others; that she herself, perhaps, did not once suspect she had them."

"Tell me who she is and where she came from," I said, "if you know. Did she marry this unappreciative husband in Grape Valley?"

"No," answered Ward lover-like eagerly accepting the opportunity to talk about her. "They were married three years before the Grape Valley experiment was inaugurated. She was a poor girl working in this Trenk's shop, reduced to poverty by the loss of her father. This man offered her marriage, and, although she tells me she did not know what love meant, she accepted him. He gave her comfort where she suffered hardship before, a home instead of the wretched tenement in which she and her invalid mother had lived. He enabled her to surround her mother again with the elegancies of life, and make the few months which the poor widow had to live, happy ones. Mr. Trenk was very much interested in industrial reform, and an

extreme radical in his ideas, so he came with his wife
to Grape Valley. Here they have lived ever since.
Although other men have sought to win her love she
has been faithful to her husband. She enjoys the freedom of social intercourse afforded here, and which, she
says, makes women far brighter, something beside
household drudges and nurses for children."

"Has she any children?"

"Yes, two. She spends most of her afternoons with
them at the nursery. I think for that matter," continued Ward, "I never saw mothers more tender
toward their children, or more happy with them than
the women here. The little ones are no longer burdens
or cares. The mothers do not dread their advent, or
bewail their number."

Verily my friend Ward's eyes were being opened.

"But I was telling you," he continued, "how true
she has been to her husband, in spite of all temptations."

"Possibly she has had no temptations," I suggested;
"a woman not in love is not like a man — uneasy until
she is."

"I do not believe she would do a wrong thing under
any circumstances," said Ward, very decidedly.

"Then you think it would be wrong, do you, if she
fell in love with some other man? If love is a matter
of mutual attraction and sympathy, she ought not to be
blamed if it befall her."

"Her offense would not be in loving another man,
but in yielding herself to the dictates of her passion;
that I am sure she would not do," insisted Ward.

"Aren't you in error there?" I demanded. "Does
a wife remain faithful to her husband when she loves
another, instead of him? Is it not the withdrawal of
the love which really breaks the marriage relation and
commits the unfaithfulness, instead of the withdrawal
of the wife's presence merely?"

Ward was apparently preparing himself for a reply

which should take to task the whole sexual relation of
the valley. But before giving him an opportunity to
reply, I said:

" By the way, why is it you have been avoiding me
lately? You and I have not been friends for ten years
to be separated by any trifle now. Have I trodden on
your toes without knowing it? What have I said or
done?"

I might have suspected that Ward could have but
one reason for his altered manner, and have known
that by asking for it I was inviting him to open fire
with all the arguments in his logical armory.

" I should not have presumed so far on our friendship as to have volunteered what you now invite me
to say. I felt shocked by your remarrying. You were
not at fault because Kate deserted you, but when you
married your second wife, you destroyed my confidence in you — almost my respect for you. You are
breaking laws which have prevailed in society since the
dawn of history. I would not have expected such
recklessness of you."

I straightened myself in my chair, and prepared
for the battle. I was determined that my friend
should not believe that I had transgressed what he
called eternal laws through weakness. " I am glad
you have spoken frankly," I said. " I will speak just
as frankly. So far as the transgression of laws goes
you must not forget that I am acting in accordance
with the laws of the settlement where we live. This
is a State within a State, making its own laws touching all matters, without reference to the constitution
or statute book of any central authority whatever.
You may consider, if you please, this settlement as
in a state of rebellion against some central authority
claiming but not enforcing jurisdiction over it. Grape
Valley pays no taxes to other governments, votes for
no representatives or governors, and recognizes no
courts or codes except its own. This is an inde-

26

pendent State, and laws passed by it are of as much force upon the inhabitants of this State, as laws passed by the law-making authorities of any other State elsewhere. As other States have a right to regulate the marriage and divorce laws for their people, so the constitutional authorities here have the same right over the people of Grape Valley. In some States divorce is granted only for adultery or cruelty, desertion, intoxication or failure to support. In others divorce is so easy to obtain that it is little more than an unpleasant process, merely leaving a stigma on those availing themselves of it. The State of Grape Valley being *de facto* independent has the same right to. regulate marriage and divorce for its people as the government of any other States."

I could see my friend was somewhat surprised at my line of defense. He had apparently expected nothing of the sort. I resumed :

" If I regulate my life by the institutions and laws of the *de facto* independent State I abide in, what more can be asked ? You may still insist that if those laws are inexpedient or wicked ones, they provide no excuse for the moral being. You will claim that, as it has often been a duty in the course of history to disobey wicked laws, so laws, unless justified by our own conscience and reason, do not justify us in what we may do. As to the religious aspect of this question I will merely say that the eternal principle of Christianity is universal brotherly love. So far as specific social injunctions in the gospel go, they may be regarded as intended for application to the state of society existing when promulgated. Under the conditions of society existing when the gospel was promulgated, and, indeed, under the conditions of society existing in the outside world to-day, divorce is most dangerous and destructive. Here we have done away with those conditions, and through freedom of divorce we are able to fulfill the essential doctrines of Christ

infinitely better than without it. If you still insist on
confining society to what is known as scriptural divorce, I must send you to the law-making powers of
the so-called Christian States and nations, many of
which have a State church, but most of which have
laws on their statute books contrary to this very
scriptural limit to divorce. At the courts of those
Christian governments which nullify the injunctions
of the head of their church, you may serve as a
prophet to turn them from their heresy. But here we
have carried the Christian principle so infinitely beyond the example of the rest of society, that, as the
greater includes the less, so the spirit overrules the
letter."

Ward was prepared, as I paused to catch my breath,
with an objection on the general ground of morality
and reason.

" But you are violating the practice of civilized people since the Christian era," he said. "That practice
was not founded on laws nor religion alone, but on
the general sense of what was best and most expe-
dient. The laws permitting divorce have been only
to a very limited extent availed of, and the stigma of
shame and obloquy has rested in a great degree upon
those who have taken advantage of them."

" Most certainly," I continued. "But do you not
see you are supplying an argument for me instead of
presenting one against me? If I appeared in the outside world as an advocate of free divorce you might
well quote the unwritten law against me and my dangerous doctrines. You might say that the feeling of
all virtuous people was sufficient proof that I was
wrong. I might, if on such a mission, well be regarded
as a social incendiary, as a corrupter of society, an enemy
of the family and of the home. But please remember
the feeling of the best people of a community against a
course of behavior is an argument against that course
only in that community. It is not among the old social

institutions, which are so much like a pile of children's blocks, that if you removed one at the base all would topple to the ground. that I would urge a system of free divorce. I agree with you that the family is the sub-stratum of the old social order, and that sub-stratum is only protected by preserving marriage as practically indissoluble. The violations of morality are innumerable, but better those than worse which would follow the license of free divorce. Marriage is called a failure because in so many families husband and wife are little more than business partners at best, and love, which hopeth all things, believeth all things, understandeth all things, only a vague dream of the past, or a maddening possibility with some other man or woman as its object. But better that, than that society should crumble and social anarchy set in; better that than that infinite suffering be brought on innocent children, that women be left without means of livelihood and men without home influences or social restraints. The old civilization is doing wisely in fighting for an indissoluble marriage tie. If I were in its bounds now, no one would fight harder for it than I. But here everything is changed. The woman is equal to the man in her capacity for self-support. Children are taken care of by the State, full privilege to enjoy them being allowed their parents. All the members of this society, married or unmarried, have homes, comforts and entertainment. So it is here for the first time in history that the marriage relation may be regarded as temporary, if the inclinations of the parties are temporary. For the first time love is admitted to its full scope and power as a chief agent for happiness, for education, for progress. For the first time women are relieved of the domestic burdens and motherly cares which in the world at large shut them in as with a black veil so soon after the white veil of bridal. For the first time their education and enjoyment of life in its broader scope, and their influence upon society continue after marriage. For the first time are men always kept under the stimulating influence of love. As is so seldom the case in the outside world, children are brought forth here under conditions most conducive to intellect and elevation of soul; offspring of an affectionate father, and of a mother in a state of mental culture and activity, such as only the favored mothers of all the centuries past have possessed. All the conditions which exist in the old world are changed here. What would have been and what would be mischievous, even fatal under those economical conditions, becomes useful and progressive here. What would have been wrong there becomes right here."

I glanced at my watch. It was 10:30, the hour at which the reception in the hall below closed. I rose, bade my friend a hasty good-bye, and went down to join Gertrude.

# CHAPTER XXII.

After Gertrude and I had returned to our own home that night, and she had laid off her hat, she seated herself by my side and turned her bright face toward me.

"Now tell me all about it," she said, as she took my hand in both of hers and leaned toward me.

My mental attitude toward her was all admiration. Her delicate features illumined with splendid life, her lithe but well-proportioned figure pleased my eye as nothing I had ever seen before. That I should have won her love, that I should be the object of her new born passion, was very delightful to me. Every faculty in me responded to the flattery, and there are few emotions more agreeable than those engendered by flattery. I was not filled with a worship for her, I was not agonized with that longing to be nearer to her, to bathe my soul in hers, which is at once the pain, the proof and the purpose of love. I could coolly observe her varied beauties, her intellectual graces, her spiritual charms, and say they were good. I could study each symptom of her novel experience of love, and analyze each manifestation of the rising and subsiding movement of her emotions, as no rapt lover could do.

Her hands that clasped mine and fondled them caressingly were as soft as silk, as pliant, as full of vitality as if they had a life and soul of their own. How delicately the fingers tapered ; the pink tipped crescents at their ends were more like shells than nails. Her wrist, slight, but perfectly rounded, was a model of delicacy and strength, and as her lace sleeve fell back, now and then was revealed the blue-white gleam of her exquisite forearm. Then the proud arch of her neck expanded at its base into the perfect curves of the ideal woman's shoulders and bosom; her hair coiled low on the back of her queenly head, was as black as night and as smooth as a southern sea before a hurricane; her forehead broad between the temples, was unruffled by line or wrinkle, like the front of Jove, I thought. Then I looked calmly into her eyes, a dark hazel in color, with capacity to show the slightest shade of feeling, to burn with unutterable passion, to soften in pity, to dilate in sympathy, to brighten with interest, to repose in intense thought, to leap in conversation like the dancing rivulet over its bed of gray-brown pebbles. She was mine in all her perfections, the most complete example of womanhood I had ever seen. She had lacked but one thing before, the enthusiasm of love. Now that had come and I was the object of it.

I think her love for me was that night at its culmination. We were nearer to each other than ever before. She was happy in her passion for me. I was so delighted and proud that it was almost like love.

For a long time we sat there while I told her all I had learned from my friend Ward, and all I had said to him, and we talked of him and his future, and then passed on to other themes. She had never impressed me as so marvelous a woman before. She seemed to understand everything before I had half expressed it. She seemed to guess my meaning before I spoke. It was as if our minds had thrown away the weak intermediary of words and dealt directly with each other.

But from that night I began to notice a change. It was a slow change. The average infatuated lover might not have noticed it. But my judgment was not touched nor my blood overheated so I should be unable to compare, discriminate and determine.

One afternoon, not many weeks later, as we met at our house, after returning from the forenoon's work, I

reached out my arm to draw her to me for a customary kiss. But instead of answering to my touch, like
an intricate mechanism whose controlling spring is
pressed, she gave a movement of repulsion. I released
her with a sense of injury. Had she recovered so soon
from her dream of love ?

"What does this mean ? " I asked, gravely.

Her eyes trembled before mine and then sank to the
floor. "I do not believe you love me," she said.
"As I think it over, it seems to me that I am the
lover and you the patient recipient. It was you who
tempted me from my unemotional heights or depths,
whichever they were. But I feel now as if you had
deserted me."

I had not dreamed but that I was in love until that
moment. A sudden revelation broke upon my soul
and so clearly that I was only anxious not to let my face
express it. With the instinct of self-protection I tried
to recall some of the gibberish of initiates. For centuries men and women had been reproached by each
other for lack of love, and a whole cyclopedia of catch
phrases and evasions have been invented.

"You are not yourself this noon," I ventured. But
it seemed to me that I had used the poorest phrase of
all. Gertrude's was quite too frank and clear-sighted
a nature for any sort of imposition. Her face flushed,
but it was not with the glow of reviving confidence.

"You are confessing everything," she cried, her
slim fingers clinching at her side as she spoke. "There
was but one answer to my reproach, to have disregarded
it and only have drawn me to you the closer. You
should have stifled my doubts with kisses and answered
my misgivings with a more tender embrace. But instead you release me at my first syllable of complaint;
at my first movement of shrinking you look at me not
in amazement, not in misery and sorrow, but in cold,
self-conscious displeasure, and say 'You are not yourself.' "

She stood, flushing, trembling, in her awakened distrust, in the first agony of doubt of what she had thought the perfecting of her life. There was yet time for me to have healed the breach between us, if I had loved her as she craved. She had leaped upon the outgoing boat. I stood upon the dock watching the gap between us grow wider and wider. There was but one power could reverse those mighty engines of character, the power of love. Alas, I had not suspected how bare my heart was until now. To her realities I could only answer combinations of words, to her passion only cool common sense, to her disappointed love only conventional excuses.

"I did not want to force you," I said weakly, and despised myself as I said it. It seemed as if she read me like an open book. She turned and rushing to the sofa threw herself upon it, face downward, and burst into tears. For nearly a minute I stood looking at her there. Her weeping disturbed but did not fill me with misery. Her emotion made me uncomfortable, but did not touch my heart. I wished myself a thousand miles away. I regretted I had ever seen her. Then I seemed to separate from my own individuality, and to look back upon myself and despise myself. What contemptible specimen of manhood, or what poor order of creature was this standing here and looking coldly upon the agonies of the woman who loved him? Shamed by my own self-consciousness, I went to her side, and, with new awkwardness, laid my hand upon her bowed head. She ceased sobbing, as if to study how much of love there was in that touch. Then she brushed away my hand and sat up.

"Oh, you have nothing for me," she cried with streaming eyes. "I knew it. I knew it. Leave me to get used to it."

What could I say that could dry her tears, that would still those wild heart throbs? If I had loved her I should not have needed to think. But I felt conscious

27

of a terrible hollow where love should be. I admired her, I enjoyed her, but that was all. One empty form of words after another came to my tongue's end, only to be rejected as too utterly shallow and impotent. At last I said, forcing myself to look into her piteous eyes:

" I am sorry you are so miserable."

" But you can do nothing for me," she answered with lightning readiness. " No need to tell me that. You do not love me. Oh, why did you tempt me to give you all when you had nothing for me ? No, do not distress yourself to say more. I am not weeping to induce you to utter lies to me, but only in regret for what I have lost. Yet how can I have lost what I never had ? "

Then she sank upon the sofa once more, and I once more leaned over her. I was ashamed that my heart did not yearn for her, disgusted at myself that I had to study for some way to comfort her. I tried to take her hand, but she caught it quickly from my clasp, moaning from the cushions :

" Leave me."

Then she raised her face for an instant and cried :

" Do you not understand ? It is not that I want you to pet me. It is because I am in agony for the love I have missed, for the joy never guessed before, which I feel now as if I could not live without. Leave me with my sorrow."

So I left her, and for that afternoon I was only sorry I could not get away from myself too.

There was no doubt in my mind now. I was sure that I did not love her. I had not for her what she wanted. She had read me aright. But why was it ? Was she not everything a man might love ? Where was there a more beautiful, a more responsive, a more amiable woman ? Men love beauty. Why did I not love her ? Men love grace, delicacy, refinement Why did I not love her? Men love intellect, brilliancy,

sympathy; men love to be loved, passionately, enthusiastically. I had all these in Gertrude, but was conscious I did not and could not give her what she was
weeping for. She had seemed to be every thing I
could desire in a wife, so I had done my best to evoke
her love. Apparently perfection was not enough for me.

I was out of temper with myself and with human
nature, so I made my way to the mountain side and
lay there in gloomy reverie for hours. I made no progress in my meditations. I began with the fact that
perfection in womanhood had been given me, and ended
with the admission that I was a most unreasonable creature not to be overwhelmingly in love with my wife.
But what could I do about it? I could resolve to be
tender and considerate. But I had been that and she
was unsatisfied. She demanded an ardor of passion
which, with all her lovableness, she could not inspire
in me. It was not enough to make me love her madly,
that I wished to do so. I could not lash myself into
the lasting enthusiasm which a lover has for his mistress. A great passion cannot be made by main force.

It was just before the time for going to dinner, that
I again entered the little house which had been assigned
to Gertrude for our home. It was with very pro-
nounced uneasiness that I opened the door and stepped
into the little sitting-room. But if my wife persisted in her cross-examination, what could I reply?
If she continued to reproach me, how could I offer new
proofs of a love I was conscious I did not have for her.
Gertrude had apparently been watching for me. For
how many hours? I guiltily wondered. Women have
infinite capacities for these long watches. As I entered
the room she rose quickly and came toward me with
something like the old light in her eyes. I opened my
arms and she threw herself into them.

"Forgive me," she said, with a new gentleness born
of her suffering. "I must have been tired and sick to
have spoken as I did."

I kissed her forehead and stroked back her hair.

"I know you love me," she added in a moment. "Tell me so once more," she raised her beautiful eyes to mine, "and I will not doubt it again. Oh," and she sighed, "I cannot, I dare not doubt it."

This was the hardest of all to bear. Her faith, to which I knew I was not entitled, had risen triumphant after its trial. I do not wonder that the faithful of all religions are women. Then I murmured some commonplaces, which, in her new forgiving and trusting mood, sounded to her like words of devotion.

For a week Gertrude's manner to me was very pathetic. She seemed so anxious that I should forget that she had doubted me, so eager that I should not suspect for an instant but that I was making her happy. I tried to be loverlike but was conscious I was only kind. I tried to be tender but could feel that I only succeeded in being awkward. The hours when we were alone together and when she would most naturally expect an interchange of endearments, a renewal of vows, I endeavored as much as possible to abridge, and to avoid when I could invent any semblance of an excuse. Not that the most cold-hearted of men could regard as disagreeable the moments passed in affectionate relations with a beautiful woman like Gertrude, if there were no after consideration. To be kissed by sweet lips, caressed by soft hands, to be told of one's engaging qualities, reminded of one's virtues and graces, cannot but be delightful if implying no responsibilities and incurring no reciprocal obligations. But I felt sure that my wife would look for a depth of devotion which I did not have, that she would seek for the presence in me of the absorbing passion which she craved. It was more intolerable, too, than open reproaches when I saw her face grow strained with the disappointment she tried to conceal, when an expression of agonized doubt was quickly followed by a forced smile.

It was a hard week, but there was no succeeding one like it. After that she helped me to avoid these suggestive hours. She would make excuses to go home earlier than I from entertainments, and then would feign to be asleep when I returned. I knew it was only feigning, for I could see the color come to her cheeks as I looked at her, and her eyelids flutter beneath my scrutiny. I noticed that while she continued to offer me a welcoming and parting kiss, she now drew quickly away as if to spare me the trouble of caressing her further. I could not but be oppressed by the change I saw in her, nor could I rid myself of a consciousness of guilt. But the one thing needful for her happiness I could not give her. It was my misfortune, I believed, as much as hers, for Gertrude's nature was one to reward a lover most munificently.

Ward called frequently on us and in his presence Gertrude was more than her old self. I could see Ward was amazed at her intellect, but the instant he had left us Gertrude's vivacious mood had passed like the energy of a spent spring. If I tried to make further conversation with her the responses were such as to make short shrift of it, and as soon as possible she would make some excuse to leave me alone. On one occasion I asked my friend what he thought of her.

" She is the most brilliant woman I ever knew," he answered, enthusiastically. " You have a prize, however wickedly you may have won it."

" But don't you think her manner toward me is changed?" I asked.

" Why no, I should think she was a model of wifely consideration. She neither exposes your mistakes, nor points her jokes with your foibles."

But I felt that Ward was more to be pitied, at this stage of his own experience, than I in my trouble. I had every reason to believe that he was falling deeper in love with Mrs. Trenk every day, and with his rigid condemnation of Grape Valley divorce and marriage, I could see no future for him except a broken heart. If Gillette had been home I should have gone to him with my perplexity, but as my own judgment seemed incapable of working on the subject, I had simply to let my relations with Gertrude drift. Then came the end of it all.

One noon as I entered the house I found a note in Gertrude's handwriting addressed to me. I opened it and this is what I read:

"Dear Mr. Vinton—I think we have proved ourselves unfitted to make each other happy, and when you read this I shall be at the clerk's office filing my record for a divorce. You know I did not believe that love was for me. For a few weeks you made me feel that I had been mistaken, and they were the happiest weeks I have ever known. Do not forget that. But I have since found I was the subject of a delusion, an ennobling delusion, but once detected it could entertain me no longer. I do not blame you for not adoring me, as I was foolish enough once to believe you did. After my little dream was over I became as incapable of love as you. It was only a matter of time when I should awake, and if so, the sooner the better. Don't you think so? GERTRUDE."

That night I slept once more at the phalanstery, the little I slept. Much of the night I sat by the window in loneliness of soul. I felt that something bright and beautiful and very dear had been taken from me; something that I ought to have been able to keep. I tried to strain my vision so as to embrace the little house away to the east, where she who had been my wife was alone. Was she sleepless and miserable too? To be sure we had seemed incapable of inspiring each other with that compelling ardor of mind, soul and body, known as love, but had we not enough for each other to make it cruel to part?

# CHAPTER XXIII.

One afternoon of the following month I stood on the steps of the phalanstery watching my wife of yesterday walk toward what was once our home and alone. She had given me a smile as she passed me. Why should I not follow her and offer her my heart anew. My loneliness was surely an indication of love. Perhaps it needed but a shadow to make me conscious of the light. Certainly I was earnest enough now in my longing to be with her. To kiss her again, to clasp her in my arms while we told each other that this little trial was all that was necessary to make our mutual love what it should be, would be a glorious experience indeed.

I had resolved to follow her and had even taken my first step in the direction she had taken when I noticed that I had been anticipated. I recognized a very familiar form. It must be Gillette, who, suddenly returning from a trip east and coming up the street, met her. He stopped to exchange salutations, and then doubtless asked her for me. Now she was answering him. He seems astonished. He gesticulates. Probably he is expostulating with her, telling her that she has been hasty, that if she had given me a longer trial I would have proved to be the man most able to give her the complete response she desired. Now they pass out of sight together. I will go to my room. Gillette will soon return and seek me there. Perhaps he will be the bearer of the good news I so much desired.

But once in my room, I began to recover my senses. I recalled the memory of the change in Gertrude since she had assured herself that I was only her friend, not her lover. Wise woman that she was she had not sought a divorce until, from constant association with me, she had forced herself to see that I did not love her, and had cured her own temporary infatuation. I might as well try to melt once more the solid lava from volcanoes extinct centuries since.

It was more than an hour later that the expected knock came at my door, and I welcomed, with a warm clasp of the hand, my friend Gillette.

As soon as the first customary questions and answers had been disposed of, and our cigars lighted, Gillette began with some hesitation :

"Your second marriage has not proved a permanent one, I see."

"I saw you talking with Gertrude," I said. "I suppose she gave you the explanation."

I thought he colored. "Your eyesight is good. Yes," he continued, "Gertrude talked very sweetly about the whole affair. I am very sorry for you both. Ward, she tells me, too, is in the toils. Do you see any way out for him ? "

"I cannot," I answered. "But he will not even admit that he is in love," I added. "He thinks his feeling for Mrs. Trenk is mere friendship, an inversion of the mistake Gertrude and I made, you see."

"It does not seem as if such a mistake were possible," remarked Gillette. "A friend is actuated in what he does by a sense of fealty, of obligation; a lover considers the favor is his if permitted to do anything for his mistress. The friend likes because in accordance with his ideas. The lover adores because he can do no less. The lover thrills at the sight of his mistress's dress, at the perfume of her gloves. He expands in her presence, even if she be unconscious of him. The sound of her voice makes him as full of joy as a robin when the sun breaks from the clouds. Her words seem to eclipse all other language. Her breath intoxicates him like an oriental drug, the touch of her hand sends the most mighty of all magnetic influences through his body. When he is with her, hours seem as minutes; to look at her face, merely to be conscious of her presence, fills the time with occupation. When she leaves him, it is as if sweet music suddenly ceased, or as if a curtain had dropped between him and his own soul. When he goes to her, his very feet seem instinct with an eagerness of their own to make good speed, and he feels strong enough to tear up mountains by their very roots if they be in his way."

I had never known my friend so eloquent before. "I believe you must be in love, you describe the passion in such detail."

"Did you love Gertrude like that?" almost demanded Gillette.

"Ah, no, but that is the sort of love she wanted."

"Well," he broke out, impetuously, "I have loved her in just that way since I first met her. Even my brief infatuation for Mrs. Blakesley hardly made me, for a minute, less Gertrude's adorer."

I looked at him in astonishment. "And you never told her?"

"Indeed, I have told her scores of times, but she only answered me as she did all the others before you. You, doubtless, wooed her more boldly than we, her real worshippers, and hence you won. But I shall yet win her." And he rose excitedly and paced the floor. "Such passion as mine must mean that sometime it will meet full return from her. Her dream of love shall be realized and mine, at once."

I could not wont myself to Gillette's anouncement. "Your friendship for me must have been severely tried when I married her."

"No," he answered, calmly. "I was simply amazed at a man who could not be happy in paradise. Marriage is not here the hopeless dead wall which shuts away the true lover, that it is in the outside world.

If we are conscious of the reality of our own love, lovers never despair in Grape Valley. He is sure that the woman he sincerely and continually longs for will some time fly to her home in his heart."

Then came another knock at the door, and I admitted Ward. Gillette and I glanced at each other significantly. There had certainly been a marked change in Ward's face. It was not that it showed illness, but a new sensitiveness. The eyes had a new gentleness in them; a new light. The lips once so firm had attained a certain mobility, and when in thought showed a slight curve downward at the corners. The impression of repose he once gave had forever disappeared. His face was more interesting, yet I could not but feel sad as I looked at him, for I was sure I knew what had made the change. I felt that my friend must experience all the wild unrest, the agonizing longing, the loneliness of love, but without hope of that glorious fruition which vindicates all the labor and anguish it has caused. After a few minutes of general conversation Gillette asked Ward a most extraordinary question :

" Why don't you marry one of the bright particular specimens of womanhood we cultivate in Grape Valley, and become one of us ? "

Ward almost gasped to be so roughly handled. It was as if Gillette had reached out with harsh hand and was tearing all his finer sensibilities. For a moment Ward did not reply. Then it seemed to occur to him that after all Gillette could not see his heart, and he finally replied in nearly his ordinary manner.

" When my two years' probation has expired, I shall leave Grape Valley forever."

" That will be in two months," I broke in. " You don't mean to say you will leave us in two months ? "

" You say ' us,' " repeated Ward. " Am I to understand that you expect to remain here ? I should think, of all men, you would be the most willing to leave a state of society whose marriage institutions have left you twice bereft."

Gillette glanced at me with interest.

"My marriages did not bring love with them," I answered, without hesitation, "so I ought to count it a blessing that I am not held for life to an unnatural bond. If I had made either of these marriages in the outside world I should have made some woman miserable, and deprived my own life of the attainment it most craves."

"You should not have made such mistakes," said Ward.

"Nor would I if I had been infallible," I replied. "But human nature is prone to err. Temporary feeling is taken for lasting passion, interest for sympathy, liking for love. To prevent the misery and perversion of the best portions of our lives which result from mistaken marriages it is not enough to warn men and women to be all knowing. What is needed is an opportunity to correct their mistakes."

Then Gillette found an opening.

"Try it yourself, Ward."

"Not I," answered he, with some excitement. "When I marry, I marry for life."

"Let us hope, then, that your first choice will be the woman to whom you can be everything, and who can be everything to you," remarked Gillette. "But if it happened you found you made your wife miserable instead of happy, if she found you were eating your heart out for another woman, would not the eternity of such a relation be a curse? I tell you human beings ought not to be held forever to the consequences of a decision which according to the laws of probabilities in human affairs, is extremely likely to be erroneous. You know it is estimated that ninety-nine out of a hundred business ventures fail, hence the necessity for courts of liquidation. Why then should a man be expected to be infallible in his choice of a wife, a choice usually made at a time of life when his judgment is untrained, and always under more or less excitement?"

"There is no use for you to urge me," exclaimed Ward, in what might have seemed to a casual spectator to be uncalled for temper. "If all the houris of paradise tempted me I would not marry here. When I marry I want to feel that my wife is mine forever, that nothing but death can take her from me."

Then he rose and hurried from the room without the formality of a good-bye.

"His prejudices will ruin his life," commented Gillette. Then after a pause he changed the subject. "I have something to propose to you, my friend. Your two years' probation does not expire for two months, but I know there is no man in Grape Valley more devoted to our institutions than you."

I said nothing, and he continued: "Next week I start for the East once more. You have just passed through an experience that must have been very trying to you. No man can separate his life from that of a woman with whom he has been on intimate relations without suffering something of a shock. Time and subjection to different influences are the best palliatives. A month's trip east with me will benefit you and our cause at the same time."

"What can I do for the cause?" I inquired.

"I will tell you," he answered. "This is a proselyting trip of mine to New York. There are several men and women whom I believe are ripe for conversion. Between us both we ought not to return to Grape Valley empty handed. Will you go?"

The proposal was a complete surprise, but it has always been a habit of my mind to come to a quick decision. "Yes."

A trip to New York would at least provide me with an opportunity to send my record of the Grape Valley experiment in marriage to the editor who had promised to publish whatever I wrote.

# CHAPTER XXIV.

The night before my departure east had come, and I went into the general hall, a little late, to find a debate in progress. Those who took the leading parts sat on the platform, though, after they had been heard from, it was the custom for people in the audience to join issue on one side or the other. In these discussions women had as much to say as men. With equal leisure for study and all the stimulating influence of unrestrained social intercourse, the women of Grape Valley were as active in their mental processes, as logical in their reasoning as the men.

It was the custom first for an essayist to lay down the general features of the subject to be discussed, to state the question broadly, fully, and without bias. Then one disputant took the affirmative and another the negative, before the general voice was called out. The essayist of this evening, no other than Gertrude herself, had nearly finished her contribution when I entered. I would not on any account have been late if I had known she was to take part. As I entered the hall the clear and bell-like tones of her voice met my ear, and gave me a very strange impression, strange and yet familiar. It was a voice out of my past, the forever past. Every inflection at once reminded me of my intimacy with her and that she was henceforth eternally cut off from me. I seated myself on the first convenient chair, without noticing who was next to me, just in time to hear her concluding words.

"Men are often attracted toward women by other qualities than those which are sufficient to constitute a basis for lasting attachment. Women are drawn toward men who can answer to but one small and insignificant trait in their characters. These inclinations are undeniable. In the outside world a large proportion of the marriages are founded on these partial attractions, only to be found wanting, at a later period, in the essentials. In Grape. Valley the same human nature exists, with the same susceptibility to attractions which are insufficient to support a true and lasting love. Love is the nearest approximation to a complete harmony between a given man and woman, but it is always probable that some other individual may excel either one of this ideal pair in some single attractive quality. Sometimes this partial attraction is merely sensual. Sometimes it lies in purely physical attributes, expressive features, perhaps a graceful carriage, or an artistic form. More often it lies in some peculiar intellectual or spiritual individuality, some piquancy of disposition, some unusual development of a winning trait, perhaps in the possession of a certain exceptional potency which appeals to the one affected and to that one alone. What shall we say of these incomplete love relations, these partial passions, these temporary attractions which crave closer association and more intimate relations, but still are not enough to make a basis for lasting marriage relations? Are they unmixed evils or not?"

The first speaker was Mr. Harvey, the mining expert who had visited the placer mine the year previous with Gillette, Ward and me. He had certainly had an experience of a most significant kind with Mrs. Blakesley. Had he learned any thing valuable from it?

Mr. Harvey said much more than I can attempt to reproduce here. But I will give a few of his more noticeable utterances.

"I believe these partial attractions are an unfortunate inheritance from the ill-assorted marriages and the unsatisfactory love affairs of our ancestors. They had to make the best of partial attractions. Their love affairs were almost always incomplete, and we are the offspring of them. The women for thousands of years have had to make the best of the few agreeable qualities in their husbands, husbands to do their best to exaggerate the pleasant characteristics their wives might happen to exhibit. So we are born amenable, in a most mischievous degree, to these partial attractions. They break up the most harmonious marriages by drawing husband and wife after some ignis fatuus. They can give nothing lasting, nothing satisfying, but they fire the fancy, excite the passions, make permanent relations unlikely, and are the most destructive forces of the sexual world."

The speaker proceeded to quote illustrations:

"The man of intellect and soul meets and marries a woman who is worthy of his fullest love. She enjoys him and he her. They are devoted to each other. A woman crosses his path who is attracted by an elevation of character she cannot understand, and which merely piques her curiosity. She smiles upon him, and he is attracted in turn by the luxuriance of her physical nature, an aspect of personality to which he is not accustomed. Being deficient in his sensual nature he is peculiarly interested in the new connection of such a nature with his. His relations with his wife, whom he can love with his whole being, are disturbed and perhaps destroyed by a transient attraction for a woman whose nature touches his but at one point. Often the wife of an ascetic disposition, whose husband returns her love, is overwhelmed by the animalism of a man whose soul is as far removed from harmony with hers as the antipodes. Often it is one phase of a character which attracts an individual of the opposite sex who is entirely out of sympathy with it otherwise. The serious man is attracted by a witty woman; the poetic woman by the dull realism of some male acquaintance; the man of sensibility is infatuated with the cold woman ; the woman of versatility by the man of one idea, and that a probably wrong one. Sometimes totally unsympathetic men and women are attracted by some peculiarity of face or of voice which in some way appeals to an occult inclination. Quite frequently the pure are drawn to the impure, the sober to the riotous, the good to the wicked."

When he concluded it was with these words : "I see no good effect these partial and counter attractions can have. They must be regarded, as far as I can see, as among the everlasting curses of our human nature. In the society of the old world they are the provoking causes of the large proportion of unhappy marriages, and of most of the unfaithfulness of husband and wife which in that society yields such plentiful harvests of ruined homes, accursed children and misery untold. Even in Grape Valley this eternal susceptibility of our nature is very mischievous. To be sure, we can correct mistakes in marriage relations caused by it, but it is the fatal peril ever threatening the true marriage when attained, which, with all its moral beauty and its possibilities for the happiness and development of husband and wife, breaks like a dead branch under the destructive force of some partial attraction."

Mr. Harvey had suggested a line of thought I had not taken before, and I was very much impressed by what he said. But I had noticed a tall, spare gentleman with uneasy black eyes and a narrow forehead sitting on the platform, and it was he who arose to present the other side of the case.

"Who is he ?" I said, turning for information to the woman who sat next to me.

"It is Mr. Trenk," she answered, and, as she turned her face toward me, I discovered that my neighbor was Mrs. Trenk. Doubtless she had saved for Ward the seat which I had hurriedly taken. I cast a quick glance around to see if he were near.

"You are looking for your friend," she remarked with ready apprehension. "I do not think he is here." Then before I could think of a suitable rejoinder, she continued : "I know you are Mr. Ward's best friend. I must talk with you."

"Certainly," I answered in some mystification, "I am at your service whenever you suggest."

"Thank you," she said, simply. But, as she made no movement to go out, I concluded I should have the privilege of hearing what Mr. Trenk might have to say.

"There may come a time," he said, "when each nature shall be so broad in its scope, so rich in its development, that the fancy of husband or wife shall not flit from its first object. That will be, however, when human nature is far more fully cultivated and educated than now. If each of us does his best to select for the object of his love that person who is best endowed, as our institution of free divorce and our custom of unrestrained social intercourse permit and encourage, thus we are each of us doing our utmost to bring about that completeness of character in our children or at least in our descendants. Meanwhile these partial attractions will continue to cause divisions in families, followed by less satisfactory remarriages. Men and women who have enjoyed as nearly harmonious relations as possible at this stage of the evolution of character will be often drawn apart by influences which are in their nature temporary. Neither can I so bitterly deplore these partial attractions, in their influences on men and women. I regard them as educating and broadening. Only through the close intimacy which marriage gives the two sexes, can a man understand the quality or attainment in a woman which attracted him. Only through marriage to a sensual woman can a man of partially awakened senses enter into his full physical state. Only by marriage to a man of refinement can a woman disposed to grossness obtain the education she most needs. We are attracted in these side directions because we there find something our characters need for their complete equipment. I could wish that each man and woman might pass through the experience of the more potent of these side attractions before making the marriage which approaches to the ideal, before meeting the one who shall inspire the deepest and most stimulating love. If these partial attractions have their sway in succession no damage is done, the education of the man and woman is completed, and their culture attained; not only without risk to their future and lasting happiness, but eminently assisting, assuring and enhancing the ideal marriage when it comes. So, instead of regretting the frequency of divorce and the large number of successive marriages under our institutions I have only to complain that their number is so small. These brief sexual intimacies are the semesters of school life for the sympathies, the passions, the understanding. Sometimes the ideal man and woman meet, understand and recognize each other at once. But generally it is in proportion to the completion of the education attained through the preceding marriage relations that the ideal marriage becomes probable for the man and woman. To be sure it is not seldom that a man and woman, ideally united to each other, are separated by an influence brought to bear on one or the other which previous experiences have not educated the unfortunate to withstand. But even in this instance I fail to see anything fatally disastrous. If the attraction which has drawn one of the married pair away — let us say it is the husband — is a partial one, it must be temporary. The deserted one may grieve for a while, but she may be sure to have her own back again if his place is there, all the safer and better for his wandering. Their second marriage will be more perfect than their first."

"Shall we go now?" whispered Mrs. Trenk. "I will not keep you away long."

I was very sorry not to hear more of what the speaker was saying, but I also felt curious to learn what possible confidences Mrs. Trenk could have with me.

"I want to speak to you about Mr. Ward," she began, turning toward me her face, which looked wan in the light of the full moon. "I have learned that you are going away to-morrow, and I felt that you, as his friend, were the only one I could come to."

How did I ever think her face dull in its beauty? "Is there is any way I can help you?" I asked.

"I don't know whether you can help me or not. I am afraid not." And she clasped her white hands unconsciously. "I believe Mr. Ward loves me, but he will not say so. He looks upon me as forever sealed to another man, and I think he would die before he spoke."

She paused, expecting me, perhaps, to reveal to her some tender secret my friend might have imparted to me. But I could only listen in silence. Then she continued :

"I think he would rather that I died, too, than that I should confess to him what he believes would be a shame to us both. But he should not have been with me so much ; he should not have talked with me as no other man could. He might have known I should love him, he is so wise, so good, so kind, so true. I am a different woman since I knew him. He has awakened my whole soul. It is all for him, but he will not ask for it ; he will not take it."

"My dear Mrs. Trenk," I began.

"Ah," she interrupted, "I know by your tone that you have no comfort to bestow. He must have talked to you then, of his prejudices against the divorce law which might make me his. Of course I know he has done so. Probably you have heard him say he would not marry a woman here even if he loved her? You do not deny it?"

"I cannot deny it, but I hope——"

"Don't say 'hope' as if you meant 'fear.' I can see you believe as I do, that he can never be anything to me."

"If there is anything I can do, Mrs. Trenk, I shall be most happy," I said earnestly. I wondered less every minute that Ward had fallen madly in love with her, especially if she had blossomed out for him into this splendid flower of womanhood. "Wouldn't you like to have me tell him how much he is to you? It might melt even his iron resolution. He is human."

"Oh, not for worlds," she cried. "If he were to be told, it is I who should tell him, or he would despise me doubly. I did not come to you for that. You will promise not to tell him. Do not even let him know we ever had this conversation."

I promised, and she continued: "I only wanted to learn from you whether he has ever told you, whether he has ever — you are his best friend I know, he has told me so many times — ever said to you that he — that he loved me. I know now he will never tell me, never ask me to make him as happy as I could make him, as I would die to make him. But I think it would be a sweet consolation to me, after he has gone away, to know — to know from his own words to you, that he loved me."

I was silent.

"You have nothing to tell me?" she asked, faintly.

"You forget what a reserved man my friend and yours is. You forget, too, how peculiarly delicate he would feel in talking, even to me, about a woman he thought he could not marry. But I have believed from his changed manner that he was deeply in love, more so than I have ever seen a man before."

The woman fairly laughed in delight.

"Oh, you are sure of that? How happy you make me. 'Deeply in love,' you say, 'more than you have ever seen a man before.' I surely ought to be satisfied. As you say, he could not have put it in words to you, if he could not to me. I must go now." And she took a step or two down the street. "No, you need not come with me. I am going home, where I can be alone, alone with my joy. If he comes late to the hall he will be sure to look for me. You will see him. But he will not know how happy I shall be, and in spite of him. You could not be mistaken — oh, of course not. 'Deeply in love,' you said." And she passed rapidly up the street.

# CHAPTER XXV.

The next morning Gillette and I set out for the East. It is unimportant for me to go into details as to our exit from Grape Valley. It will be sufficient to say that as soon as we had reached the railroad line we came East as fast as the latest modern appliances for killing time and annihilating space could bring us. My impressions as I alighted from our train were most peculiar. It was as if I were walking in a dream. The thought that this terrific bustle, this stupendous activity, had been going on for the nearly two years which I had passed in the peaceful valley, was inconceivable. It seemed to me it must have commenced just as I set foot in New York.

"Hello, old fellow," a sharp voice sounded in my ear. I turned to find my hand clasped by one of my old companions at the club. Many were the dozens of champagne we had broken together over late suppers and dinners to celebrate occasions. It was as if a hand was stretched out from another life, as if the voice was from another world, which exclaimed:

"Where have you been for this age?"

Men in New York do not wait for answers unless returned very speedily, and he continued: "But you shall tell me all that later. Dine with me at seven to-night. In the old corner, you know."

I muttered some excuse.

"Well, come around to the office when you have time and we will talk it over." And he was off.

"I am glad you sent him away," said Gillette, as we mounted the stairs to the elevated railroad station.

" The less you see of your old friends, just at present, the less liability there is to embarrassment."

We passed through the station and took our seats on the train.

" It is just four o'clock," he said, looking at his watch. " Now let us lay out our plans between here and Third avenue. I have an errand up town, but will meet you at the " Fifth Avenue" at seven o'clock. We will dine, and then I must take you with me to-night to a party of advanced thinkers. Don't fail to be on time."

Gillette had hardly finished his directions when the train reached the avenue, and my companion left me. For a few minutes I stood on the platform at a loss what to do. The strands of my destiny were being woven very rapidly then. One train after another passed down town, but the cries of the conductors did not move me. " South Ferry " had no special attraction for me. " City Hall " suggested no motive for me to step aboard the succeeding train. Then something within me said : " Why wait longer ? " And as the next train swept up to the platform I boarded it, careless whither it took me. I had, then, more than two hours to dispose of. It made little difference, I thought, what I did with them. But who will say there was no hidden force drawing me toward this very train ? Who can pretend that my destiny hung in the balances of chance, and was decided by the merest whim ? I entered the middle car and took a seat between a man much the worse for liquor and a plainly-dressed young woman. I had been so long removed from the stimulating influences of metropolitan life that the mere sight of so many strangers, each on his own errand, each oblivious to the rest of mankind, each an epitome of life's history and tragedy, was quite exciting to me. I remarked peculiarities which I had not observed in the days when I was a constant patron of these trains. I was especially impressed, at first, by the complete ab-

sorption of every passenger in his own interests, his
total indifference to the sorrows and joys of others.
Then I undertook to study the nearer passengers in
detail. Directly opposite me was a man of middle age,
ruddy, alert and prosperous. He was probably a
business man going down town to buy or sell something. He had no thought except how he should
manage to drive a sharp bargain with the other business man who awaited him. His whole life was taken
up with these sharp bargains. He reckoned his day's
work each night by the number of victories over less
shrewd competitors which he had won, and every day
his heart grew less generous and his soul dwindled.
Beside him was a woman on a shopping expedition.
She was generously powdered and extravagantly bedi-
zened with jewelry. She was busy calculating the
number of yards it would positively require for a summer silk dress, and trying to make up her mind whether
she should spend for the dress all of the money she
had wheedled from her husband, or, buying something
cheaper, save the difference for her private account.
How miserable the man who was her husband. At
my right was the drunken man, a mechanic, to judge
from his dress and hands. His eyes were set and
glassy, his head sunk forward on his breast. Some
good genius would doubtless see him home; one always attends on such drunken men. I examined him
closely. He was in his shirt sleeves and still wore the
paper cap donned while at work. His hands were
black and oily and had left their mark upon his face.
It was clear enough that he had left his work to pay a
visit to some saloon. There he had met some boon
companions and had drunk so many healths that he
was advised by the friends which a drunken man always makes not to attempt to return to work, but to
make the best of his way home. So home he was
going, to a sorry welcome from his wife, I feared.
At my left was the plainly-dressed young woman,

and my sensibilities were so far uncalloused by New York associations that I was immediately touched by what I, alone of all the carfull, seemed to notice. She looked intensely miserable. I have always observed that the faces of people in great cities are more expressive of the mind than in small communities. It is the very multitude of spectators which relieves the consciousness of being observed. They think no one notices, that no one interests himself, and so do not take the trouble to smile when they feel sad, or to affect gaiety when suffering misery. Perhaps I would not have been so impressed by the evident unhappiness of this woman, if her face had not been singularly attractive to me. It was very dark, and the features were strong in the profile, but the mouth, red and perfect in its bow shape, was all womanly in its beauty and its sensitiveness. She was a large woman, almost as tall as I, and with arms and shoulders in full proportion, a rare specimen of a type of womanhood which always appealed to my taste. But her attitude now was one of complete dejection, and the sadness in her eyes, looking in dull hopelessness straight before them, touched me exquisitely.

I immediately forgot every one else in the car, and only busied myself in devising some excuse for addressing her. Surely it was not decent that I should sit there, cold and indifferent, while she suffered. As it happened, if there is such a thing as chance, every one except us two and the drunken man, had left the car before we reached Thirty-second street. Then in a sudden inspiration, I turned to her.

"You are very unhappy. Can you trust me sufficiently to tell me why?"

As she turned her face toward me, I was astonished at my own temerity in inviting the scorn of a woman of such force and dignity. She seemed to study my face for an instant before replying.

"I suppose," she answered slowly, in a sweet contralto

30

voice, "that I ought to refuse to answer you. Yet I
see nothing but kindliness in your face, and I do not
know why I should not satisfy your interest." Hers
was the voice and speech of a woman of education.
"I am wretchedly and hopelessly poor. Isn't that
enough to make me miserable?"

She paused for me to speak. But I was wise enough
to observe the silence which is golden, and she continued: "I don't know that I could choose a safer
confidant than a stranger, and it may relieve my misery
a little if I put a part of it into words. Certainly your
audacity in addressing me ought to have some reward."
And she tried to smile.

By this time the car was half full again, and she bent
a little toward me as she spoke in a lower tone. "My
father was that most hapless of men, an inventor. He
came to New York from a little Massachusetts village,
where he had enjoyed a good position and a fair income, hoping to make his millions. He managed to
get rid of his patent, poor, dear man, but he was paid
only in promises, and, when he fell sick and died, even
the promises were denied to mother and me. We found
some poor employment for a while, and then I lost her
too. I am now supposed to be supporting myself on
three dollars and a half a week."

"That is terrible," I ejaculated, hastily. "The man
who pays you such a pittance ought to be drawn and
quartered."

"Oh, no," she answered, bitterly. "The man who
gives me that pittance, saves me from starvation. You
asked me why I am so unhappy. I think I have given
you sufficient reason."

This conclusion to her sentence was plainly intended
as a dismissal of the subject and of me.

"I am going to ask you to dine with me," I said
hurriedly, trying to look unconscious of her surprised
look. Then I hurried on: "To be sure we have
not been formally introduced, but I do not know as

that is a reason why I should sit down to my dinner alone."

A sudden rush of color made her face positively brilliant for an instant. Warned by the signal, I made haste to drop my unwisely frivolous manner and to add, more seriously : " What you tell me of yourself and of your life interests me extremely. I shall regard it as a kindness if by accepting my invitation to dinner you prolong our interview for a few minutes more."

She made no reply, which of itself was a favorable sign. Poor girl, doubtless the gnawings of hunger were pleading more powerfully than any words of mine could do. Prompt to make the most of my temporary advantage, I rose as the guard opened the door and called the number of the street.

" Here is our station," I said in a matter-of-fact tone. As she stood, I noticed what a faultlessly powerful figure she had. We descended the station steps and, without further attempt at conversation, I conducted her to the nearest restaurant and ordered dinner. As the plates containing the soup were set before us, she gave me a pitiful, appealing glance, as if in apology for the uncontrollable expression of hunger which was on her face. My eyes moistened and my food choked me. If I had not offered this poor gift of a dinner, she would at this moment have been suffering as it is worse than heartless to permit a creature of the shambles to suffer.

I did not attempt to talk with her, except in the most desultory way, until dessert was served. Then she said : " I do not quite understand why you make the peculiar impression which you do on me. You seem familiar with New York and yet there is an air of strangeness about you."

" You are very discerning," I replied. " I feel just as I look, familiar and yet strange. I am an old New Yorker, but have been away for two years."

" Are you going to stay in New York, now that you have returned?"

" Only for a short time," I answered. " New York
has too much unhappiness. I think it would break my
heart to live here."

Then there came a pause, after which she said : " I
am afraid I am not entertaining you. You forget your
excuse for asking me to dinner." Her eyes were downcast as she added, in a new and softer tone : " But I
now know it was only a pretense. You saw I was
hungry and it made you miserable."

" Oh, but I assure you ——," I began.

"Ah, there is no need to apologize for your courtesy."
Then she rose from her seat. " But I must detain you
no longer. Believe me I appreciate your delicacy as
well as your kindness. It is not so often they are
united."

As we reached the sidewalk again she held out her
hand to me. " Good-bye," and she smiled with a sweet
sadness. " You are a fairy prince to work such miracles for me, and then disappear forever."

" Yet I do not propose to disappear just now unless you command it," I said with sudden resolution.
My relation with my new acquaintance was so unusual
that it was already stirring my imagination danger-
ously. To be a *deus ex machina* for a lovely woman
is indeed a most fascinating position for any man.
Thoughts of what her life would be when I was once
more taken out of it came over me, of the wretchedness which must be her daily portion with no one to
relieve it except at the price of her honor.

" What then ? " she asked, without looking me in the
face.

" To begin with," I said, "I want to know where
you live."

" I am ashamed," she began. " But why should I
be ashamed ? I will show you my home, if that is the
proper name for the place where I sleep and weep.
But it is some little distance from here." Then she
turned her face toward me with a new, bright expres-

sion in it. "But you haven't even asked my name yet. It is Ruth."

"And mine is Harry Vinton, at your service," I said, as we slowly walked along together.

"Have you written a novel?" she asked with new excitement.

"Four of them, if I remember aright," I answered.

"Then you are not a stranger to me after all," she exclaimed, with a low, sweet laugh. "Why didn't you tell me before?"

This was very gracefully said, and my heart gave a new thrill as she bestowed that last confiding look upon me.

As we at last reached the narrow hall way she said: "Here is my home. Good-bye." And she reached out her hand.

"Not quite yet," I said with a laugh. "I suppose you must live in some one of the upper rooms here. But I do not know which. I may want to find you again."

She did not smile nor indeed look at me as she replied: "You will not have occasion to see me again. But I shall always remember you. Such kindness, such gentleness and such delicacy, who could ever forget them?"

"Doesn't it seem," I said, "as if some influence beyond our knowledge, but none the less real, had brought us together just when you needed me most?" I asked, and she turned her dark face toward me with new interest, as I continued: "I had a few hours to spare, and had waited at that station while several trains passed. Finally, at a venture, as I thought, I took the train you were in, entered your car and seated myself by your side."

"Yes," she answered, her voice vibrating with feeling, "and how strange that I should have been on that very train? There was no work for me in the box factory this afternoon, and I had taken the opportunity to apply, in answer to an advertisement, for a position as nurse maid up town. Unsuccessful, and with only a few pennies in my pocket, which was my world, I took the train which you were to board. I was on my way to the poor chamber which now awaits me up stairs. I should have been weeping there in hopeless, friendless misery during the hour I have spent so happily with you."

A young woman, slatternly in dress and brazen in aspect, stopped on the sidewalk and stared at us for an instant. Then she brushed against us on her way inside, and went up stairs. At the first landing the woman paused to look at us again, and catching my eye she gave me a significant smile. I knew what was in her mind, and flushed with a sense of insult. But I noticed my companion was unconscious of it all.

"Is it so impossible," I asked, "that I might have felt your need of me before I even knew of your existence, and was drawn by that potent influence to take the train which carried you, to seat myself by you, and then, when I saw the unhappiness on your face, to make so bold as to address you?"

"I should like to believe it," she said, softly. Then there was a pause, and she added: "But I must not detain you longer."

A sort of impatience with her seized me. "Do you really mean that we shall see each other no more?" I demanded; "that I shall go my way, and you go yours to hopeless poverty?"

"What else can I expect?" she said, in that low tone of hers. "Our lives will never cross each other again. But I shall not be quite as unhappy again, I think."

A sudden thought struck me.

"Let us live one day at a time," I said. "Can't you get away from your work to-morrow?"

"I shall have nothing to do," she answered, sadly. "Work is so dull that I was not to go back until Saturday."

"Then I have it," I exclaimed, laying my hand lightly on hers as I spoke. "What do you say to a day with me at Coney Island?"

A flush of undeniable pleasure suffused her olive cheeks and then faded away.

"I don't think it would be well."

"Why not?" I insisted. "You can trust me. You said that since you knew my name it made me an old friend."

"I would doubt everything else first," she said, slowly. "But think yourself how much better for me not to have such a happy experience, how much blacker by contrast it would leave my life afterward."

I was still touching her hand. But now I took it in both mine and pressed it gently. "Do it to please me. Meet me at pier No. 1 so we can take the half-past eleven o'clock boat. Promise," I said. Then she hurriedly caught her hand away as she answered : "I promise then." And she left me.

It was a few minutes after seven o'clock that I entered the corridor of the "Fifth Avenue" and saw Gillette walking up and down evidently in some impatience. He came up to me at once.

"I was afraid something had detained you," he said. Then taking my arm : "Let us go in to dinner at once. We shall have none too much time afterward to dress and reach where we are expected."

"I have dined," I remarked. "But I have no objection to watching you follow suit."

"Dined? Well, that was considerate I must say. But I'll excuse you this time. I suppose you met a friend."

"Yes," I answered, slowly, as we made our way to a table. "I met a friend."

Gillette ordered his dinner in a careless style which would have broken the heart of that accomplished student of the menu, my friend Ward. Then turning to me: "I hope, though, that you will try to keep clear of entangling alliances while in New York this time."

I smiled at the very apt advice Gillette was unconsciously giving me, but thought it well enough to change the course of the conversation. "Where are you going to take me to-night, by the way?"

"To a west side reception. The hostess is a dabbler in all sorts of radicalism, and radicals of both sexes meet there. I have obtained an invitation for you and for myself, and hope we may be able to drop a little good seed. But let me eat now."

When at last we were in a carriage and riding rapidly across the city, Gillette found more time to tell me something about the class of people we should meet.

"But," I objected, "don't you think that we could do more good both for our community and for the world by seeking a different line of converts? Why can't we make a hundred proselytes among the unfortunate and those suffering from want while we fail often among these advanced thinkers and theorists?"

"I don't know but there is something in what you say," said Gillette, thoughtfully. "We will talk about it later, but let us do what we can to-night."

I imagine Gillette did very little. As for myself I could not induce any one to listen to me long enough to make the attempt of proselyting judicious. After a few ineffective efforts to inculcate my ideas I gave up in despair. Everybody seemed to have a cult to urge, a theory to expound, a scheme of religion, science or philosophy to set forth. It was only out of decency that they listened to others while eagerly waiting an opportunity to discourse each of his own peculiar doctrines. One after the other we were all taken into corners and labored with by this or that radical, and expected to grow enthusiastic as the beautiful points of the different theories were brought out. The women indeed were the most inveterate proselytes of all. They argued

with their beautiful eyes as well as with their tongues,
and a gentleman felt that he was very unchivalrous
unless he appeared, at least, to be convinced. There
was the spiritualist and the theosophist, the material-
ist and loudest of all the agnostic, the old-fashioned
atheist, too, and the Darwinian, the Swedenborgian,
the humanitarian, the positivist. Each one said many
true and suggestive things, but all were extravagant
in their intolerance, and furious in their confidence
that if the world would but open its eyes to the truth,
as theorized upon by its expounder, the millennium
would be at hand.

All varieties of social reforms were represented. A
man was at my ear at one minute who believed that
by a modification of the land tax every inequality
would be cured and each one insured his deserts.
Then I was taken in hand by the advocate of a system of profit sharing, as the long-awaited panacea for
human ills. Then would come the prophet of woman
suffrage claiming that, when women were enfranchised,
good laws, and those only, would be passed, and a new
moral tone and trustworthy public opinion would be
formed. Another man looked to the regeneration of
the world through the universal banishment of alcoholic liquors; another expected it from some new
scheme of universal education; another, from some
change in the machinery of government. Each and
all had ear for nothing but talk of his own patent.
They tired me. They disgusted me with logic itself,
which could be made to prove so many inconsistent
theories. I had found one unpretending motherly little woman who was inclined to talk to me about her
wonderful children. With her I retired into a peaceful corner, and was glad to be treated to the smart say-
ings of her precocious babies until Gillette came to
take me back to the hotel.

"It is a wasted evening," he said, as we parted for
the night. "These men and women are not the sort

31

we could touch if we offered them a paradise ready made. Each one must have reform brought about by his own scheme or he will have none of it."

"Surely," I said, "it was not from such people as these your colony was first made up?"

"No; we saw to-night only the charlatans of the radical world, those who make a show of their ideas, who preach them only to gratify their personal vanity. I have never tried before to proselyte what should be called the society radical. I shall not need to repeat the experiment. There may be a good deal in what you suggest, to seek further additions to our community from those who have come to ideas like ours through experience and suffering."

"That would be practical philanthropy, too," I answered, "and on the grandest conceivable scale. Let us make Grape Valley a haven of rest for the suffering and the distressed, and when Grape Valley becomes too small, search out new valleys or isles of the sea, which shall serve as the promised land for the happy multitudes we shall yet lead out of the land of bondage."

Gillette seemed plunged in thought, but made no reply.

"By the way," I exclaimed, "what are your plans for to-morrow?"

"I have business which will occupy me all day to-morrow," he answered, "fill out your day to suit yourself. The next day, that will be Saturday, I will call you in again, and I hope to more purpose."

# CHAPTER XXVI.

At eleven, the next forenoon, I was at Pier No. 1. It occurred to me that Ruth might be early. Women are divided into two great classes by the standard of promptness. Those of one class are always late at their appointments, those of the other class are ahead of time. There is no third class, I think. The few hours of my acquaintance with Ruth had not been sufficient to classify her, and I went early myself, so that, if it happened that she belonged to the class of those who anticipate their appointments, she should experience no uneasiness in waiting for me. I walked the full length of the waiting-room, and made sure she was not there. I took the opportunity to buy tickets, and then sought a position where I could see her when she entered. How strange our meeting had been. How unusual the interest she had inspired in me. But would it outlast so thorough a test as that to which this day would subject it? In the forenoon a man is disposed to take rather prosaic views of life, and I now began to be sceptical as to the reality of the charms of my new acquaintance. It was very natural that I should have been interested the previous afternoon in my protege. To occupy the attitude of a kind Providence toward a young woman is most pleasing in itself. A man is apt to regard a woman, under such conditions, with feelings of marked complacency, even if she be quite ordinary. But doubtless I had been indiscreet in arranging for so long a time in her society. She would weary me. It would have been far kinder to her if I had insisted upon leaving her some generous present, and then

wished her good evening, and more considerate of myself, too.   In all my previous years in New York, I
had not done so injudicious a thing.   My experience
at Grape Valley must have increased my susceptibility,
or else my common sense had been suffered ·to run to
seed.

With a yawn I glanced at my watch.   It was twenty
minutes past eleven.   The girl was due now, if she were
coming.   I examined with closer attention the faces of
those who entered.   I must be careful she did not pass
me unrecognized in the crowd.   Probably my idea of
her and her actual appearance were quite different.   I
finally took a position on the sidewalk, where I could
see up and down the street.   But there was no figure
like hers in sight.   Her sound judgment had reminded
her how foolish it would be to pursue my acquaintance
further.   She must have decided not to come.

Then I glanced most anxiously at my watch.   It was
twenty-five minutes past eleven.   My indifference was
all gone.   I looked with painful impatience in all
directions.   But everybody seemed going from the
pier, instead of approaching it.   There was no use to
look any more.   The last bell would ring in a moment.
I turned away from the street and stood staring with
envious eyes after the men who had ladies with them,
as they hurried up the stairs.   One fact was clear.   I
should never see Ruth again.   Ruth—I did not even
know her last name.   I had been thoughtless enough
not to insist that she give it to me.   I could not find
her, of course, without knowing her full name.   She
was lost out of my life forever.   She must suffer all her
sorrows, bear all her burdens alone.   It was denied me
to bring a smile to her lips again or to gladden her eyes.
The fate that seemed so kind yesterday shut us apart
to-day with an eternal barrier, which it seemed impossible to overleap.   But I would find her.   I could describe
her, and with her first name to help me, I would inquire of every tenant in the block where was her poor

room. I would not submit to losing her. I would force myself upon her. Suddenly a thrill seemed to pass over me. I turned to my right and saw almost touching me, but still unconscious of my nearness, Ruth, at last.

"We have just time to catch the boat," I cried, and taking her hand, I added: "if we run."

And run we did, and so well that though we were the last ones through the gate before it closed, yet we were aboard the boat when the paddle wheels began their noisy revolutions.

"That was a close race against time," I said, breathlessly, as we passed through the cabin on our way to the deck. "But I felt as if to catch that boat was worth risking our lives for."

"It is all my fault. I shouldn't have been so late," she answered, as we took our seats on the shady side, and looked out upon the most beautiful harbor on the Atlantic coast.

"How did it happen?" I asked.

"I am almost ashamed to tell you," she said, giving me an apologetic look. "Last night I lay for hours thinking, and then dreaming how happy I should be to-day; but when I awoke in the morning, it seemed to me that happiness had no place in my life and I decided not to go."

The harbor lost its interest for me and I looked into Ruth's dark, sensitive face.

But I said nothing and she continued: "I thought, too, that you must have repented of your rash invitation, and would be only relieved that I did not come and would say: 'Ah, she was a sensible girl after all.' Wouldn't you have said so?" Her black eyes scrutinized my face very keenly.

"I should have been intensely disappointed,' I answered, speaking of course for the latter part of my period of waiting. "You know, I concluded you had failed me, and so I can speak from actual experience."

She smiled with winning sweetness and continued: "Just why I dressed myself for the trip I cannot tell. I kept telling myself that it was only because I was going in search of a new position. But something made me dress myself, even to the ruffle at my neck, just as if I were to go with you. But all the time I reminded myself that I had made a firm and unalterable determination not to come and so not see you again. I sat down to my sewing where I could see the old clock which I had kept when almost everything of my mother's was sold. For two hours I did not appreciate the full measure of the sacrifice I had decided to make, because it was far from the time when I needed to set out for the boat if I were to come. I remember now that once I let my sewing fall in my lap while I nicely calculated that it would take me just half an hour to walk to pier No. 1. It was only half-past nine then. But I am tiresome. Excuse me."

"Tiresome?" I exclaimed, with one of those great heart throbs which are so full of pain and yet of rapture. "I cannot tell you how intensely you interest me."

"Well, when it was half-past ten o'clock my heart began to sink. The full meaning of what I was sacrificing came over me. The day was the finest, I thought, I had ever known. I used to so love the sea, but I had never been down New York harbor." Then she lowered her voice, and looked far away over the water as she added: "And I so wanted to see you once more. I felt I had but half thanked you. I wanted to tell you that I should always think you the grandest, the truest, the best of men. I then threw my sewing upon the floor. I would go after all. A wild, exultant joy filled me. I pitied the whole world beside. I thought of the hundreds of thousands of girls bending at that instant over their ill-paid tasks, and pitied them because they could have no delight like mine. I pitied myself of a moment ago sitting at my sewing with tears in my eyes and an ache in my bosom. I put on my hat, made the last few adjustments in the room where I had passed such miserable hours in the forever past, as for the moment I strangely regarded it. I had even reached the door when I gave a last glance around the room. Then my fancy relentlessly pictured my returning there to-night, my only too brief holiday over, my one joyful day past, and I back again to take up my wretched life like that of so many millions more. I could imagine myself groping for the mantel, and, finding there a match, striking it, and lighting the kerosene lamp which stood on the table. Then I would look about me, at the bare walls, at the carpetless floor, at the poor, torn working dress on which I had been sewing, at the ill-furnished bed where I should soon lie sobbing in uncontrollable desolation, ten times more intolerable after my one day of happiness."

The tears came to my eyes in spite of myself. What an accursed mechanism was the human heart to be capable of such sickening misery as this of hers. I could not trust my voice, but I took her hand as it lay on the railing, and, unconscious of what I did, carried it to my lips and then released it. I do not think she appreciated what I was doing, as she continued her story without change of voice.

"I returned to my chair, and bowing my head over my hands, resigned myself to my fate, and bade you good-bye forever. How long I sat thus, I cannot tell, but when I looked at the clock again the hands pointed to quarter-past eleven. It was now too late. It required at least a half hour to reach the pier, and there were but fifteen minutes. Even if I changed my mind I could not reach the boat in time. Then, womanlike, I upbraided myself for my folly. That I must be miserable hereafter was surely no reason why I should refuse a joy for to-day. Would I not be miserable when night should come, as it was, and with a fresh

sorrow, a new torment because I had thrown away
a chance for a day whose pure delight would furnish
my memory for a life-time. Something in my throat
choked me. A deadly congestion seemed settling
about my heart. I wished I might die. I wondered
whether it would make a quick end of me to leap from
my window. It was at this moment that I heard footsteps in the hall and a man's voice calling to some
questioner up another story. 'What do you want?'
I heard a shrill voice call down the bannisters: 'The
clock has stopped. What time is it?' Alas I knew
too well the time. My own solemn-faced clock said
fifteen minutes past eleven, but the man answered
crossly: 'You always forget to wind it. Well, it is
five minutes past eleven.' I leaped to my feet in sudden response. But this was a mockery. The man
must be wrong. Then I heard the querulous woman's
voice call down once more: 'Are you sure?' I held
my breath. My fate hung on his answer. It came
sharp and clear: 'Sure? Of course I am. I set it at
the jeweler's an hour ago.' Then there was yet time to
catch the boat, if I ran. And, without stopping even to
lock my door, I rushed down stairs. I was so nearly
blind in my excitement that I collided with foot passengers right and left, but I did not look behind me, nor
stop to make excuses. It had taken me but eight minutes to reach Broadway, and my heart beat high with
hope. But there the street was densely blockaded.
Drays, street cars and private carriages were packed so
close that they made almost a solid wall. I waited for
a few seconds for a passage to be opened, but, seeing
none, I started to force my way through. I ran
under the heads of snorting horses, dodged the poles
of truck wagons, and was half way across the street
when an absolutely impenetrable blockade shut me
in. I could not go forward, I would not go back.
So I took refuge on the platform of a street car, and
waited it seemed almost a life-time. At last I could

see light between me and the farther sidewalk, and hurried through the perilous and uncertain alley, in spite of the warnings of drivers and the gesticulations of policemen. I drew a blessed breath of relief and walked rapidly on my course. It was now that I glanced at a clock in front of a jeweler's store, and read the terrible time. It was twenty-four minutes past eleven. A carriage happened to stand by the curbing, and I cried hastily to the driver : ' What will you charge to get me to the Coney Island boat before half-past eleven ? ' The driver took out his watch. ' It will be a close call to do it. Well, one dollar.' I drew out my purse and counted out two ten cent pieces and a twenty-five cent piece. ' This is all I have in the world,' I said. ' Will you take me for this ? ' He gave me a sharp look, and I think believed me. He reached down and took my money. 'In with you, quick,' he said, and before the door had fairly closed we were in motion. The awful suspense, the cold terror I felt at the prospect that I should be late after all, were the most agonizing experiences even I had ever had. A score of times, in imagination, I saw the carriage stop, the driver open the door for me, give a quick glance at the dock, and I seemed to hear him say : ' We are just too late, Miss, but I done my best.' Then a mist seemed to come before my eyes, and a woman who looked like me but who was fairly staggering with the intoxication of despair, walked slowly back. Surely there could be no worse suffering in store for me after that. Then came the sight of the masts, and I knew the end was at hand. The carriage stopped. The driver stood at the open door with just that dreaded expression of regret on his face. Then came the very words: ' We are just too late, miss. I am sorry, but I done my best.' Even the bad grammar was what I had anticipated. But as I leaped out I heard the bell ringing. There might be a chance yet. I rushed inside the door, felt your hand

32

upon my arm, saw your eyes look into mine, and all
my misery was turned into joy."

If ever a man was made that could listen unmoved
to such a story from a woman's lips it was not I. Yet
I managed to say as she concluded :

" But I would not have missed seeing you again."

" You didn't know which was my room, or where I
worked, or even my last name," she said. " But I
must tell you my name now. It is Ruth Gordon."

" But I would have moved heaven and earth to have
found you."

" Would you ? " she asked, loooking in beautiful
surprise at me. " You forget I was almost a stranger
to you. All that you knew about me was that you had
befriended me. But there are a hundred thousand in
New York as poor as I — why is the steamer stopping ? "

" This is the iron pier," I said, in a more practical
tone of voice. " We are at Coney Island."

As we made our way from the boat I said to her:
" Now I want to make this the happiest day of your
life. Shall we begin by taking a sea bath ? "

" Nothing would please me more," she answered in
a voice that was full of a new excitement, and within
a very few minutes we were clad in the ungraceful
costumes of the country, and I was teaching her how
to make the most of that mighty playmate, the Atlantic. At first the scantiness of our dresses seemed
to fill her with overpowering shame. Her eyes were
downcast, her cheeks aflame, and she seemed anxious
to release her hand from mine as we walked out to
meet the breakers.

" Oh, let me go back," she murmured. " I shall be
ashamed all day to look you in the face."

·" Why, only look at all these other bathers," I said.
" They none of them are abashed. You will forget it
all when the first big wave strikes you."

And so she did. She became as wild with delight

in her new sport as any child, and no nymph could have taken more kindly to the rough embraces and the frequent complete falls the foaming rollers gave her. But I could not keep my eyes from her faultless and yet powerful figure, her magnificent arms, her statuesque curves, her grandly arched neck. Ruth Gordon was the most perfect specimen of physical womanhood I had ever seen.

It was as if we left in the ocean our recollections of past griefs, drowned care, indeed. And when she came out from her bath-house with a new glow on her cheeks and a fresh vitality in every movement, I felt more in the mood for a gay holiday than ever in my life before. We devoted ourselves to amusement pure and simple for the next hour or two. For people who wish to be entertained without effort of their own this famous Vanity Fair has the most varied devices. The attractions had long since become an old story to me, but to-day they all pleased me as never before, because I acted as the guide and cicerone of Ruth Gordon. To experience pleasures together always puts two people on familiar terms, and we grew to be intimate so fast that when we sat down to dinner on the piazza of the Brighton it seemed as if we had known each other many months.

I think I distinguished myself in ordering that dinner. It was a sea food symposium; a marine study. No variety of seafish, bivalve or crustacean was missing. We had a bottle of champagne too, of course, although no wine ever made could enhance my exhilaration or I think hers, and the ice cream and sweets which womankind are supposed most to like.

"You make me feel," she said as she tasted the wine, "that there is nothing so rare or delicate but you would offer it to me to-day."

"There is no woman on the earth," I replied, bending toward her, "with whom I would be so happy to dine."

"Really?" she asked, curiously. But she did not redden in self-consciousness as I had expected. As she continued, I understood how her modesty shut her in from my compliments as with a veil.

"How chivalrous you are. Do you know," she said in that peculiarly low, thrilling tone of hers, "that I have wondered many times since I first met you yesterday — it seems ages ago — how I dared to accept such kindness from you? But now that I know you I do not wonder any longer. There was, I think, some unknown finer sense in me which recognized how noble and magnanimous your nature is."

"You make me ashamed," I said. "If there is anything fine in my behavior to you, it is because it is impossible for me to be with you and show poor or cheap traits. A man is what a woman inspires him to be."

"I am glad I came," she said, simply. I, too, was glad that she came, intensely glad. As I sat there at the table with this woman whom yesterday at this hour I had not yet met, I felt I was tasting perfect happiness at last. It seemed to me I would ask nothing better if I could but have hoped to sit with her before me listening to her sweet voice, drinking in the light from her dark eyes, forever, if the sun would but stand still and time and change be suspended. Even when she was silent I seemed to commune with her. It was as if our spirits had recognized each other and kept whispering their mutual secrets, and answering confidence with confidence.

But the tables came into great demand as the afternoon boats brought new arrivals from the metropolis, and I said at last:

"We must make place for other hungry people." I offered her my arm and for a little while we walked up and down the broad piazzas. To entertain her I directed her attention to the men and women at the tables, or sitting by the railings listening to the concert, and to still others walking as we were, or occupying the seats below. I tried to show her how they bore the marks of their characters upon their faces, how their history was much of it written in their features, history for the most part of perverted natures, of distorted tastes and of disappointed hopes.

" You do not think very highly of human nature," she said, looking reproachfully at me.

" Ah, yes, I do think very highly of it, but human nature has small chance to show its glorious attributes in modern civilized society. It is our lower capacities which are stimulated into excessive activity by the demands upon them. Our higher faculties, our fraternal sentiments, our power to love and all implied in that power, are left nearly dormant."

" What a pity that society cannot be changed, then ! Do you think that men and women would grow to be better and nobler if different influences were placed about them ? "

" Why not ? It is debasing influences and temptations to do evil which make men and women low and bad. Is it not plain that if these influences were for unselfishness ; if the temptations to overreach our fellows, to anticipate them in greediness, were removed, that we should grow to be better ? We are not bad because we want to be, but because we have to be so or go to the wall."

She sighed deeply. " It is because there is not enough for all, I suppose, and that only by being craftier than others, can one win what he wants."

I had made a sudden resolution.

" Let us draw some chairs back into a retired little nook. There we can talk and listen to the music at the same time."

" That will be delightful," she answered, both with her voice and with her eyes.

We found just the corner which I wanted where we could talk without likelihood of being overheard, and I began my story by asking a question.

# CHAPTER XXVII.

"You seem to be a woman without curiosity," I said. "Don't you care to know where I live, or any thing about me more than the fact that I have written a poor novel or two?"

"It is only your present in which I have any concern," she said. "Your past and your future are equally out of my world."

Another of those waves of emotion which this girl had power to stir swept through me.

"You do not know what you are saying," I cried, breathlessly. "Do you think I shall let this day be our last together?"

She grew pale and her breast heaved magnificently.

"Don't talk in that way," she murmured, "it is cruelty."

Did her heart-beats hurt her, too? Did she fear me and my influence over her, or did love seem to her maiden soul a terrible power whose masterly spirit she dreaded with vague alarms? I tried to put a curb upon my emotions and to speak in the proper tone of a dispassionate historian, if there is such a thing.

"But this is a part of my past, which will, I am sure, interest you. For two years I have been in the far West, a member of a community founded on the brotherhood of man. There no man spends his strength in efforts to deprive his fellow of the good things of life. All work for a common end, the welfare and comfort of all. There are no rich men there, and no poor men or women. All alike work, all alike enjoy. The hate and ill-will which have been perverting and distorting human nature for so many centuries have nothing there to feed upon. Envy, selfishness, covetousness, meanness, and all the soul-destroying influences they breed have no scope in that society. It is a noble thing that the people of that valley are assured all the comforts of life and the leisure for enjoyment. But these luxuries, I and tens of thousands of favored men and women, have enjoyed before. The most glorious achievement of this society is that human character is at last given field to fulfill its capacity for good; men are permitted to look upon each other as friends; upon loving kindness as a disposition which they are no longer forbidden by the laws of self-protection to cherish."

Her eyes, big with wonder, were fixed upon me as she exclaimed:

"Are you dreaming aloud? Surely there can be no such place in this world as you describe?"

"Why not?" I asked. "Man is not selfish because he likes to be, mean because it is a pleasure to him to be mean, cruel because he delights in cruelty. To make his way in this state of society he must be so. To draw his income, if he be rich, he must cause the sick and the weary to toil for him, the poor to go hungry, children to lack the pleasures even the wild beasts give their young. To earn his bread, if he be poor, he must show scant pity to those as needy as he, fight like a wolf and trample on other hungry men to keep his poor place in the industrial ranks; his heart consumed all the while with bitterness at his lot, his soul burning with hate for those who profit by his ill-paid labor, with envy of the happy and of the prosperous who have their paths made easy and their burdens light while he toils early and late and feels himself unable to bring a smile to his wife's wan cheeks or a laugh to his children's eyes. In this place I speak of, however, the evil passions, which have killed out the manifestations of brotherly love for so many centuries, have gone so far

toward stifling even the wish to be unselfish and toward
throttling generous impulses at their birth, are no longer
engendered.  Even the seeds of them will soon die out
in the human heart.  Henceforth men can be all the
immortal longings of the soul have drawn them to be."

She did not speak, but her glowing eyes urged me to
continue:

"In that valley the subjection of women, too, is forever past.  She works as does the man, and shares alike
with him.  If she chooses to marry it is not for support,
since she continues after marriage to earn her livelihood,
nor is it for a home and companionship simply, since
each person there is assured a home where all the
society which could be desired is offered.  If she marries, she marries for love, or what she thinks is love,
and if she finds she has made a mistake, her bonds, for
such they must have become, are dissolved at will.
Her life is not wrecked because of mistaken judgment.
The ideal in that valley, between men is fraternity,
between each man and some woman, perfect love.  If
a man really loves a woman she must love him as much.
Their souls and minds cry out for each other as do their
lips.  If that love ceases to bind them together the true
marriage is in fact dissolved.   In this valley the law
merely records that fact.  To deprive them of the enjoyment of true love, and its ennobling, inspiring influences,
would be to do them intolerable injustice.  If men and
women were all-wise and incapable of making mistakes,
the first marriage would be the best marriage.  But since
mistakes are more frequent than ideal selections, the
laws of that valley permit frequent divorces and remarriages.   Women there are growing into a life their
sex never conceived of before.  The burdens which for
so many centuries have rested upon them have been
lifted.   They are wives, but only when they love and
are beloved as they desire.  They are mothers, but the
care, nurture and education of their children are taken
from their shoulders, while their joy in their little ones

is not at all abated. So their progress and development is not arrested with the advent of the first infant; a book whose first pages only have been turned. They have homes, but not confinement at hard labor. Their life is as free of care as a man's, as open to influences for culture, for education, for that development which we live for, and which we must have ourselves before we can hand them down to our children."

I waited an instant to hear what she should say, but as she did not speak, I said:

"I will take you there if you desire it."

For a moment she seemed as if she could not believe her ears, then her eyes melted in gratitude. She opened her lips to speak, but it was a moment before she whispered:

"What miracle is this?"

For the last hour before our boat sailed for New York, we walked along the beach, as happy creatures as the moon shone upon that night. I answered her hundred eager questions, which were like those of a child on the eve of a delightful journey. I told her all about myself, too, and my relations with the women of Grape Valley. I had expected some signs of irritation, I had thought to see an expression of displeasure cross her face. But so poor and cheap an emotion as that of jealousy was not possible to this woman.

"And your love story," I said, at last, as, our return journey over, we stood on the steps of the hallway of the block somewhere on whose upper floors was her room. "You have not told me of your lover."

"I have had no love story," she answered, slowly. "I do not know what it is to love."

Passionate words started to my lips, but I still held them back.

"Now you are sure you understand," I said. "This is your last night here. To-morrow morning I will call early, and we will breakfast together. Then I will take you to some quiet boarding-house, and bring a

33

friend to see you. Then we will arrange our plans
for taking you to Grape Valley."

"How good you are," she said, dreamily. "What
desert is there in me for such an interference of destiny
in my behalf? What good have I done or thought
that I should be singled out of the ranks of the unhappy women of New York for translation to Ely-
sium?" Then she seemed to recover her grasp of the
practical present. "But I must go to my room. It
is long past midnight." And she held out her hand.

"I cannot bear that you should stay here even to-
night. It is such a horrible place," I exclaimed, without releasing her hand.

"Oh," and her smile was more sweet and gentle
than ever, I thought, "but you say it is only for one
night. Besides it will be so wonderful to go into my
room again and compare my happiness, oh my rapture,
why was such joy ever given to me? — with the misery,
the despair, which I expected would await me at my
door when I returned."

"Just think," she continued, letting her hand stay
in mine, "I shall grope through the room to find the
mantel piece, and the poor little bonbon box which
did duty as a match safe. Then I shall strike a match
and crossing to the table light my old lamp. Do you
know the shade of that lamp always seemed nearly
human to me. When I used to sit in my chair by it
and work late at night repairing my old dresses, I used
to think it watched me with solemn sympathy. When
I cried I used to feel as if it looked a shade more melancholy than before. There I have made a pun. You
can see how much in need of rest I must be. Really
you must let me go," and she looked significantly at
my hand as it imprisoned hers.

"But you were going to tell me how different your
feelings would be from those you had dreaded," I insisted, wondering whether I was going to be able, after
all, to keep back my declaration of love until to-

morrow as I had intended, she was so bewildering to-night.

"Haven't I told you before? Well, there on the floor beside my chair, I shall find my old dress just where I threw it half mended when I decided to come to you. Ah, just there, as I touched it the waves of desolation would have swept over my soul. As I must put on that old dress to-morrow, so, I would have remembered, I must put on my old life. As I must lay off the dress I have worn to-day so I must put away all the joy from my life. Then I would have heard the terrible tick of the clock sounding sharp and clear, as it always does when I feel most desperate, and I would have straightway invented some gloomy sentence and imagined that it was what the pendulum was articulating. Perhaps the sentence would be: Why—did—you—go? Why—did—you—go? in dreadful rythm. Then I would take one more look at the bare walls and a deadly sense of suffocation would come upon me. I would have rushed to the bed, and burying my face in the poor little pillows, sobbed and wept and longed for death."

"Oh, I cannot endure it," I cried, coming closer to her.

"But to-night I will laugh that you have cheated giant despair of his prey, my noble knight, *sans peur et sans reproche.* Please let me go — you really must let me go."

"Come into the street first, and show me where your room is," I said, drawing her with me down the steps. "I must know where to come for you in the morning, you remember."

"Why, to be sure," she answered lightly. "How stupid of me." Then pointing above the hall entrance she said : "Look up to the third story. The window next to the left opens into my room. When you come for me you will only have to climb two flights of stairs, and make ready to climb the third flight but stop right there. Turn around, and knock at the door which will stare you in the face. As it opens to your knock you will see me ready and waiting, and oh, so happy." Then with a quick movement she released her hand and ran up the steps.

"Good night," she cried, as she passed into the dimly-lighted hall and up the stairs.

I was sorry I had let her go. Why should I have permitted this woman who had suddenly filled out the measure of my whole life to stay in this repulsive place even for one more night? Who could tell what dangers might lurk here? This very night fire might break out in the pawnbroker's shop beneath and Ruth, my sweetheart without knowing it, yield up her life in agony. My plan had been to take her on the morrow to some private boarding-house and let that be her home while she stayed in New York. If she promised to marry me, she would, of course, want time to make preparations. That is one of the dearest privileges of her sex. I reproached myself now for not taking an earlier boat home which would have given me time to have found a more suitable place for her to sleep to-night. Then I blamed myself for not having taken her to a hotel when we returned; late as it was I should have sacrificed the proprieties rather than have taken the risk of sacrificing her on the altar of my own fussiness.

Then I stepped well into the street so that I could see her window. Ah, it was the one-half way to the roof. She was doubtless at this moment climbing the second flight of stairs. In a minute more she would enter her room, find the match on the mantel and light her lamp. Perhaps it would then occur to her that I might still be watching below and she would step to the open window for a last glance or wave of the hand. Women seldom forget these sweet little bits of sentiment.

But what should I do to protect her to-night? I might, to be sure, go up to the stairs opposite her door and sit there through the long hours on guard. But that would give her too good an opportunity to laugh at me in the morning when the danger was past, and the sunlight seemed to laugh too at the terrors of the night before. It would provide her with a convenient method of pointing her jokes at my expense all the rest of our lives, if she married me. But would she marry me after all? One can never be sure of a woman. Gratitude and love are very different things, and the love I wanted from her was the grandest grade of the grand passion. I must not be too hasty with my wooing. Women are always displeased at being thought too easily won. I was convinced that she had not yet thought of me as a lover. She regarded me as a friend, as a benefactor, almost as a worker of miracles. It would really be more magnanimous of me, under the circumstances, if I carefully abstained from breathing a syllable of love until we were both in Grape Valley. It might seem to her as if I was, in a way, making conditions for rescuing her from her life of misery and unhappiness. But what lover is magnanimous?

Ah, there was a gleam of light in her bedroom. She had struck a match. I wondered if she were as happy as she thought she would be. Was she thinking of me or was she thinking of Coney Island; or more likely still, of the tempting picture I had drawn for her of Grape Valley? Perhaps, as she crossed the room, she was wondering why I had seemed so fond of holding her hand. Women in their solitude recall our behavior, of which they seemed quite oblivious when with us, and show wonderful analytical powers in dealing with it.

Now the room became somewhat lighter. She had touched the match to the wick. Now it was brighter still; she must have placed the chimney on the lamp. In an instant more she would be at the window if she remembered me. There she is. Would it be indiscreet of me to call to her?

Then came a muffled scream and she suddenly disappeared from the window.

# CHAPTER XXVIII.

For an instant I seemed incapable of moving, even of thought. Then there came a flash of memory. The smell of the salt air was in my nostrils again. I was sitting with Ruth by the rail of the boat, while she told me of her sudden decision to come. One sentence of them all sounded with new significance in my ears. 'Without stopping to lock my door I rushed down the stairs.' During her absence some creature had entered her room, and for hours had crouched there in the darkness for his victim. While we had exchanged gentle words and gentler wishes, he had plotted his treachery and violence. Then a consuming heat filled my breast. My heart was bursting with rage for her assailant were he man or beast, or both in one. I longed to be at his throat, to tear his life out for causing the girl I loved so much as one first faint qualm of terror. My stunned will had recovered its power, and driven by an instinct as strong as that of a tigress springing to the defense of her young, I leaped into the doorway and up the stairs. I caught the bannisters to aid me and took four steps at a time.

For guide to Ruth's room I had only the directions she had given me a few moments before. Little she knew how speedily I should use them. Now I stood facing the door of her room as it stood just ajar. She had doubtless waited before she should shut it until her lamp was lighted. Within all was silent, horribly silent. My heart almost stopped beating as I pushed the door open, and saw a man and a woman engaged in a deadly struggle. The man was slight of figure, and bore the marks of dissipation upon his face. The woman — my own Ruth — was very pale, and her features were set, as if in *rigor mortis*, as she knelt upon the chest of the writhing creature. His arms she held flat upon the floor upon either side. She must have thrown him down in her first spring, and now, with straining muscles and tense nerves, she was striving to hold him there. It was her only hope. The marks of his fingers were yet upon her throat, and her dress was torn open at the neck, revealing beauties which she would rather have died than that this wretch should see. How villainous was his white, sneering face, how devilish the smile of expected triumph which yet lingered about his lips. Well he knew her strength would soon fail her.

Neither of them had noticed my entrance, so absorbed were they in their terrific struggle. But before I could decide how to act, alternate waves of fury for this man, and of admiration for the woman, passing over me, her strength began to fail. His arms drew up in spite of her agonizing attempt to hold them. With a pitiful cry she sprang to her feet, for the last and hopeless struggle, and he faced her with a new flush of hateful delight upon his cheeks.

My time had come, and I leaped upon him like the tigress, whose ferocity would be gentleness compared with mine, and catching him by the throat strangled him almost into unconsciousness. He must have thought it was Nemesis who had flown in at the window. He was like a child in my grasp as I forced him to the door of the room which he had profaned, and to the stairway. Then lifting him over the railing I dropped his vile form far down below, as I hoped, to his death. I hardly waited to hear the crash before I returned to the chamber of my beloved. The room seemed strangely familiar to me, until I remembered it was from her description I had been able to picture it. The solemn-faced clock was an old acquaintance,

the round table, with ink-stained cloth, the lamp with
its companionable shade, even her working dress as it
lay on the floor where she had dropped it in her haste,
all attracted me with a pathetic sense of recognition.
But oh, the bareness of the walls, and of the floor, the
scantiness of the furniture! Poverty, loneliness, misery,
were written everywhere. From all these I could save
this girl, but who would save the millions of others
as unhappy, as innocently ground beneath the pitiless
heel of a fatal industrial system? How could men of
heart and soul sleep by night, or be at peace by day,
while there was one human being whose hourly cup
of bitterness is such as millions drain in our Christian
civilization?

Ruth sat in a semi-faint upon her bed. It was clear
I had not come a moment too soon, but I do not
think she yet knew what had saved her. She had
drawn together her dress to conceal the fair vision of
her bosom, but more in instinct than in appreciation of
my presence, I thought.

"Don't you know I am here, dear Ruth?" I said, seating myself by her side, and supporting her with my
arm.

I thought she tried to smile. "I have come for you,"
I went on. "I shall take you away from this place
this very night, if you will go."

Her lips moved to form the word "Yes."

"Do you know," I said, "what it is that I want you
to do, and this very night?"

She opened her eyes at last and gazed at me in wonder. How did I come here, in her chamber? she
seemed to query of herself. Then she must have recalled her terrible struggle and her mysterious rescue.
She closed her eyes again, and nestled toward me with
an unconscious movement which filled me with wild
joy.

"I am going to take you away with me; so we must
be married, and this very night."

The pallor had left her cheeks now. The rich colors painted on the woods in Autumn were dull to the living glow of her cheeks. Her eyes, too, fairly blazed with a new consciousness and beauty. Then she drew away, and rising, stood facing me.

" I marry you ? " she asked, in a voice I could not interpret.

" Not if you do not love me," I answered in sudden wretchedness. " But you must let me ask you again, many months from now, when you know me better." I rose to plead with her more persuasively. A strange look was in her eyes as she listened.

She said at last : " I dared not dream that you loved me. To be offered life instead of a living death; to be given hope, instead of despair ; to be assured that I should be an honorable and useful woman, and no longer an enemy even of my own toiling sisterhood, competing with other poor girls for bread; these were enough. Should I expect your love too? Was there no one in the world to be made happy but me? Should I greedily ask for all the beautiful things I saw ? "

I took her in my arms in the first wonderful embrace of love, and as she raised her lips to mine for their first kiss, I was filled with amazement that in a world so full of misery, such ecstasy as mine could be possible. Then, still in my arms, she drew back her head, and, leaning away, looked into my face for a moment as she said, in a voice like one just yielding to the potency of powerful liquor : " And did you think I could love you better bye and bye? That would be impossible. Now that I have entertained for a moment the thought of being loved by you, I love you with my whole soul. I think I would die without it."

" We will start for the happy valley to-morrow." As I spoke the clock struck two. " Not to-morrow, but to-day."

" Where you are, is my paradise," she answered.

**34**

"We must go at once," I said. And without waiting for so much as one parting look behind, she went out from her old dark life forever.

As we went down the stairs we saw that help had been attracted by the cries of the degraded wretch who had so nearly paid with his life for his attempted villainy. Barely noticing that he was not fatally hurt, I drew Ruth's arm closer to mine, and we hurried out into the air.

It was a half hour before we found a carriage, an hour more before we secured an audience with the minister we desired, and the blackness of night was giving slow place to the gray of dawn when I could use to her that tenderest of names : "My wife."

"Shall we go to the bridge," I suggested, "and see the sun rise?"

The drays had already commenced their slow procession as we entered the bridge, but we were the only foot passengers in sight. The attendant policeman, to whom the welcome hour of release was drawing near, watched us somewhat suspiciously at first, but when he perceived that we were mere lovers, he yawned contemptuously and gave his thoughts once more to the tempting picture of the soft bed and darkened chamber which would soon be his solace.

"Let me tell you just what we shall do to-day," I said softly, my voice lingering over that delightful plural. "We must breakfast early, perhaps in Fulton market, that will be convenient. Then we shall have to take an early morning drive through the park to refresh us. It will fill the place of the night's rest which we both have missed. It will be nine o'clock when we return, and I must present Mr. Gillette to you. Then you shall go shopping until noon."

"And you?" she murmured, sweetly.

"I will finish the last few pages of my two years' experience in Grape Valley. This I must send to a friend, a New York editor. He is to make a book of it. All this must be done before we start for the West this afternoon."

"And shall you put me in your history?"

"I must, my darling. You it is who give completeness to it."

"And if you tell the miracle which has befallen me, all poor girls, too, may hope. Oh, why cannot we come back from our happy valley, now and then, and gather up others whose lives are as black as mine was, and save them for themselves and for happiness?"

"We will," I answered, as we reached the highest point of the bridge, and seated ourselves upon the same bench where Ward, Gillette and I had sat that other night, almost two years ago.

The sun was just gilding the east for his rising, and with my arm about my wife and with her head upon my shoulder I felt that all the beauties of the world would henceforth have a new and fuller meaning for me. The gold, the red and the blue outvied each other in the marvelous monocromes they painted on the clouds, then blending all in one perfect picture, made my eyes fairly tremble with the revelation. Then the sun himself sent his first rays glancing over land and sea and there came the answering gleam from the white sails and from the vanes and domes of glistening gold and shining steel.

I looked at the three mighty cities with their teeming millions of men, women and children, mostly miserable, although formed for happiness; mostly selfish although inclined to fraternity; mostly wicked although yearning for the good. The poorer of those millions, the ones with their faces crushed nearest to the earth, were already astir. Sleep, the only boon undenied them, has left their eyelids and with sighs, whose united breath would sweep whole navies from the sea, they begin to drink their daily cup of misery. In a few hours more their masters, the well-to-do and the rich, will come forth from their white sheets to another day. But it seemed to me the masters were hardly more happy. Were not both, indeed, slaves together to industrial and social institutions which forbid all real development and progress? The few cannot attain progress unless the many share in it. Happiness lies in the fulfillment of the capacities of our nature for good. Civilization is based on principles of selfishness, and selfishness begets all ignoble and degrading tendencies. Who, in civilization, unless he gives all his goods to the poor and his life to the service of others, can be happy? And even if he did that, the still unflagging revolutions of the wheels of our murderous system of society, must tear the tendons of his sensitive heart. The sop the philanthropist throws to Cerberus is all in vain.

Could those miserable beings be made happy? Could the people of thousands of cities and towns besides be led into the higher possibilities of their moral and spiritual natures? How little a leaven indeed was that community in Grape Valley to effect this stupendous work. Yet we could search out here and there a few even now, and point them to the promised land which sooner or later awaits all humanity.

I caressed the white hand that lay in mine but there was no response. I pressed the yielding form closer to me, but there was no answering movement like a returned caress. In sudden solicitude, I bent forward to look into the face that rested on my shoulder.

Ruth's eyes were closed, and the long lashes lay on her cheeks in perfect lines of beauty. Her lips, slightly parted, revealed the tips of her white teeth and her breath, sweet as mountain breezes, came in even and regular respirations.

My wife was asleep.

### NOTE FROM EDITOR.

The foregoing pages, from chapter IV to chapter XXVIII inclusive, were the contents of the packet sent me through a district messenger by my friend Vinton. The first three chapters, it will be remembered, I had prepared myself from the story of Ward and Vinton given me at Delmonico's. I had promised to make a book of the matter, and, it will be seen, was doing my best. The whole twenty-eight chapters had been at the printers for six weeks, when Ward returned to town and called upon me. He was a changed man. His old cheerfulness and ready good humor had disappeared, and he brought gloom into my room when he came. He would not talk about his two years' experience nor let me talk about Vinton's history. When I tried to induce him to help me correct the proofs and decide on a name for the forthcoming volume, he not only flatly refused to do so, but, apparently fearing urgency on my part, he did not call upon me again.

But it happened that just as I was reading the last proofs of Vinton's history, a district messenger came to my room with a packet, similar in general appearance to that which Vinton had sent me a few weeks before, but very much smaller. I soon found it to be manuscript, but as there was no signature, and as no letter of explanation came with it, I was forced to read it before I could assure myself who was its author, and what was his purpose in sending the sheets to me. It was clearly from Ward, as the reader will at once see, and was intended as a supplement to Vinton's history, at least so I gathered from one of the concluding paragraphs. There was no time to lose if Ward's contribution was to go into the same volume as the preceding chapters, so I sent it at once to the printers, with directions that it was to be added. It seems to me to have been written in a somewhat injudicious frame of mind, but I have not taken the liberty to so much as alter an adjective or suppress an adverb. The sort of a book I should write is so entirely different from this, that if I began to expunge and revise there would not be enough left of the original to hold the pages together. In the succeeding chapter I give it to the reader as it was given to me.

I have fulfilled my responsibilities to both of my friends, and I hope have incurred no new ones so far as the world at large is concerned.

# CHAPTER XXIX.

## PART I.

It was the week after the return of Harry Vinton with his extremely attractive wife that the two years of what might be called my novitiate in Grape Valley expired. In spite of the persuasions of Gillette, and notwithstanding the arguments of Vinton I had announced my irrevocable determination to leave the valley and forever.

The last evening of my stay had come. At dinner—the dinner is always a banquet in Grape Valley—I had been called up and had made my adieux. Of course that was not the place nor was then the time for criticisms, if indeed I had felt disposed to make them. But in fact my heart was quite too much touched with sentiments of good-will toward the kind friends I was to leave on the morrow. I felt, as I rose from my chair to address them, as if it were a big family of brothers and sisters which I was about to leave. The social intercourse of Grape Valley was so much more free and complete than I had thought possible, the cultivation of the genial instincts and of the fraternal spirit was so remarkable here, owing, I suppose, to the absence of conflicting interests and of the evil passions bred of them, that I felt myself upon intimate and tender relations with almost every one at the table.

I much fear my farewell address was not a success as a forensic effort. My impression is that I repeated a great many of my sentences a quite unnecessary number of times, and that there were frequent intervals when my voice became nearly inaudible from my emotion. I remember, too, that I could not keep my eyes from wandering to the place where sat Lydia Trenk, and that, when I saw her eyes filled with tears and her lips quivering, something seemed to choke me. It was only by a very great effort of will that I recovered myself sufficiently to make even a poor show of continuing.

When dinner was over I felt that I could endure no more leave-taking. It had taken me many years to attain the reputation of a man of self-poise, and I wanted to leave something besides a maudlin memory behind me. I thought to spend the evening in walking about the little city. The woman whose tearful eyes had met mine at the table least of all could I endure to meet again. Good-byes with women are dangerous things at best, but if one is conscious of being in love with a woman, and at the same time thinks he is bound to leave her, then a farewell scene is worse than dangerous. Although it made my heart ache to come away without a last touch of her hand, and a last whisper of that tender yet cruel word, "good-bye," I was still relieved at feeling that I had escaped without meeting her face to face.

But as I passed the piazza I heard a voice calling me in her soft, caressing tones.

"Wait," she said, rising from the bench, "I have been watching for you." Then as she came down the steps and laid her hand upon my arm, she added: "You see how well I knew you."

Instead of being displeased, as I should have been, that she had come, I was unreasonably happy. What I had honestly tried to avoid, a last meeting with Lydia, had come about, yet I was fully content. I drew her arm through mine and we walked slowly down the silent street.

"This will only make us both more miserable when I am gone," I said. But I did not release her arm.

"So you are really going to-morrow?"

" Yes, to-morrow," I answered.

" And never will return ? "

" Never will return," I repeated, thickly.

" Is there nothing I can say or do which would keep you ? "

" Nothing."

" Then," she hesitated, " then, if I wanted to say something which was very unwise, I need not be timid about it ? You would be in no danger of staying to make me ashamed of it ? "

" I do not understand what you can mean," I said in painful excitement, expecting I knew not what, at loss whether I hoped or feared it most.

" I mean," and she hung back a little on my arm, " I mean if I should want to say something which women do not generally have to say to men, something men usually say to women, there would be no fear of my seeing you to-morrow and thinking you despised me ? "

" I shall never see you after to-night, Lydia."

" Oh, you have called me Lydia for the first time," she cried. " I have so longed to hear you speak it. I cannot keep back my secret any longer from you. I have already told it to the moon and to the stars, to the river and to the mountains, oh, so many times."

I could not speak. I seemed suffering for breath.

Then came her voice again : " I love you so. I love you morning, noon and night. You are my life, but not my hope, my all, but yet you leave me forever."

How I wanted to take her in my arms. I felt as if I would be willing and glad to give my life if I could but press her to my breast for one moment. I could see, too, that she perceived my emotion, that she felt in some mysterious way how much I longed for her. Her eyes dilated, her bosom rose and fell, her form seemed leaning toward me in mute invitation. Suddenly I recovered myself, remembering how I had re solved that no temptation should ever cause me to give

35

the first caress to this woman who was another man's wife.

"Lydia," I said, "I must not take you to my heart, though you would not believe me if I told you now that I do not love you. It is because I love you that I am going away to-morrow, forever."

She gave me a hurt look like that in the eye of some gentle and tormented creature of the chase. I can never forget it. It was a minute, I think, before she spoke. "Is that the way to show your love for me, to break my heart?"

Then I tried to lash myself into a holy fury. "Duty comes before love. I must be sacrificed and you too, if necessary, to the duty you owe your husband."

But she then became really angry, and more beautiful than ever. "What duty can I owe him except kindness and honesty, unless it be the duty to leave him when I find I do not love him as he deserves to be loved by some one? I wrong him if I consent to maintain the hollow form of a marriage after I have ceased to love him, and a hundred times more if I have learned that I love another."

"But has he no rights?"

"Am I his slave, that my body is his when my heart is another's; that I must submit myself to caresses when I do not return tenderness? That would be pollution indeed."

"But you should not give your heart to another," I answered brutally, nerving myself to scourge the woman I worshipped.

Her lips curved magnificently. "Can a man or a woman love by rule or measure? Can I say to myself: 'You must like this sort of mind, that sort of intellect must please you; you must be delighted with this spiritual power, that type of physical manliness must thrill you with magnetic force?' Can I force myself to long to lay my head on a breast whose touch does not warm me? Can I make my heart melt in tenderness at will for a man because he is my husband?"

As I did not reply at once she continued : "Perhaps I never loved him, Perhaps I married before I was capable of knowing what love is. Perhaps I have grown away from him. All I know is that I do not love him now, but you, with my whole nature ; and to do what you call my duty to him would be to desecrate me as with a mortal sin, to shame me before my better nature, to do violence to my woman's purity and honor."

"But do you not consider that he may yet love you, and his happiness depend on you ? "

"I think my first obligation is to my own higher womanhood and sense of honor ; to fulfill my capacity for that best development of soul which comes with perfect love. But even if it were right for me to think first of him, I am still sure that I ought to leave him. Love is not simply desire, although the training of countless generations makes many of us think so. Neither is it admiration, nor yet esteem ; brothers and sisters and friends have these for each other. Physically, it is a magnetic attraction between a man and a woman ; mentally, it is responsiveness and mutual power to excite and stimulate and refresh ; spiritually, it is mutual inspiration and inarticulate sympathy ; a harmony of the inner and immortal natures beyond all other joy, beyond all other education. Love is mutual in its every essence ; so when a woman ceases to love her husband, or finds she has never loved him, her duty to him, as much as to herself, calls upon her to leave him free to form a new and perfect association. Even if he does not appreciate the fatal lack of a mutual love, it is still her duty to him to dissolve what has become a false marriage. So she will bless him in spite of himself."

"I only wish I could believe you."

She gave a sigh which might have been the fluttering of the wings of hope as it left her bosom forever, "I see all I have said is in vain. Your mind is so steeped in prejudice it will not believe your heart, which I know is pleading with me. I shall now go to my home never to see you again. But before we separate I must tell you that long since I have revealed to my husband that I love you, and you only. What he said to me and I to him; how gently, how sacredly, he has treated me since that moment, I shall not betray. He has the heart of a true knight. The only reason why I did not file my notice of divorce before was that I was afraid of shocking you. But this afternoon I made the record. My husband that was is my husband no longer, even in name. I return now to my home alone."

Then she walked rapidly up the street away from me and I stood watching her. Once or twice, I thought, she almost stopped. Once I am sure she partly turned as if she imagined that she heard my voice calling to her. But I neither called to her nor followed her. If her heart ached, did not mine ache as much? If she suffered agony, did it not seem as if a ragged blade of steel were piercing my bosom? By sheer force of will I rooted myself to the spot. Passion bade me pursue her. Love, touching with immortal flame every faculty of my soul and spirit, bade me call after her. But will held me back, and only when she turned into her door and became lost to my view, did I move, and then it was to walk back to the phalanstery to occupy my room for the last time.

Next morning I started east.

## PART II.

I was very unhappy on that journey to New York, and very ill-tempered. With considerable trouble I had secured the title deeds to a miserable remnant of life. I had rejected the love of the only woman who had ever stirred my heart. I had inflicted upon her a sentence as severe as I accepted for myself. I would have preferred the joy of a future with her

to all the other delights of a life-time. I would have
thought I was attaining the highest ideal of existence
in living in her presence and expanding under her
brooding love. But I sacrificed that joy, that ideal,
and so chose the very refuse of life. I kept telling
myself that it was duty which impelled me, a sense
of right which enabled me to resist temptation. But
never did duty seem so cold and unalluring. Never
did right seem so wholly, so eternally wrong.

Of course, I was thoroughly out of temper, and disposed to see only what encouraged cynical reflections,
but as my observations had some fruit it may be
well enough to record a few of them. In the seat
in front of me, when I took the train from St. Louis,
I noticed a young man and a young woman. He
was reading a newspaper, she examining her purse,
to make sure that the checks and tickets were safe.
When she spoke he had only curt replies, which he threw
at her without deigning to raise his eyes from his
newspaper. I immediately concluded they were married. She was pleasant-looking, and of graceful figure,
deferential and timid in manner, evidently anxious to
say what should commend itself to her husband, but
nervously conscious of failure. His face bore an ill-
tempered expression, his mouth showed impatience, the
lines running from the eyes to the chin showed weariness. She did not want to tire him, but she could not
help it. Poor little woman. She was married to a
man she could not make happy, and he retaliated by
shutting her out of all possible joys. They had only
reached the first station, when, without a word to her,
he started to go out, not even looking back to see if
his life companion were coming. I watched them as
they entered the waiting-room, he striding along as
if there were no woman at his heels, she ever watching
his face to anticipate his slightest wish or change of
mood, hungry for the smallest attention.

Their place was immediately taken by another husband and wife. This time, too, the second seat in front was turned so as to accommodate three children of ages from two to seven. The woman was large and sturdy, the man spare, and, perhaps, consumptive. Here it was the woman who was sharp and impatient, the husband who was deprecatory and eager to please. He was blamed for a number of discomforts experienced, as it appeared, since they had left the farm that morning, for things that had been left behind which he should have brought, for things brought which should have been left behind. The sun was too hot, and he should have taken a covered carriage. It was not going to rain, so there was no use for bringing those big umbrellas. Occasionally she bent forward and jerked some child's hat forward or back, pulled the little ones this way, or pushed them the other way. Her husband did not make her happy, and her children were a burden to her. As for the husband, I was sure that he must look forward to his death as a happy release. But then, there were the children who would be left unprovided for, and without a comforter, if he were to die.

The next station was a city of consequence, and the same two seats were occupied by a husband and wife, evidently in very prosperous circumstances, if one may judge by the character of their parcels. This man and woman were of a rank which is supposed to be above rudeness of speech, but a more unpleasant connection than theirs I cannot imagine. Both were young, and good-looking. Both were bright and educated. She began by telling him how thoughtless he was of her wishes and of her tastes. He was taking her to spend the remainder of the summer at a place she detested, and which he knew she detested. It was only because there were some men there with whom he could drink and play cards. So it was he always sacrificed her, she said. He was very cool in his replies, and so much more subdued that I heard very little of them. But I

could see there was a barb behind the point of each
sentence. Probably these bickerings were daily episodes
of their private married life, and among strangers on
a railroad train they saw no reason for restraining themselves. Finally he asked her, with a mockery of polite-
ness, if she would excuse him as he went forward for
a smoke. She answered that she knew very well that
there would be gambling too; at which he took off his
hat to her with a most graceful effect, and went on his
way. The woman very hastily opened her bag, and
taking out a novel, made a brave pretense of reading,
but when, in a few moments, she turned her head
toward the window, I saw her eyes were full of tears
of vexation.

I thought there must be something untoward about
those particular seats, and I looked about me for a new
location. I found it in the rear of a man and woman
whose faces seemed fairly shining with amiability.
Here at last I would find my happy married pair. I
took my seat quietly, but the man and woman were so
much absorbed in each other that they did not notice
that the seat behind them was now occupied. I heard
the man tell the woman how long he had hoped for this
meeting, and her reply by asking what he thought her
husband would say if he knew they were together. So
it appeared they represented two unhappy homes,
instead of exemplifying, as I had expected, one harmonious family. My heart turned sick. I made such
a commotion that, after a frightened look behind from
each pair of guilty eyes, they carried on the rest of
their conversation in whispers.

Once arrived in New York I spent my first evening
at the club, and fell in at once with several of my
old friends. After they had concluded that I had no
confidences to impart as to the reason of my long absence they left me to the silent role I preferred, and
entertained each other in their own way. Most of them
were married men, and nothing of course was said to

reflect upon the connubial bliss much less upon the sanctity of their particular homes. But the secrets of no other fireside were respected. I heard how Mrs. B. had intercepted a letter written to her husband by a former governess, that for a time there was a loud talk of separation, but everything had been finally smoothed over with a proper regard for appearances. Then I was informed that C. had quarreled with D. for visiting his wife so preferably during his absence, and had forbidden him the house. At this, it seems, however, C.'s wife showed her fangs, and by certain unpleasant threats induced her husband to swallow his grievances. Another of my companions told of a quarrel between E. and his wife, overheard from the hall where the narrator was left waiting by some servant's mistake. There was no scandal, so far as he heard, but any amount of infelicity. She wanted gaiety and show, he did not. She liked the people he hated; what interested him bored her. Neither seemed to care for the other, except as a butt for sarcasm; a target for slings and slurs.

I could endure no more of this depressing conversation from representative men of the higher society, and I went out into the street. It was too early for bed, and I took a walk along the Bowery and side streets. The evening being very warm, families had moved out in full force upon the steps and sidewalks. The children barefooted, and clad in dirty garments, played or fought, it was hard to tell which, in the gutter. Fathers in soiled shirt-sleeves and stocking feet, with strong-smelling pipes in their mouths, mothers in flowing and shapeless wrappers of what were once prints, but now masses of indistinguishable and faded colors, and older daughters with frowzy hair and cross faces, occupied the upper steps. The husbands and wives did not sit together, or appear to have the slightest common concern. They looked everywhere except at each other, and seemed to think of everything except of each other.

At first all these sidewalk groups looked alike to me. Each one was an epitome of human misery, an example of the wretchedness of the poor man's home, an illustration of how separate are husbands and wives, fathers and mothers, who are harassed by daily want, how cut off from tender and joyful relations to each other or to their children.

But, as I passed along, I became able to discriminate among the examples of misery in the family relations. In some cases the woman had grown coarse and corpulent; her femininity had been worn away. She was no longer a wife, but a rude companion, a partner with as strong an arm, as rough a soul as the man's. In others the man showed marks of alcoholic deterioration. His hard fate had driven him to seek the false sense of power which liquor gives, and in his cups what wife and children could not be to a poor man. In other cases the husband showed maudlin fondness for female acquaintances sitting near him, giving them the interest his wife should have claimed, which the neighbors seem to take quite for granted, and to which the neglected wives were as indifferent as the neighbors. I saw no case where the wife was enjoying the attention of any man, her husband or another. The married women had too generally lost their attractiveness through the terrible plague of poverty to be able to tempt men to do them honor. Their voices had lost all the gentle cadences which lovers like to hear. Their lips had forgotten how to smile, far more to kiss. Their hands, hard and callous, would have felt any thing but pleasant to the touch of a manly gallant.

Sometimes a father would hold one of his smaller children on his knee for a few minutes, or a wearied mother would be seen tossing a wizen-faced baby to and fro to still its moans, or exposing her shapeless breasts without a trace of modesty, seeking to soothe the baby moans with such poor nourishment as could be found there. But for the most part, the parents seemed as indifferent to their children as to each other.

Then I crossed Broadway and walked up Canal street, full of painted women and wretched girls eager to sell themselves to the lowest of men for money or for food, and then to Sixth avenue, and up to Haymarket. I looked into the faces of what should have been pure and happy womanhood, with eyes still beautiful, which should have stirred the heart of some lover, with cheeks, pale and wan for all their disguise, which should have been pillowed on the shoulder of affection. Then I dared to wonder how much less shameful, how much more honorable and happy would have been their lot if married, as the women in the poor tenement region, with such homes as those.

I slept very little that night, and the next morning made my way to the Tombs police court, and listened to the charges against the men and women of the poorer classes. A wife had complained of her husband for beating her; he urged as extenuation that the home she made for him was no better than a pig-pen. There were half a dozen cases of women, most of them married, who were sent to the work-house as common drunkards, curses of some men's lives. Then a wife asked that her husband be forced to support her and their child. She told me her story very graphically afterward. Two years ago he had married her, promising that they would be the happiest pair in New York. She had not known him very long before marriage. A few picnics, a dance or two, and three evenings at the theater, had furnished all their courtship. He was always well dressed when she saw him then, and very gentlemanly in his manners. She had thought he was the grandest man in the world. When they were married, she left the store where she was saleswoman; he bought some furniture on the installment plan, and everything looked well. But it cost a good deal to buy food, and there were no more entertainments for them. He had no money to spend for cigars and beer, as long as he kept up his comfortable style of living, and was obliged to spend his evenings at home, soon afterward beginning to sulk and mope. Then he began to let his bills go unpaid, and to spend his time and money on his own amusement. When the baby came he was better for a few days, but the new care only made his demeanor more disagreeable and his habits more dissolute than ever. At last the furniture was taken away, and then the rent being unpaid, they had to move to a cheaper tenement. Now he was not even buying her enough to eat. She loved him no longer. If she could but get along until the baby was old enough to leave, she would go to work again. Women who wanted marriage could have it. Every poor married woman in the tenement where she lived was miserable, and so were their husbands. Marriage might be well enough for the rich, but it was not meant for poor folks.

For a week I hunted up old friends who had married, and I accepted invitations to their homes. I did my best to worm the secrets of their matrimonial successes or failures from them. Some I appealed to as a bachelor who wanted advice. Others I accused of looking careworn, and thus induced them to tell me more than they would like their wives to have known. All began with "Of course I am very happily married." So much out of chivalry for their wives, but with this proviso they spoke very freely. The common course of feeling on the marriage question was intensely cynical. Even those who I believed were still in love with their wives had so much to say about the ill success of their neighbors, that they contributed more to my prejudice against modern marriage, than did those who were living warnings. Aside from lack of what they had thought love would give, the loss of liberty, the deprivation of former companionship, the increase of care, were the general objections. Then for particular instances, there was

the man who had pleased his taste at nineteen and had
been repenting since twenty-five, and the man who had
married because he thought a girl overwhelmingly in
love with him, and found her sentiment wearing out
faster than her trousseau. There were the husbands
whose wives had been so bound up in the care of children
and under household burdens that they have been shut
as much away from their husbands, as if the heads of
the families were nothing but agents to pay the rent and
buy meat and groceries. The verdict seemed to be that
the sentiment of love as exhibited in courtship did not
usually long outlast the marriage ceremony. Sometimes it was the husband's fault; sometimes the wife's.
More common were the cases of men and women simply
mismated, or who had lost all adaptability to each other.
In the instances where the material for a love match
seemed to exist it usually happened that family or
financial cares, and deprivation of social pleasures, prevented enjoyment of each other. There were of course
husbands and wives whose relations were ideal, but even
their happiness was clouded by the misery they could
not but see all about them. They must needs weep for
others between their smiles for each other. They could
not but feel that joy was almost out of place in a state
of society where selfishness was the rule of life.

Exactly at what point I experienced a change of will
I cannot tell. All that I can say is that one morning
I awoke with the conviction that if, by any labors of
Hercules I could make my way back to Grape Valley,
and to Lydia, I would shake from my feet the dust of a
civilization which has made a failure both of the industrial and social relations. Unfortunately, however, I
was in possession of no data which could enable me to
reach Grape Valley unassisted. My only chance lay in
meeting Gillette. He made frequent business trips to
New York and was accustomed to stop at the Fifth
Avenue hotel. So much I knew. I calmly resolved
to go to that hotel and stay until the fortunate day

when I should see his name on the register, whether
it should be this summer or in the fall, or in another
winter.   When I had found him I determined to beg
him to take me back with him to Grape Valley and
to happiness.   He could not resist such arguments as
I should use.   He might remind me that a man who,
having his choice between good and evil, chose the
latter, deserved to suffer.   But the tide of my eloquence would overwhelm him.

As soon as I had eaten my breakfast I began packing
my trunks.   In a few minutes they were on their way
to the "Fifth Avenue."   Then I visited my lawyer and
arranged my business affairs, leaving strict orders to
convert all my property into cash and to send all the
proceeds to my address at St. Louis. I had determined
to devote all my property to increasing the number of
colonists at Grape Valley.   I was not content in
achieving happiness for myself, while millions were
suffering in ignorance from the ills of a civilization
wholly barbarous.   As soon as I reached the hotel I
seated myself in the reading-room and began to write
this little sketch of my recent experiences.   My long
fight against the light and my final conversion to the
truth may not be without good effect if published to
the world.   I only hope that my friend the editor will
deign to look at it when put into his hands and——

It is decided.   Fate is with me.   I had just written
the lines above when a hand was laid upon my arm.
Looking up impatiently—a man is always provoked at
being interrupted just as he is rounding a sentence—I
saw Gillette himself.

"I hope you are not sorry to see me," he said with a
surprised air.   Then I recovered my senses and, leaping to my feet, I wrung his hand with fervor enough
to more than satisfy him.

"Sorry?" I exclaimed.   "I am the happiest man in
the world."

"So anxious to bid me good-bye?   It was a mere

chance that I saw you at all. I had passed through the room and was just at the door when I happened to look back and saw you writing here."

" You are going back this morning — back to Grape Valley?" I cried.

"Yes; Vinton has been gone a month you know, and I had my work to do, besides what I had laid out for him."

" And may I go with you?" I asked, and waited in an agony of suspense for his reply.

"For another visit?" he smiled.

"No, for life. I am a convert. Don't refuse me."

"Refuse you indeed," he replied. "I am only too happy to accept you. How long will it take you to get ready?"

" My trunks are in the baggage-room now. My affairs are all settled," I answered with wild gaiety. "I only want to finish this letter and despatch it by a messenger. Then I am ready."

THE END.